Maine Birding Trail

The Official Guide to More Than
260 Accessible Sites

Bob Duchesne

To Sandi:
The next time I say the words,
"You know what Maine really needs?"
please talk me out of it.

Cover photograph used by permission

ISBN: 978-0-89272-783-4

Printed at Versa Press, East Peoria, Illinois

5   4   3

BOOKS·MAGAZINE·ONLINE
www.downeast.com
Distributed to the trade by National Book Network

Library of Congress Cataloging-in-Publication Information: Available on request

CONTENTS

INTRODUCTION

I started working on the Maine Birding Trail in 2003. As it advanced toward its official launch in 2009, the project was embraced and supported by Maine Audubon, Maine state government, and scores of local birders. I personally visited and evaluated hundreds of sites. Today, the official state trail reflects the best of the best. Abbreviated information is widely available. This guide describes all of the official sites and a great many more–a complete guide to the state, plus the Canadian islands of Campobello and Grand Manan.

In the late 1980s, Maine entered a period of transition. Intense development pressure and rapid changes in forest ownership spawned two citizen-supported counter-strategies. Land trusts sprang up nearly as fast as subdivisions. In 1987, the state launched Land for Maine's Future–a publicly financed program to purchase and conserve some of the remote places in the eastern United States. The program expanded in 1999 and has received the strong support of Mainers ever since, with new sites continuing to become available to the public. A companion Web site has been created to provide updates on the information contained in this book, keeping current with the latest opportunities and changes. Visit www.mainebirdingtrail.com.

The official Maine Birding Trail will evolve beyond the date of this guide. This guide coincides with the launch of the official trail, but history shows that new sites will be added to the list and a few original sites may be downgraded or restricted according to the needs for habitat protection. Additionally, community initiatives and private landowners will certainly provide new chances to enjoy the birds in some of Maine's most spectacular surroundings. Birding trails take on a life of their own as communities come to realize the value inherent in the nature around them. Signage and landmarks will improve over time, beyond what is described in this book.

For better or worse, the regions defined in the chapters of this guide correspond to Maine's official tourism regions rather than habitat zones. This organizational decision makes trip planning easier for visitors because information in other books, guides, and Web sites regarding accommodations, dining, sightseeing, shopping, and adventures are typically organized according to these tourism regions. It also facilitates one of the chief goals of this book: the use of the Maine Birding Trail for the encouragement and development of nature-based tourism within the state, so that wildlife and natural resources may be better conserved, protected, and enjoyed for generations to come. The drawback is that the habitat zones don't always line up with tourism zones. Visitors seeking specific birds may be challenged to figure out which area is best for chasing Spruce Grouse or Bicknell's Thrush. The appendices in the back of this guide should help make those decisions easier.

General Information

Maine is a diverse state. It is dead center in the temperate zone: the 45th parallel runs through the heart of the state. There are several key transitions that happen in Maine.

Northern deciduous forests are characteristically found in the southern and central interior parts of the state, as well as on the lower elevations of most mountains. Boreal forests take over in Baxter State Park and at the higher elevations of the western mountains. Boreal forests also exist in the cedar swamps of the North Woods, Down East through Washington County, and on many of the wooded offshore islands. All of these forest types mix at transition points and birds of different habitats can be found in relative proximity.

The coast, too, is a transition zone. The extensive sand beaches of southern Maine give way to the "rocky coast of Maine" in Portland. There are enough stony capes along the coast of southern Maine, however, that many species overlap. It is possible to find a beach-loving Sanderling with rock-loving Purple Sandpipers. And though the salt marshes and estuaries of southern Maine are extraordinary for shore-birds in late summer, the mud flats uncovered by the huge tides of Down East Maine are their equals.

Glaciation has produced much of the diversity. 12,000 years ago, the weight of mile-thick ice depressed the earth. When the glaciers retreated, the sea advanced, depositing marine clay into areas that would eventually lift and become peat bogs. Alluvial deposits of sand from the same retreating glaciers formed gravel eskers. Thus, systems of well-drained and poorly drained soils exist right next to each other. Kennebunk Plains in southern Maine and the blueberry barrens of Down East Maine are good examples of sand plains that are close to nearby wetlands.

Salt marshes and freshwater marshes coexist along the entire coast and many species are equally at home in both. Saltmarsh Sharp-tailed Sparrows and Nelson's Sharp-tailed Sparrows both breed in the state. They overlap, and even hybridize, in places like Scarborough Marsh and Weskeag Marsh. In fact, Maine is the northern limit of many southern species and the southern limit of many northern species. Some offshore islands, and even a few mainland parks, are notorious migrant traps. Monhegan Island is the destination of choice for international bird tours because of its propensity for attracting off-course migrants.

Maine is well known for seabird watching opportunities. Offshore islands provide nesting for Atlantic Puffins, and for Common, Arctic, and Roseate Terns. Colonies of Common Murres, Razorbills, and Black Guillemots dot these islands. Leach's Storm-petrels nest offshore and Wilson's Storm-petrels move into these same waters each summer, along with three species of shearwaters, Northern Fulmars, Northern Gannets, migrating jaegers, and even rare skuas.

Warblers:

Maine is rich in warblers. Yellow-rumped, Black-throated Green, Northern Parula, Black-and-white, and Magnolia Warblers are all so common that it is hard to imagine a day in the field without them. So are American Redstarts, Common Yellowthroats, and Ovenbirds. Yellow Warblers dominate city parks and the brushy open areas of the coast, river bottoms, and logging cuts. Chestnut-sided Warblers favor secondary growth areas. Large stands of white pine, especially near lakes and rivers, are bound to contain Pine Warblers. Black-throated Blue and Nashville Warblers are relatively common in mixed forests, just as Blackburnian Warblers are likely to be present in the canopies of more mature forests.

Other warblers share a more limited range or season. Canada Warblers skulk in damp, wooded tangles. Wilson's Warblers favor the live alders around wet areas of small ponds and streams. The Northern Waterthrush prefers the upright dead trees of beaver flowages. Blackpolls are relatively late migrants and may be found in the boreal forests and mountains of western Maine, Baxter State Park, and spruce forest tracts along the coast. Palm Warblers are one of the earliest migrants, arriving in the state in mid-April. By mid-May, they settle into their boggy breeding grounds where Tennessee Warblers are also infrequent breeders. Cape May Warblers prefer the tall conifer forests and edges more common to northern Maine. Bay-breasted Warblers choose the boreal spruce of bogs and mountaintops, but tolerate nearby hardwoods. Mourning Warblers are difficult to find, but should be looked for in regenerating clear cuts on the edge of boreal areas of northern Maine. In contrast, the range of Prairie Warblers barely extends into southern Maine and they are seldom encountered north of Augusta. Blue-winged Warblers recur in small numbers in southern Maine. Sightings of Orange-crowned, Hooded, Worm-eating, Golden-winged, and Kentucky Warblers are rare events.

Red-eyed Vireos are common in all mature woods. Blue-headed Vireos prefer mixed forest. On a day of spring birding, neither can be missed. Warbling Vireos are present in open deciduous areas, especially bordering farm and pasture land, and wetland areas. Philadelphia Vireos are encountered in migration but they are hard to find outside of their breeding grounds, which in Maine lie primarily in Baxter State Park, the Bigelow Range, and the Mahoosoc Range around Grafton Notch State Park. Yellow-throated Vireos breed in a few areas of southwestern Maine, especially Brownfield Bog.

Gulls:

Herring, Ring-billed, and Great Black-backed Gulls are widespread. There are also plenty of Laughing Gulls, though they prefer oceanic habitat to the mainland. Island trips and ferry rides turn up plenty. Bonaparte's Gulls are common locally after breeding. There are several good spots for locating Iceland and Glaucous Gulls in winter, and these spots are noted in the text. The culprits that qualify for local Rare Bird Alerts are the Common Black-headed Gull, Lesser Black-backed Gull, Little Gull, Thayer's Gull, and—once in a blue moon— the Ivory Gull.

Seasons:

Maine is a four-season state. Even though natives argue that winter lasts longer than all other seasons combined, in reality the seasons are about equal. Each season has a dramatic effect on birding opportunities. Surprisingly, winter is one of Maine's best birding periods.

The busiest birding season begins in April. Expect mud and standing water. Migrants arrive in southern Maine and Portland about a week ahead of Acadia and Bangor, which in turn are nearly a week ahead of the Katahdin and Aroostook regions. The eastern coastal areas melt faster than the western mountainous regions. On average, by April 1, American Robins and Song Sparrows have returned and started singing. Most rivers are flowing freely, attracting diving ducks, including Barrow's Goldeneye. By the second week of April, ice on the lakes and ponds has begun to disappear. A variety of ducks move into open water and flooded farm fields. Wilson's Snipe and American Woodcock return. Purple and House Finches also reappear in greater numbers about this time. By the third weekend of April, Tree Swallows and the earliest warbler species begin to show up, specifically Yellow-rumped, Pine, and Palm Warblers. Calls of the first Eastern Phoebes and Yellow-bellied Sapsuckers enliven quiet mornings in late April. Hawks also return in April. Many of Maine's wintering ocean ducks use the Kennebec and Penobscot Rivers, as well as the Allagash and St. John Rivers farther north, to reach Hudson Bay. It's common for eiders, Buffleheads, and scoters to show up on inland rivers and adjacent lakes in migration through mid-May. Before the foliage thickens in April is a good time to see Spruce Grouse.

About the first of May, the remaining warbler species begin to return, peaking by Memorial Day. Ruby-throated Hummingbirds can be expected around Mother's Day. Some migrants such as Bicknell's Thrush, Nelson's Sharp-tailed Sparrows, and Black Terns may not return until early June. As an example of geographic diversity, Maine Audubon Big Day teams typically achieve species counts of around 150 in southern Maine and 125 in eastern and central Maine, since Portland is the northern limit for some species. Warbler season is richest between mid-May and mid-June. Black-backed Woodpeckers are noisiest around the nest in late May and early June. Conversely, Boreal Chickadees are typically hushed while on nests in late June.

By July the woods are more quiet as the parents raise their broods. In August, southward migration begins again, starting with shorebirds. Though most shorebirds use the ocean beaches and marshes, a surprising number can be found on river and lake mud flats. Peregrine Falcons and Merlins follow the shorebirds, so either may be encountered at these places. Pelagic activity picks up dramatically in August. Wilson's Storm-petrels and Greater, Sooty, and Manx Shearwaters increase. Atlantic Puffins, Common Murres, Thick-billed Murres, and Razorbills disperse to open water. Jaegers mix with gulls and Northern Fulmars. This activity peaks in late September, though Northern Gannets straggle southward from late July through Christmas.

The bulk of hawk migration occurs around the middle of September, and in October the sea ducks start to return from Hudson Bay. By November, Maine begins to discover what kind of winter it will have. Each year, some species that normally winter in Canada irrupt into northern New England. Common (and sometimes Hoary) Redpolls, Pine Grosbeaks, White-winged and Red Crossbills, and Bohemian Waxwings may turn up anywhere, some after an absence of several years. Snow Buntings may be common or scarce in any given winter. Snowy, Great Gray, and Northern Hawk-owls are rare, but in the right winter they can be found in unpredictable places.

In November and December, wintering sea ducks flood the coasts. Common Eiders, Long-tailed Ducks, Buffleheads, Common and Red-throated Loons, Black Guillemots, Common Goldeneyes, Horned and Red-necked Grebes, and all three scoters are findable just about any-where. Harlequin Ducks are regular in several places and uncommon in several more. Purple Sandpipers are common and easy to spot for the experienced eye. In fact, it is estimated that 80% of the world's popula-tion of Purple Sandpipers winters in Maine. King Eiders and Pacific Loons are found sporadically. Look for freshwater ducks in the ice-free water below dams. Snow Buntings and sometimes Horned Larks frequent beaches, particularly Reid State Park and Popham Beach State Park. It is possible to spot a Lapland Longspur in such flocks, too. Northern Shrikes turn up anywhere in winter but prefer the edges of open areas along the coast.

The DeLorme Maine Atlas is a helpful tool when roaming the state. They are available in every convenience store, and many Mainers have one. One caution: logging roads throughout Maine's forests are well marked on the DeLorme maps, but the smaller roads are subject to change even in a single season. Do not rely on the atlas alone for negotiating Maine's remote logging roads. Checkpoints for the North Maine Woods will provide updated local maps.

12

THE MAINE BEACHES

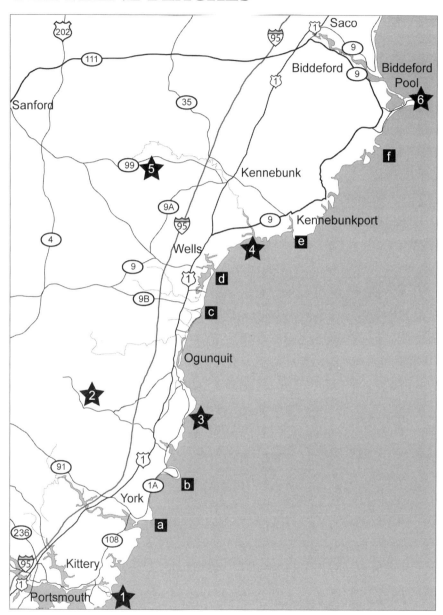

York County in southern Maine has some of the most accessible birding in all of New England. The coastline is dotted with parks and refuges. There are vast stretches of public sand beaches. Even birding hot spots that are not on the coast are within fifteen minutes of main routes. Interstate 95 and US Route 1 enable quick transit from site to site. York County also boasts the highest concentration of lodging, dining, and amusement in the state. Because of its proximity to urban markets, it maintains a high regard for creature comforts while retaining the ambience of a small town, fishing village, all within a two-hour drive of major airports in Portland, Boston, and Manchester, New Hampshire.

Because York County is the southernmost county in the state, it boasts a greater number of species than elsewhere. Kennebunk Plains is a lingering remnant of a grassland habitat that has all but disappeared in the northeast. Look for Grasshopper, Vesper, Field, and Savannah Sparrows, and Upland Sandpipers. Laudholm Farm and the Wells National Estuarine Research Reserve protect a breeding population of Piping Plovers and Least Terns that scurry nearly underfoot. The Rachel Carson National Wildlife Refuge shelters breeding Saltmarsh Sharp-tailed Sparrows.

Migration season also has its share of pleasures. Several of the migrant traps in spring and one of Maine's best hawk-watching mountains in autumn—Mount Agamenticus—are in York County. Biddeford Pool is noted for its surprise finds.

Unlike frozen portions of the Maine interior, winter birding in York County equals, and sometimes surpasses, the excitement of summer. This is because many of Maine's sea ducks breed in arctic Canada or on offshore islands. Common Murres, Thick-billed Murres, and Razorbills don't stray far from their nesting islands during the warm months, but in the winter all may show up close to shore. Even Dovekies appear occasionally. Subarctic breeders triple their numbers along the Maine coast in winter. Birders can find Black, White-winged, and Surf Scoters just about anywhere, often on the same stretch of coastline. They are joined by scores of Horned Grebes, Red-necked Grebes, Red-throated Loons, Long-tailed Ducks, and Buffleheads that are largely absent in summer. Common Eiders triple their numbers and at a couple of well-known spots, a King Eider may join them. Harlequin Ducks are seldom seen from shore in Maine except in York County. Purple Sandpipers and Great Cormorants return to the coast in large numbers each winter. Gull watching becomes more interesting because Iceland, Glaucous, and Lesser Black-backed Gulls turn up regularly. Large concentrations of Bonaparte's Gulls occasionally contain a surprise Common Black-headed or Little Gull. Best of all, the ocean's effect modifies the weather so that snow and ice along the shoreline is less of a problem here than farther up the coast. The tide cleanses the sandy beaches free of snow.

Southern Maine contains the bulk of the state's human population and therefore it also contains the highest number of birders. Rare and unusual species seldom go unnoticed. The York County Audubon Society is particularly active; its members lead interesting field trips and volunteer their expertise at Laudholm Farm and the Wells National Estuarine Research Reserve.

Trip planning: www.MaineBeachesAssociation.org or 207-363-4422

Official Maine Birding Trail Sites

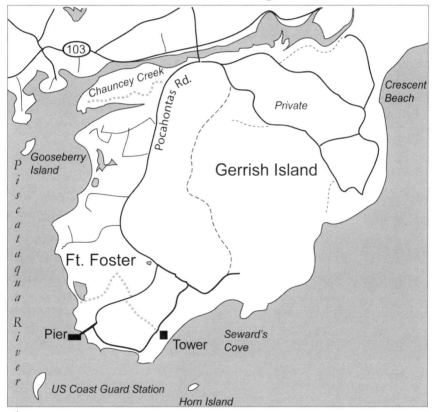

⭐ **Fort Foster** is at the southernmost tip of the Maine Birding Trail. It sits on Gerrish Island overlooking a large expanse of ocean and tidal river. Habitat on this 88-acre site is diverse, offering mature hardwoods, evergreens, and freshwater marsh. This is a good migrant trap in spring and fall, so look for all of Maine's warblers, thrushes, sparrows, and other passerines. In winter, this is a good place to look for alcids and sea ducks offshore, and Purple Sandpipers on the rocks. The fort, built in the early 1900s, protected the Portsmouth Naval Shipyard in both World Wars. The town of Kittery operates Fort Foster. The park gate is closed from late fall to late spring, but visitors may park at the gate and walk in during the off-season. It can be icy in winter.

Directions: from Route 1 in Kittery, follow Route 103 east 3.5 miles. Turn right onto Chauncey Creek Road, follow 0.5 mile, turn right onto Pocahontas Road, cross the Gerrish Island Bridge, turn right and follow Pocahontas Road 1.2 miles. A fee is charged in summer.

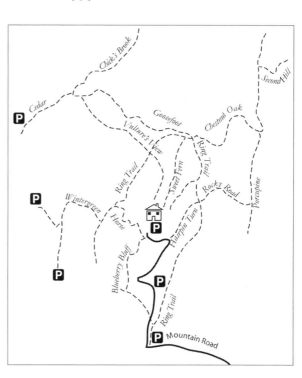

2 Migrating hawks are drawn to **Mt. Agamenticus**, making it one of Maine's best hawk-watching sites. Rising almost 700 feet a mere five miles from the ocean, this monadnock stands alone in a section of the state dominated by low plains. At one time, the peak was an active ski slope and the lodge is still used as a recreation center. Its deck is ideal for 360 degree viewing. In breeding season, the surrounding woodlands make good habitat for many of Maine's songbirds. Hawks are best seen on southerly breezes in spring and northwest breezes in autumn.

Directions: from Route 1, turn south onto Clay Hill Road. Drive 3.9 miles, bear right at a T intersection, and continue another 1.6 miles. Drive 0.6 mile to the summit, or park below and walk the trails or road.

3 **Marginal Way** in Ogunquit is a narrow, paved, mile-long footpath that hugs the rocky shoreline. It is extraordinary at any time of year. In winter, Harlequin Ducks and Purple Sandpipers can be plentiful and sighting any of the sea ducks is possible. The path is lined with low bushes and shrubs, making it attractive to sparrows, mockingbirds, and cardinals any time of year and migrating passerines in spring and fall. There are thirty-nine park benches spaced along the route. Dogs are prohibited in summer. Beware of ice in winter. Start at Perkins Cove where there are pleasant shops, restaurants, and facilities.

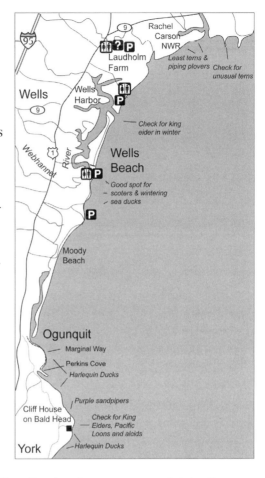

Directions: from Route 1 in Cape Neddick, follow Route 1A south 0.9 mile, turn left on Shore Road in Ogunquit, proceed 4.6 miles to a hard right turn onto Perkins Cove Road. From Route 1 in Ogunquit, follow Shore Road 0.8 mile south to the entrance of Perkins Cove Road on the left.

4 **Wells National Estuarine Research Reserve** at Laudholm Farm is one of Maine's best birding destinations year-round. A trail system provides seven miles of hiking that meander through fresh and saltwater marshes, mixed forests, fields, beaches, and dunes. Eastern Towhee and Brown Thrasher are uncommon elsewhere in the state, but flourish here. Because of limited access and posted admonitions to avoid disturbing the nesting Piping Plovers and Least Terns, the beach is underused compared to the stretches of sand to the north and south. On the northern end of this beach there is a natural jetty of shallow rock that extends into the sea just past the Little River outlet. This area is a magnet for gulls and terns, including occasional rarities. First settled in 1642, the Wells Reserve also preserves many historic farm buildings on this site. The slight elevation and open farm fields near the buildings make this a good place for migrating hawks in September. The visitor's center maintains a bird-sighting log and is open all year except for the four weeks surrounding Christmas. The Wells Reserve is one of twenty-seven national estuarine research reserves that promote the protection of coasts and estuaries through education, research, and conservation programs.

Directions: from Route 1, turn onto Laudholm Farm Road. Follow the (small) signs a half mile to the entrance.

---

5 Kennebunk Plains is owned and managed in part by the Maine Department of Inland Fisheries and Wildlife and The Nature Conservancy. The sandplain grassland represents a human created, early successional stage of pitch pine barrens. Great drainage on these gravel-sand plains makes them ideal for development, one reason why they are

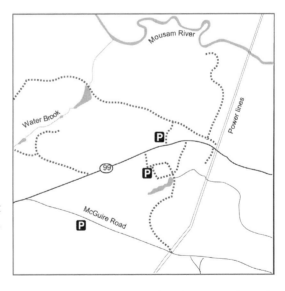

fairly rare. This remnant is home to breeding grassland species found almost nowhere else in the state, including Grasshopper and Vesper Sparrows, Upland Sandpipers, Prairie Warblers, Eastern Towhees, Bobolinks, Eastern Meadowlarks, and Brown Thrashers. Plants are sensitive to foot traffic, many grassland birds nest on the ground, and ticks are present, so stay on the roads and paths. Start from the parking lots on Route 99, but allow ample time to stroll along the edges of the McGuire Road as well. Both ponds can be quite productive, especially the flowage pond of Cold Water Brook, a dependable water source for passerines.

Directions: from Route 1, turn west on Route 9A (High St.), then in 0.3 mile turn right onto Route 99. Follow for 4.2 miles and look for the parking areas on both sides of the road.

<hr />

6 Biddeford Pool is another of Maine's exceptional year-round hot spots, though parking is very limited in summer. There are four key areas.

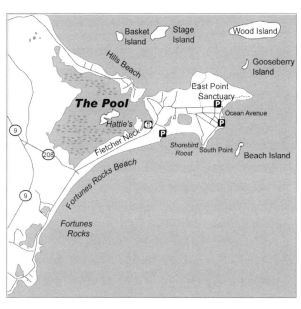

1) The mile-long tidal pool dominates the area. It is surrounded by private property, but Hattie's Restaurant has traditionally been supportive of birders, especially if they are also restaurant patrons. Those respectful of the restaurant's limited parking can usually get permission to access the edge of the salt marsh for ducks, waders, and shorebirds. In fact, most local birders will look for any excuse to eat at Hattie's. Across the street from Hattie's is a municipal parking lot that is reserved for locals in summer, but is available all other times of year.

2) East Point Sanctuary is a small Maine Audubon property with paths that wander along the cliffs over 30 acres. There is limited parking near the entrance gate.

3) Ocean Avenue lies at the end of Main Street and abuts the point and its seawall. Parking is very limited. Scan the water for sea ducks—King Eiders occur occasionally—and the rocks for shorebirds in season.

Pay close attention to the islands. Snowy Owls and Rough-legged Hawks are recurring rarities.

4) Hills Beach is the spit of land on the north side of the tidal pool. This beach has always been productive for terns. Common, Roseate, and Arctic Terns occur regularly, and terns such as Caspian, Royal, and Sandwich Terns have made historic appearances. In recent years, it has become a good spot to look for Lesser Black-backed Gulls.

Directions: from Route 9, turn onto Route 208 and follow 1.8 miles to an intersection at the southwest corner of the pool. (Turn right for the southern half of Fortunes Rocks Beach.) Turn left and follow to Hattie's Restaurant on the left. Then continue ahead, bearing right onto Main Street, and following to East Point. Turn right again onto Ocean Avenue and follow it around South Point to return to Main Street. For Hills Beach, turn onto Hills Beach Road near the University of New England and follow to the end. Parking is very limited.

Additional Sites:

a **Nubble Light** at Cape Neddick is one of Maine's most popular lighthouses. It rests on a small island just off the point of land occupied by York's 3-acre Sohier Park. In winter, it is a good place for Harlequin Ducks and occasional King Eiders. Many other sea ducks, occasional alcids, and Purple Sandpipers turn up from late fall through spring. It's also a good spot to see songbirds in migration.

Directions: from Route 1 in York Village take Route 1A north 5 miles, turn right onto Nubble Road, and follow 0.9 mile to the park.

b **The Cliff House** is a large resort that sits on Bald Head. It is private property, though the owners have traditionally been accepting of birders. Its exposure to open ocean always invites unusual sightings, and some of the best birding is in winter when the resort is closed. Park out of the way and avoid icy and construction areas. This is one of the best mainland locations to see Harlequin Ducks and one of the better places to look for a King Eider. A good variety of other sea ducks, loons, and alcids are possible here. Purple Sandpipers are frequent, especially on the left side of the motel units on the northern end of the resort.

Directions: from Route 1 in Cape Neddick, follow Route 1A south 0.9 mile, turn left on Shore Road, proceed 2.9 miles to the Cliff House entrance on the right. From Route 1 in Ogunquit, follow Shore Road 2.5 miles south to the entrance on the left.

c **Wells Beach** is one of many beaches along this section of coast. Because of a barrier of low islets just off shore, it is better than average for sea ducks. In winter, all three scoters may be present and Purple Sandpipers may be roosting on the islands. Sanderlings are often on the beach at any time of year. Moody Beach and upper Ogunquit Beach, reached from the parking lot at the south end of Ocean Avenue, can be good from late fall to spring and provide views of the upper Ogunquit River marsh. Driving south from Mile Road and around Moody Point, you'll find several productive pullouts.

Directions: from Route 1 there are three access roads leading east to the beach. The best for birding is Mile Road, which leads 0.9 mile directly east to a small town parking lot. Scan the beach and islands from here. Just before the lot, look for Webhannet Road going south where limited roadside parking may be found in one mile. Look for Atlantic Avenue going north where a large town lot provides parking and beach access for residents.

d **Wells Harbor** at the end of Atlantic Avenue provides another chance to scan for ocean and beach birds. In winter, scoters, Common Goldeneyes, and loons frequent the harbor itself, and the fishing boats draw larger numbers of gulls. Common Terns and occasional Least Terns feed along the shore waters in summer.

In tourist season, there is a fee for parking in the town lot. It is free in the off-season but facilities are closed. The harbor itself can also be reached directly from Route 1 along Harbor Road. This drive offers better mud flats and pannes that often prove productive.

Directions: from Route 1 take Mile Road east. Just before reaching the dead end at the town parking lot, explore Webhannet Road south and Atlantic Avenue north.

e **The Rachel Carson National Wildlife Refuge** protects a number of scattered salt marshes and estuaries from the New Hampshire border to Cape Elizabeth. The headquarters in Wells maintains a one-mile walking trail that meanders through white pine forest containing a good number of Pine Warblers, and a salt marsh with an equally good number of Saltmarsh Sharp-tailed Sparrows.

Directions: from Route 1 turn east onto Route 9. The entrance is 0.7 mile from the intersection.

f **Fortunes Rocks Beach** stretches just below Biddeford Pool. The sweeping half moon bay offers excellent views of sea ducks in winter, terns in summer, and roosting shorebirds in migration, especially on the north end of the beach. Purple Sandpipers are regular on the rocky shoreline. There is a freshwater pond adjacent to Marie Joseph Academy and three more adjacent to the road on the southern end of the beach, all worth a scan for ducks and gulls.

Directions: See directions to Biddeford Pool (#6) but instead turn right at the intersection.

GREATER PORTLAND AND CASCO BAY

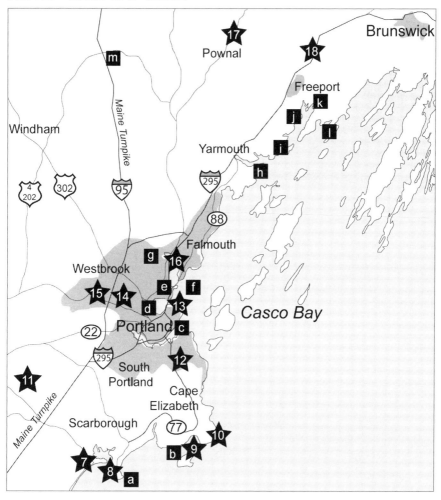

The Portland area delivers wonderful birding year round. With its variety of habitats: sand beaches, rocky beaches, granite cliffs, estuaries, fresh and saltwater marshes, deciduous and pine forests, urban, suburban, and rural parkland, Portland provides a transition point for many species. This is the northern boundary for southern warblers. It is where Nelson's and Saltmarsh Sharp-tailed Sparrows overlap and hybridize. Brown Thrashers, Eastern Towhees, and Grasshopper Sparrows become scarce north of Portland.

Portland is Maine's largest community, boasting many tourist amenities. Most of the area's best birding spots are less than 30 minutes from downtown hotels and the airport, making birding easy while on a business trip. Maine Audubon is located in nearby Falmouth and two other Maine Audubon sanctuaries are located within Cumberland County.

The metropolitan area includes several communities. The city of Portland is known for sites like Back Cove, Eastern Promenade, Evergreen Cemetery, Capisic Pond, The Dragon Fields, and Portland Harbor. South Portland is home to Hinckley Park. Cape Elizabeth encompasses Dyer Point, Kettle Cove, and Crescent Beach State Park. Scarborough Marsh dominates the town of Scarborough, where birders also spend time at Pine Point, Prout's Neck, and Fuller Farm. Falmouth lies just north of Portland, and features Mackworth Island and Maine Audubon headquarters at Gilsland Farm.

It is common for birders and vacationers to visit or drive through the northeast corner of Cumberland County. I-295 and Route 1 both carry motorists to other destinations along Maine's coast. Yarmouth is popular with sailors and is a jumping off point for several islands in Casco Bay. Freeport is the famous headquarters of L.L. Bean, and the outlets surrounding it have turned the town into a shopping destination.

There are seven local birding sites in Freeport that can be interesting. Florida Lake, Mast Landing Audubon Sanctuary, and Wolfe's Neck Woods State Park are all close to L.L. Bean and offer a little bit of general birding, perhaps while others in the family shop. South Freeport Landing and Winslow Park are productive in winter. Sandy Point Beach can be extraordinary for viewing the autumn migration and winter sea ducks. Bradbury Mountain is pleasant for hiking and cross-country skiing, but is most interesting for its spring hawk migration through April and mid-May. None of these sites take long to bird.

Trip planning: www.VisitPortland.com or 207-772-5800

Official Maine Birding Trail Sites

⭐ **7** **Scarborough Marsh** is one of the top places to bird in Maine. It encompasses more than 3,000 acres of estuarine saltmarsh, 15% of the state's total. It produces the most abundant and diverse flocks of waterfowl and wading birds. Canada Geese arrive in large numbers in mid-March, signaling the beginning of northward migration. Snow Geese follow in smaller numbers. By mid-April, American Black Ducks, Mallards, Northern Pintails, Northern Shovelers, Gadwall, Blue-winged

and Green-winged Teal congregate. Wood Ducks and Hooded Mergansers nest in boxes along the wooded edges of the marsh. Nelson's and Saltmarsh Sharp-tailed Sparrows overlap and interbreed here. Seaside Sparrows are rare in Maine but have become annual in recent years here. Flocks of Glossy Ibis forage throughout the marsh. Great Blue Herons and Snowy Egrets are common. Little Blue Herons are regularly spotted. Great Egrets and Tri-colored Herons are uncommon, but may be seen later in the summer. Black-crowned Night-herons nest offshore a couple miles away and sometimes venture into the marsh. In late summer and fall, migrating shorebirds collect in the marsh. In winter, Rough-legged Hawks turn up regularly and Snowy Owls are possible.

The marsh is very wide and the Spartina grass is thick, hiding many of the pools. This is a good place for a spotting scope. There is a seasonal Maine Audubon Nature Center midway along Pine Point Road. The center can provide trail maps, birding tips, and a bird-sighting register. It also rents canoes for access into the estuary. In season, there are regularly scheduled nature trips available from Maine Audubon.

From the Maine Audubon parking lot, scan the marsh slowly, noting the walking path and bridge to the south. Take the time to explore the pools on the opposite side of the road. This is one of the best places for a close view of shorebirds, particularly Greater and Lesser Yellowlegs, but also Semipalmated Sandpipers, Stilt Sandpipers, and Short-billed Dowitchers. In winter, scan the marsh for raptors, including Rough-legged Hawk, Short-eared Owl, and Snowy Owl.

Just a short drive farther south along Pine Point Road, Eastern Road (now a walk/bike path) provides an opportunity to stroll deeply into the marsh along some of the best salt flats in the refuge. This is the preferred place to see both Sharp-tailed Sparrows and, in some years, a Seaside Sparrow. High tide has a tendency to push sparrows closer to the path for easy viewing. Willets breed here. Red Knots, Hudsonian Godwits, and Stilt Sandpipers are regular in small numbers in August–September. Rarities occur along this path, so don't rush. Be aware that Harbor Seals swim all the way into the marsh at high tide and may be seen when least expected. Note: Facilities at the Maine Audubon Nature Center are seasonal.

Directions: Route 1 through Scarborough passes through the north edge of Scarborough Marsh. Drive south along Route 1 from Portland, cross the marsh, and turn left onto Pine Point Road (Route 9) at Dunstan Corner. Proceed to the Maine Audubon Nature Center parking lot to begin the adventure. From Saco, drive north on Route 1. Pine Point Road will be a right turn at Dunstan Corner.

———❖———

8 **Pine Point** is an often extraordinary birding site. The outflow from several streams mixes with the incoming tide of the Scarborough Marsh, then squeezes through a narrow channel to the Atlantic. This concentrates a rich food source for birds (and Harbor Seals). Gulls and shorebirds are the primary benefactors. Herring, Ring-billed, and Greater Black-backed Gulls are abundant year-round. From August through October there are often over a thousand Bonaparte's Gulls here. Common Black-headed Gulls and Little Gulls occasionally associate with them. Semipalmated Sandpipers and Plovers are plentiful in late summer, to be replaced by Dunlin later in autumn. In the height of the season, Hudsonian Godwits sometimes turn up. Stay alert for White-rumped, Pectoral, Stilt, and Baird's Sandpipers.

Be sure to check the ocean-side beach at Pine Point. From fall through spring, the waters usually contain scoters, eiders, grebes, and loons. This beach is good for Sanderlings any time of year. Where gulls flock, scan for a vagrant Little Gull among them, or perhaps roosting on its own. (Look for its small size and dark underwing.) The jetty on the far north end of the beach is attractive to terns and it is possible to find any combination of species roosting here in August and September. The jetty and channel are top sites to look for Roseate Terns, particularly around breakfast time. Forster's Tern is rare in the state, but it shows up here occasionally. At dusk in the off-season, rare sightings of Short-eared and Snowy Owls have been reported. The Lighthouse Inn at the corner of Pine Point Road and King Street is closed in winter and serves as a good place from which to scan the beach.

Directions: from Route 1 in Scarborough and Scarborough Marsh, continue along Pine Point Road (Route 9) until it bends abruptly south right toward Old Orchard Beach. Instead, turn left and follow to the town landing. There are two lefts–the first is East Grand; the second is King Street. Both end at the town landing.

⭐**9** **Kettle Cove** is well known to birders. On the DeLorme Maine Atlas, it is part of what is named Seal Cove and lies at the far eastern end of Crescent Beach State Park. Kettle Cove's advantage is that it extends into the cove, offering a northwestern view along the beach for shorebirds and

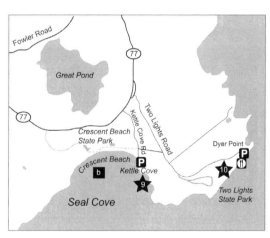

gulls, a western view into the cove, a southwestern scope of the distant fields on Richmond Island, and a southern observation of open ocean. Look for Common Loons, Common Eiders, Horned Grebes, Long-tailed Ducks, Common Goldeneyes, and any of the scoters. Mallards and American Black Ducks probe the shallows. Brant are scarce in Maine but they favor this spot, especially in late winter. Flocks of gulls usually roost on the spit. This spit sometimes attracts Horned Larks in winter, and any flock should be checked for Lapland Longspurs and Snow Buntings. There are no facilities.

Directions: Kettle Cove Road is just 0.2 mile south of the entrance to Two Lights State Park or 0.8 mile north of Crescent Beach State Park. Look for an innocuous turn onto Ocean House Road and follow the sign to "Kettle Cove Area."

10 ★ Dyer Point forms the easternmost point of land in the Portland area and is a pleasure any time of year. The point sits at the end of Two Lights Road and locals sometimes refer to the entire area as "Two Lights." The prime viewing spot is next to The Lobster Shack at Dyer Point. In summer, this is one of Maine's best eating experiences. Lobsters and clams are steamed on demand, and nothing can compare to eating such a feast on picnic tables overlooking the ocean. The rocky promontory pokes well into the Atlantic and it is possible to see every alcid in fall and winter, less frequently in summer. Expect two and perhaps all three species of scoter. Common Eiders are abundant while King Eiders are occasional. In winter, Buffleheads, Long-tailed Ducks, Black Guillemots, Horned Grebes and Great Cormorants are present in varying numbers. Scan the Common Loons for a Red-throated Loon or even a vagrant Pacific Loon. In August and September, particularly in bad weather, this is one of the best places in Maine to look from land for Greater, Sooty, and Manx Shearwaters, as well as Parasitic and Pomarine Jaegers. Northern Gannets are often visible, though usually distant. In winter, Purple Sandpipers are possible along the waterline. Facilities are seasonal.

On the return to Route 77 along Two Lights Road, some birders enjoy exploring Two Lights State Park, which has a better view to the southeast. The park offers the same oceanic possibilities as Dyer Point, but the brushy foliage and mature conifer thickets make for a good migrant trap in spring. Owls are occasional in these thickets. The park gate is closed in winter and there is no convenient place to park outside the gate. Be alert to icy and snowy conditions that can make this section of the rocky coast treacherous.

Directions: from north or south take Route 77 to Two Lights Road, and follow to the end. From the north, Two Lights Road is about 5.4 miles from the bridge in Portland. From the south, it's 5.5 miles from the intersections of Routes 207 and 77 in Scarborough.

⭐**11 Fuller Farm**, owned and managed by the Scarborough Land
Conservation Trust, is just 25 minutes and 14 miles from downtown
Portland. It is a conserved 220-acre tract with 3100 feet of frontage on
the Nonesuch River, the 23-mile stream that empties into Scarborough
Marsh. The parcel retains about 70 acres of grassland and hay fields,
ideal for Savannah Sparrows, Bobolinks, and Eastern Meadowlarks.
The rest is mixed forest with enough early succession of alders and
bushes to enable songbird variety. At least twenty-one species of warbler and thirteen sparrows have been documented. Eastern Towhees,
Indigo Buntings, and both Black-billed Cuckoos and Yellow-billed
Cuckoos work the edges between field and woods. Northern Goshawk
and American Kestrel are breeders and many other raptors are regularly seen in migration. Moose, deer, fox, coyote, and beaver may also
grab attention. There are no facilities.

*Directions: from Exit 42 off the Maine Turnpike (I-95): at the first
light, go left onto Payne Road, and left at the next light onto Holmes Road.
Continue to the second intersection marked by a blinking light and turn
right on Broadturn Road. Go approximately 1 mile to the farm's parking
area on the right. There are no buildings and the parking area is small and
easily overlooked. Look for the kiosk in the parking area next to a large field.
From Scarborough Marsh, Broadturn Road is directly across from Pine
Point Road (Route 9) at Dunstan Corner. Fuller Farm is 4.1 miles northwest of Route 1.*

⭐**12 Hinckley Park**
is a wooded hide-
away in the center
of residential South
Portland that is very
popular with dog
walkers. Its popular-
ity with birders is
due to the notable

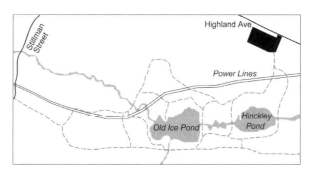

variety of habitat contained within its 40 acres. Trails surround two small
ponds at the heart of the park; one is an old ice pond. On the near side,
the terrain drops steeply from the trail to the ponds, providing scrubby
cover and changeable slope that birds relish. Power lines behind the trails

provide a grassy area bordering oak woods on one side and pine on the other. All these transition zones between field, woods, slope, and water, and between pine, grass, brush, and oak account for the habitat's richness. Expect a good variety of warblers in spring, including occasional Blue-winged Warblers, and check for Rough-winged Swallows over the ponds.

Directions: from downtown Portland, take the bridge to South Portland along Route 77. After crossing the bridge, continue for 0.8 mile along Route 77 (Ocean Street), and then turn right onto Highland Avenue. Follow for 0.3 mile and look for the park entrance on the left. From I-295, drive south toward South Portland, crossing the Fore River to Exit 4. Follow the signs to Route 1 (Main Street) in South Portland. Proceed south on Route 1 (Main Street) and turn left onto Broadway. Follow Broadway 2.3 miles to Route 77 (Ocean Street), turn right onto Ocean Street, and follow 0.2 mile to the right turn onto Highland Avenue.

13 Eastern Promenade is at the northeast end of Portland, extending into Casco Bay. There is a wide boulevard that sweeps the length of the bluff overlooking the bay. The panoramic, street-level views from Eastern Prom-enade are splendid, but the multi-use path that runs along the water is what at-tracts birders. Find Cutter Street at the eastern end of

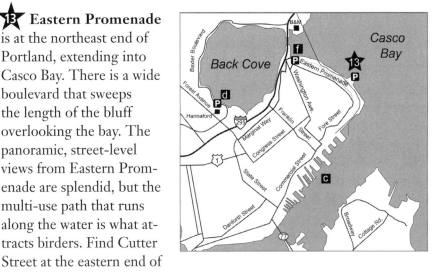

Eastern Promenade where the boulevard rounds to the south. There is a public boat landing and small parking lot at the bottom that provides a much closer look at the bay. A good scan should turn up many of the common sea ducks, a variety of gulls, and perhaps a Bald Eagle. Walk the path toward the bridges, staying alert for uncommon waterfowl and gulls. Song Sparrows overwinter in the brush along this path and other specialties such as Orange-crowned Warbler sometimes turn up, especially in late autumn. Toilet facilities at the boat launch on Cutter Street are seasonal.

Directions: Washington Avenue intersects Eastern Promenade at its westernmost point. Follow around to Cutter Street and descend to the parking and boat launch area.

14 **Evergreen Cemetery** and its surrounding 100-acre woodland are well known as the final resting place for many of Maine's famous sons and daughters. It is also known statewide as a warbler haven in May. Every warbler that breeds in Maine—and some that don't—turn up here. Blue-winged Warblers

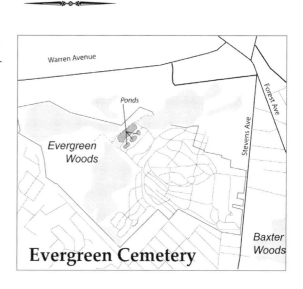

are seen regularly each spring. Blackpoll, Mourning, and Cape May Warblers breed farther north but stop here along their way. Yellow-throated, Kentucky, and Worm-eating Warblers make rare appearances. Maine Audubon leads frequent bird walks at the cemetery in May. Check the schedule at www.maineaudubon.org and follow the menu to Field Trips. The best area for birding is around the ponds at the back of the cemetery. Amble slowly around the trail behind the ponds. Be sure to guard against ticks, which can be present in the brush beyond the trail. In May, this is one of the best places to explore if on a limited time schedule. There are no facilities.

Directions: from I-295, take Forest Avenue north at Exit 6. Continue north about a mile to a five-street intersection. Make a gentle left turn onto Woodford Street in front of the Dunkin' Donuts and follow to Stevens Avenue. Turn right onto Stevens, go past Deering High School, and look on the left for Evergreen Cemetery in about half a mile. The street address is 672 Stevens Avenue. Enter through the cemetery's second gate (past Walton Street) and proceed to the ponds at the back of the cemetery grounds.

15 **Capisic Pond** is Portland's largest freshwater pond. The 18-acre park that contains the pond borders on the Fore River, and it is this combination of river, pond, and green space that is so attractive to waterfowl, wading birds, warblers, and orioles. Orchard Orioles and Warbling Vireos are uncommon breeders in the uplands. Wilson's Snipe, Sora, and Virginia Rails breed in the cattails. It's a good place to look for migrating sparrows in spring and fall, and for fruit-loving birds in winter. It doesn't take long to bird this park, and it is often done in combination with Evergreen Cemetery, which is only five minutes away. There are no facilities.

Directions: from I-295 in Portland, exit west onto Congress Street at exit 5 (5a from the south, 5b from the north). Follow Congress Street for less than half a mile, then turn right onto Stevens Avenue, which is Route 9 East. In 0.2 mile, turn left at the light onto Frost/Capisic Street. In a moment Frost Street splits left. Follow Capisic straight ahead, looking for Macy Street on the right. A small parking lot is available in front of the Capisic Pond Park sign. From Evergreen Cemetery, turn right onto Stevens Avenue and follow 1.2 miles to the right turn onto Frost/Capisic Street. Follow as above.

16 Maine Audubon has its headquarters at **Gilsland Farm** in Falmouth, just across the Route 1 bridge from Portland. The 65-acre sanctuary is open and free for visitors during daylight hours. There is a store at the visitor center that is well stocked with field guides, optics, accessories—plus

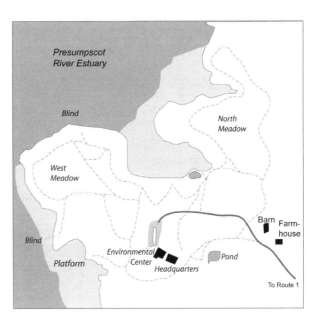

information about the most recent sightings and hot spots. Feeders around the center attract Purple and House Finches, Goldfinches, sparrows, and a variety of other seedeaters. Tree and Barn Swallows nest on site. Bobolinks and Eastern Meadowlarks populate the meadows and are seen from the walking paths.

Three trails provide a total of 2.5 miles of easy walking and birding. The West Meadow Trail winds through a small, forested wetland before circling the meadow. There are two blinds off the trail that allow good looks at the Presumpscot River estuary. Watch for waterfowl in winter and shorebirds in summer. The Pond Meadow Trail ventures through mature hardwoods and hemlocks, continuing to an apple orchard and down to a pond where wading birds keep company with muskrats. The North Meadow Trail also passes through a grove of mature red oaks and hemlocks before entering the meadow. Canada Geese frequently forage this field in winter. It's also a good place for migrating hawks and owls. Spruce, red sumac, and speckled alder border the fields and are good for warblers.

Directions: from the north: take I-295 to Exit 10 and then go left on Bucknam Road. At the light turn right onto U.S. Route 1 and continue south for one mile. After the blinking light at the intersection of Routes 1 and 88, the entrance to Gilsland Farm Road is on the right at the light blue sign. From the south: take I-295 to Exit 9. Continue 1.9 miles north on U.S. Route 1 and turn left onto Gilsland Farm Road at the light blue sign, immediately before the intersection of Routes 1 and 88.

17 Bradbury Mountain State Park is open year-round. In winter, it is known for its trails for cross-country skiing and snowmobiling. These trails are a natural for hiking in summer. Pines dominate the park and the birding features mostly common species much of the year. However, during spring migration in April, this can be one of Maine's premier hawk-watching sites on a southerly or southwesterly breeze. There are fees year round. Facilities are seasonal.

Directions: from I-295, take Freeport Exit 22 and head west off the highway. Turn left and follow the sign toward Bradbury Mountain State Park. After 4.5 miles, turn right onto Route 9 (Hallowell Road). The park is 0.5 mile ahead on the left.

18 The Florida Lake Conservation and Recreation Area is a birder-friendly property preserved by the Town of Freeport and its partners. Its 167 acres protect a small lake and surrounding uplands. Several trails wind through differing habitats, including emergent marsh, shrub swamp, forested wetland, and wooded upland. As a result, a large number of species can be found here. The lake is attractive to waterfowl in migration, and some linger through summer. American Bitterns and other wading birds frequently take advantage of the shallows. Florida Lake has also proven to be productive in winter, with noteworthy sightings of Pine Grosbeaks, Bohemian Waxwings, and Northern Shrikes.

Directions: from I-295, take Freeport Exit 22 and head west off the highway. Florida Lake is 3.1 miles from the I-295 exit. From the exit, turn right onto Route 136/125, and continue to follow Route 125 when it diverges from 136 a half-mile later. After about 1.5 miles, look for the Florida Lake sign on the right. The access road runs behind some small homes to reach the parking lot 500 feet into the property.

Additional Sites:

a Prout's Neck lies opposite Pine Point and overlooks much of the same water. (The journey from Pine Point to Prout's Neck requires a complete circumnavigation of Scarborough Marsh, so there is no quick way to get closer to birds seen on the distant shore.) The view from Prout's Neck is accessible from the Ferry Beach boat launch, preferably at high tide. There is a hefty parking fee here in summer but it is free in the off-season. The point is privately owned and inaccessible. On the west side of Prout's Neck, Scarborough Beach State Park provides another half moon beach and open ocean. Look for loons and grebes, particularly Red-necked Grebes. Rarely, King Eiders mix with the Common Eiders in winter. All three scoters are possible. Check for wintering Harlequin Ducks at the rocky northern point of the beach.

Directions: Prout's Neck is reached from Route 1 in Scarborough by way of Black Point Road (Route 207). Follow to the end, looking for Scarborough Beach State Park on the left and the turn for Ferry Beach on the right. From Cape Elizabeth and the Two Lights/Crescent Beach area, follow Route 77 south until it splits with Route 207.

b **Crescent Beach State Park** in Cape Elizabeth is a popular spot year round due to its sheltered southern exposure. The accumulation of people tends to keep the birds off the beach after early morning. In the summer, the park gate is closed until 9am, but it is permissible to park on the main road, taking care not to block the entrance. In winter, this is the only option and there can be many vehicles parked on a nice day. Sanderlings sometimes work the beach even in the dead of winter. On the fringe of the winter season, stay alert for Horned Larks, Lapland Longspurs, and Snow Buntings. The beach is indeed a mile-long crescent, so any seabirds present are easily observable. The woods and a freshwater pond make the park noteworthy. The spruce-fir mix is more typical of habitat farther up the coast, increasing the variety of conifer-loving thrushes, warblers, kinglets, and finches. There is also a trail into the woods near the entrance gate. A small pond is just west of the parking lot on the approach to the beach. Most of it is screened by cattails, but this is the domain of nesting Marsh Wrens and Swamp Sparrows. Ducks and teal are sometimes present in summer. There are seasonal facilities and fees.

Directions: from north or south take Route 77 to the park entrance.

c **Portland Harbor** is home to the state's fish pier. Gulls naturally flock to it and all the common species are present. Iceland and Glaucous Gulls are sometimes intermixed in winter. The fish pier is private property, but many gulls can be scanned from a distance, especially along the rooftops of the warehouses. Certainly the Portland Fish Pier is likely to be busy. The Cat ferry to Nova Scotia docks at the Maine State Pier and is also a good place from which to scan. The surrounding area is a commercial and tourist hub, so there are many facilities and amenities.

Directions: Route 1A is called Commercial Street through this area of the Old Port and congregations of gulls are obvious. Portland visitors can count on local maps and signs to reach the harbor. To reach it from out of town, exit from I-295 at Franklin Street and follow the signs to the waterfront.

d **Back Cove** is perhaps the most prominent landmark in Portland since much of the city is built around it. In fact, Route 1 (locally named Baxter Boulevard) is forced to circle two-thirds of Back Cove's circumference. A hiking path surrounds this large inland bay, making it readily accessible. Twice a day, Back Cove fills and empties with the tide, so twice a day the birding opportunities change. The better birding tends to be at high tide when gulls and waterfowl are present. As tide falls, the revealed flats attract shorebirds in season. At low tide, gulls congregate in large numbers on the elevated portions of the flats, often within close view of the access points. Herring, Ring-billed, and Great Black-backed Gulls are abundant. Look also for Laughing, Iceland, Glaucous, and Lesser Black-backed Gulls (in descending order of likelihood). Bonaparte's Gulls are regular before and after their breeding seasons.

Seasonal changes are just as remarkable as tidal changes. Buffle-heads, Common Eiders, Common Goldeneyes, and both Common and Red-breasted Mergansers are possible throughout the winter months. Mallards and American Black Ducks are inevitable at any time of year. Greater and Lesser Scaup are occasional. In April, any migrating duck might turn up here as it waits for fresh water to open farther north. Ironically, summer is the slow season. In the fall shorebird migration, Maine's most common shorebirds—Semipalmated and Least Sand-pipers, Semipalmated and Black-bellied Plovers, Greater and Lesser Yellowlegs—are probable. Ruddy Turnstones, Short-billed Dowitchers, and later-arriving Dunlin are less common. A few White-rumped and Western Sandpipers make annual appearances. In some years Peregrine Falcons have taken to wintering over in Portland. Scan the building tops and spires for them. The athletic fields that stretch between Back Cove and I-295 produce numerous instances of migrating sparrows and other field-loving birds, including American Pipits, Horned Larks, Lapland Longspurs, and Snow Buntings.

Directions: the public parking lot lies alongside the cove near a large Hannaford supermarket on the southern edge. From the south on I-295, take Exit 6B onto Forest Avenue North. Look immediately for a right turn onto Baxter Boulevard, then another right at the next light onto Preble Street Extension. The parking lot is just to the left. From the north on I-295, exit onto Baxter Boulevard and follow it around the cove until reaching the light at Preble Street Extension. Turn left and the parking lot will be ahead on the left.

e **The Wastewater Treatment Plant** is a natural extension of any visit to Back Cove. Most of the likely species are the same as Back Cove, but the narrowness of the adjacent inlet enables a closer view. Iceland and Lesser Black-backed Gulls appear infrequently in this cove. Barrow's Goldeneyes are sometimes seen in winter.

Directions: the plant is accessed from Marginal Way, which parallels I-295. Get off I-295 at Exit 7 and take the first left onto Marginal Way.

The plant is just over half a mile straight ahead. From Back Cove, it is even easier; just continue along Preble Street Extension and turn left onto Marginal Way. In either case, drive as far as possible and park just after the underpass, but before the gate to the treatment plant. There is plenty of open viewing area here and a small walkway along the west side of the inlet, as well as the paved hiking path that heads east around the Eastern Promenade.

f **Mackworth Island** is productive year round. The hundred-acre island sits at the mouth of the Presumpscot River overlooking a wide swath of Casco Bay. It is home to the Baxter State School for the Deaf, which dominates the high ground. A security guard is posted at the entrance, but the island is public and there is parking just beyond the guard booth. A footpath circles the island near the shoreline, providing views of rocky shores and mud flats. The mile-long path is popular, so expect a leisurely pace. Scan for waterfowl at high tide and shorebirds at low tide. In winter, eiders, grebes, scoters, goldeneyes, Long-tailed Ducks, and Buffleheads are prominent. Greater Scaup show up in some years. In spring, Pine Warblers arrive and begin singing in late April. Other migrants follow in May and a dozen different species may be encountered during a stroll. However, most passerines do not linger to breed and they move on before Memorial Day. In summer and autumn, the causeway is productive for Semipalmated and Black-bellied Plovers.

Directions: from I-295 in Portland, head north and bear right at Exit 9 on Route 1 North towards Falmouth Foreside. After crossing the bridge, look for the third right turn (Andrews Avenue) and follow the signs to Baxter School. From the north, the turn is on the left just a mile past Maine Audubon's Gilsland Farm.

g **The Dragon Fields** is the popular nickname for an old, capped landfill on the Portland/Falmouth line that has become prominent among local birders. It earned its nickname because it is behind the Dragon Cement plant and quarry on Route 9 in Portland. The capped landfill has created a weedy knoll that is maintained by the city for sparrows and specialty birds year round, particularly in autumn. Dick-cissels are vagrants in Maine but they have appeared intermittently in past autumns. Grasshopper Sparrows have turned up here, as have Lapland Longspurs. Because of the height of the mound, it also offers good looks at passing raptors. In spring, the path into the area is lined with shrubs and secondary growth, attracting to warblers. In autumn, the hill explodes with the color of blooming asters, making the site alluring. Just in front of this site, Portland has created a canine exercise area called Quarry Park Dog Run that is served by a small parking lot. Avoid the fenced area and instead follow the path directly uphill to where The Dragon Fields are located.

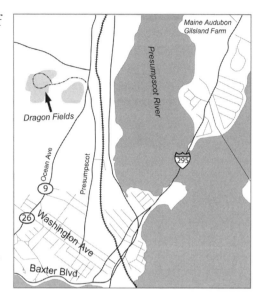

Directions: from I-295 in Portland, exit west onto Washington Avenue and proceed 0.75 mile to Ocean Avenue. Turn right, follow for 1.1 mile and look for the trail entry on the left, just past the Dragon Cement plant and the junction with Presumpscot Street. From Falmouth, take Bucknam Road at the I-295 intersection, then immediately left onto Route 9 (Middle Road). Follow 2.3 miles just past Ledgewood Drive. There are no signs, but the area is clearly fenced and there is a large cellphone tower across the street.

h The importance of **Sandy Point Beach** for avid birders has only lately become clear, since the north end of Cousins Island in Yarmouth has proven to be a migrant fallout spot in August and September. Migrating birds that have drifted out onto the offshore islands of Casco Bay find their way back to the mainland over Cousins Island and its causeway. The brushy area beneath the power lines at Sandy Point creates an attractive staging area. When wind conditions are right—northwesterly breezes are best, easterly worst—it is nice to sit in the parking lot and watch a confusing fall of warblers swarming the bushes. Expect a few passing hawks as well. This is also an excellent spot for sea ducks in winter, featuring flocks of Common Eiders and impressive numbers of Common Goldeneyes, Buffleheads, Long-tailed Ducks, and all three scoters. Ruddy Ducks and Greater Scaup recur regularly.

Directions: from I-295 in Yarmouth, exit onto Route 1 South, then bear left almost immediately onto Route 88. Follow for 1.5 miles, then turn left, following the signs to Cousins Island. The Sandy Point Beach parking lot is on the left immediately after the causeway. From Falmouth and Cumber-

*land, follow Route 88 north to Yarmouth, turn right toward Cousins Island
and follow the signs as above.*

i **Winslow Park** is best in winter. It sits at the mouth of the Harraseeket River and commands a wide view of Casco Bay. During the
coldest part of
winter, the bay may
become completely
frozen. Otherwise,
it is a great place
to view Common
Eiders. Like nearby
South Freeport
Town Landing,
Common and
Barrow's Gold-
eneyes are often
seen, sometimes in
impressive num-
bers. Red-breasted
Mergansers,
Common Loons,

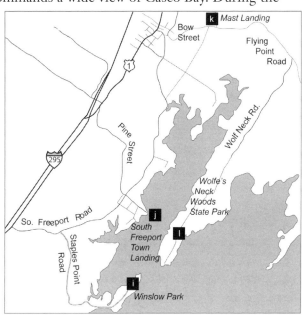

Buffleheads, and Long-tailed Ducks are all likely. Greater Scaup are
occasionally spotted. There is a seasonal campground at Winslow Park
and admission is charged in summer. Facilities are closed in winter but
the parking area is plowed throughout the off-season.

*Directions: from Route 1, turn onto South Freeport Road. Follow 0.7 mile
and turn right onto Staples Point Road. Follow to Winslow Park at the end.*

j **South Freeport Landing** is a working dock on the Harraseeket
River. It looks across at Wolf Neck and downriver toward Winslow
Park. In winter, it is one of the more likely places in Maine to find
Barrow's Goldeneyes, often close to the docks. It is not unusual to find
Common and Barrow's Goldeneyes near each other for easy compari-
son. Long-tailed Ducks and Red-breasted Mergansers also favor these
waters. Large concentrations of Common Eiders are usually present in
the distance. There are no facilities.

*Directions: from Route 1 at the junction with I-295 in Freeport, proceed
south on Route 1 and then take an almost immediate left onto Pine Street.*

Follow about 2 miles to the end. From Route 1 in Yarmouth, turn right onto South Freeport Road just before the Freeport Trading Post. Follow for 1.9 miles, turn right onto Main Street and follow downhill to the dock.

k **Mast Landing** is a 140-acre Maine Audubon Sanctuary located just a three-minute drive from L.L. Bean and downtown Freeport.

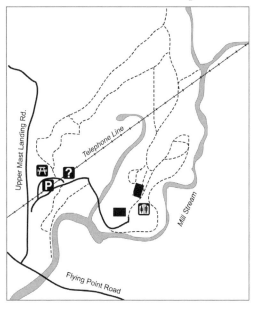

For birders, the sanctuary's chief asset is its proximity to town. It provides pleasant trails for hiking and birding while family members shop. There are a variety of trails passing through mixed forest habitat, the remnants of old orchards, and the Mill Stream Trail, which passes through riparian habitat. This is not a place to look for uncommon species, but Black-capped Chickadees, Red-breasted Nuthatches, Golden-crowned Kinglets, Downy and Hairy Wood-peckers, as well as a variety of common warblers are likely. Facilities are primitive and seasonal. In summer, Maine Audubon operates a popular day camp for children. In winter, hikers and cross-country skiers often pack the trails.

Directions: *from downtown Freeport on Route 1, turn east onto Bow Street from the middle of town in front of L.L. Bean. Follow 1.1 miles and turn left onto Upper Mast Landing Road. The sanctuary is just 0.2 mile ahead on the right.*

l **Wolfe's Neck Woods State Park** is another nice place to relax and enjoy the outdoors. This is not a place known for unusual birds but the common species, the pleasantness of the park, and its proximity to town guarantee plenty of visitors. There is a trail system providing several miles of varied hiking, including nearly one mile that is wheelchair accessible. The Harraseeket Hike is a 1.8 mile loop with some steep and uneven terrain that traverses woods and river-

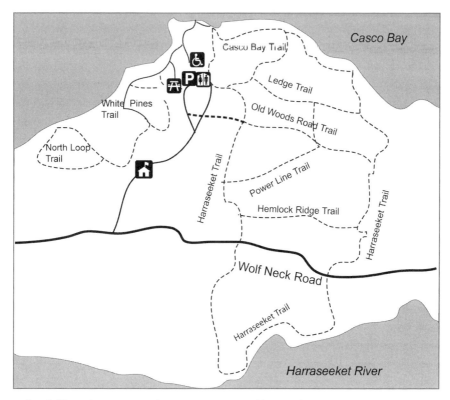

side cliffs. The 1.25-mile Casco Bay Walk wanders past salt marsh, mud flats, and an Osprey nesting island. There are stands of conifers that are more typical of habitat farther north. Admission is charged in summer. Facilities are seasonal. There are often several different spellings of this park's name. While the official name of the park is Wolfe's Neck Woods, the road through it is Wolf Neck Road. Ironically, the area is named for the first European family that settled here in 1733, spelled Woolfe.

Directions: from downtown Freeport on Route 1, take Bow Street east from the middle of town in front of L.L. Bean and follow for 2.5 miles. Bow Street becomes Flying Point Road after passing Mast Landing. Bear right onto Wolf Neck Road and proceed 2.25 miles to the park entrance.

Gray Meadow is a wetland bisected by an old trolley line. This creates a walking path directly though a sedge marsh, something that would not be permitted today but does provide a unique opportunity for birders. The first few hundred yards are through a forested woodland of tangled growth and hemlocks. Blackburnian and Black-throated

Blue Warblers are found within this stretch. As the path enters the meadow, secondary growth attracts many warblers. American Redstarts, Common Yellowthroats, and Chestnut-sided and Yellow Warblers are abundant throughout the meadow. Wilson's Warblers can sometimes be found in surprising numbers. In the middle of the meadow, Sora and Virginia Rails call, Marsh Wrens chatter, and Great Blue Herons hunt silently. When the path reenters the woods on the far side of the meadow, Northern Parula and Black-throated Green Warblers are common. The line is also used by all-terrain vehicles and snowmobiles.

Directions: Gray is located at Exit 63 on the Maine Turnpike. From the center of Gray, go south on Route 100 for 1.8 miles. Turn left on Long Hill Road. The trail is only 0.1 mile ahead, but it is not well marked and there is limited parking by the side of the road. The trail continues on both sides of the road, but the meadow is along the trail to the left.

MID-COAST

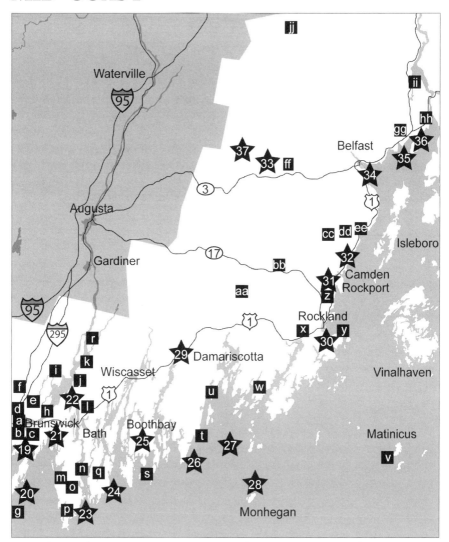

The Mid-Coast region represents the "Maine" many first-time visitors imagine: lighthouses, quaint villages, sailboats, lobster pounds, and idyllic inns. Fractured by glaciers, pounded by surf, and sliced by rivers, there is no place on America's eastern seaboard that has more bays, sounds, coves, and estuaries. These geologic features contribute to the overall excellence of birding experiences.

Because each peninsula in the Mid-Coast area extends into the ocean and away from Route 1, the communities that lie off the beaten track enjoy a slower pace than the oceanside towns farther south and those to the north around Rockland, Camden, and Acadia National Park. Boothbay Harbor is best known among these, but Phippsburg, Georgetown, and Pemaquid share similar attributes.

Two of Maine's largest rivers—the Kennebec and the Androscoggin—converge shortly before entering the ocean, joining at a place aptly named Merrymeeting Bay. This is a major migration stop for waterfowl that feed on the wild rice in the rivers. Bald Eagles are common nesters around the bay.

Pemaquid Point is a good example of the fragmentation of the coastline. Two of Maine's best birding beaches are located in this region. North of Popham Beach State Park and Reid State Park, there are no long stretches of sand beach before Prince Edward Island, Canada.

One of Maine's largest Great Blue Heron colonies is located on Wreck Island in Muscongus Bay. Black-crowned Night-herons are uncommon residents of the bay. At the outskirts of the bay lies Eastern Egg Rock, the southernmost colony of Atlantic Puffins in the world. Hog Island is located off Bremen, renowned as the headquarters of National Audubon's Field Ornithology Camp. Roger Tory Peterson was its earliest instructor. The camp still operates today under the auspices of Maine Audubon.

Maine's coast from Thomaston to Camden is a stretch of working villages. Thomaston is noted for boat building, Rockland for its fish cannery, and Camden/Rockport for tourism and windjammer sailing vessels. The towns in Knox County have been dramatically revitalized in recent years. The new Project Puffin Visitor Center is located in Rockland. Ten miles offshore from Lincoln County, Monhegan Island is famous internationally. As a migrant trap, it has few rivals. Weskeag Marsh in Thomaston presents a different experience every time you visit. Arguably, it is second only to Scarborough Marsh in Scarborough as Maine's most productive wetland, but it receives far fewer visitors. The Mid-Coast has an unusually high number of small ponds and streams that attract waterfowl in migration, and many are adjacent to the road. In spring and autumn, just a quick "stop and peek" can bring rewards.

In response to tremendous development pressure, land trusts have sprung up along Maine's coast from Kittery to Calais, and some of the most effective are in the Mid-Coast area. Dozens of precious tracts have been preserved, and some offer good birding opportunities. Quiet islands, such as Vinalhaven, North Haven, and Islesboro lay just off-shore. A few pelagic birds can be glimpsed from the ferries that serve these islands each summer.

The coastline of Waldo County snuggles against Penobscot Bay, partially screened from ocean winds by peninsulas to the east and islands to the south. In winter, this topography produces sheltered pockets of waterfowl and gulls. The area was once famous for a different set of birds. Until the 1970s, area farms provided up to 200,000 chickens a day to giant poultry processing plants located in Belfast. Agricultural is still important to the county, but the coastal villages have retooled their maritime heritage buildings. Belfast was once home to eleven shipbuilders and Searsport boasted eleven more. Ship captain's mansions are now inns and dockside warehouses are restaurants and summer theaters.

Trip planning: www.MainesMidCoast.com or 800-872-6246.

Official Maine Birding Trail Sites

Cumberland & Sagadahoc Counties

19 **Maquoit Bay** is seasonally productive. Waterfowl collect here in fall, winter, and spring, and the mud flats attract shorebirds from late summer through autumn. At Wharton Point in Brunswick, the bay is both sheltered and shallow. Where falling tides expose acres of mud, look for sandpipers and plovers. Short-billed Dowitchers are common, and on rare occasions Long-billed have been identified. Dabblers such as American Black Ducks, Mallards, and American Widgeons take over as the tide

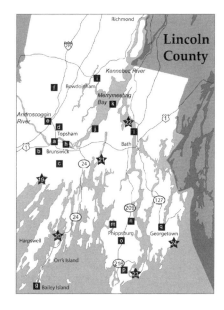

rises, accompanied by Great Blue Herons and occasional Snowy Egrets. During the colder months, diving ducks, notably Common Goldeneyes, Buffleheads, and Red-breasted Mergansers, can be found in the deeper channels at any tide.

Directions: in Brunswick, proceed south on Maine Street 0.2 mile past the intersection with Pleasant Hill Road to where Maine Street splits into Mere Point Road and Maquoit Road. Bear right at the split and follow Maquoit Road 1.9 miles to a small dirt parking lot at Wharton Point, which overlooks the bay at a good vantage point. There are no facilities.

20 Bowdoin College runs the **Coastal Studies Center**, which is located south of Brunswick on a peninsula of Orr's Island. Several different habitats exist on its 116 acres, including a spruce-fir swamp, fields, secondary growth, an old apple orchard, and communities of red pine, cedar, and oak-pine. There are walking trails throughout the forests and fields, including several trails that offer extensive ocean views. In May, there are frequent opportunities to enjoy an influx of summer warblers before the Arctic sea ducks have departed. June and July are promising for many of Maine's breeding songbirds.

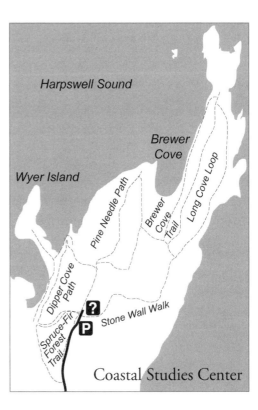

Directions: from Brunswick, take Route 123 (Harpswell Road) south 6.1 miles, turn left onto Mountain Road, proceed 2.7 miles and turn right onto Route 24 (Harpswell Island Road), proceed another 2.6 miles and turn right on Bayview Road. The entrance is 0.8 mile from the intersection and the parking lot is another 0.2 mile. From Cook's Corner on Route 1, take Route 24 for 11.25 miles to the right turn on Bayview Road.

21 Hamilton Audubon Sanctuary has a mile of trails through open meadows and mixed woodland along a peninsula beside the New Meadows River. Spurs to a freshwater marsh overlook vistas of Back Cove. Wood Ducks are sometimes found in the marsh of this former ice pond. Broad-winged Hawks and Pileated Woodpeckers move in and out of the forested areas. Bobolinks gurgle from the high grass of the meadows. Common Yellowthroats, American Redstarts, and Yellow, Chestnut-sided, Blackburnian, Nashville, Black-throated Green and Wilson's Warblers have been found here. Great-crested Flycatchers are noisy when present. The cove can be good for Common Eiders with their young in early summer and Snowy Egrets in late summer. At low tide, check mud flats for shorebirds.

Directions: take the New Meadows exit off Route 1, left onto New Meadows Road, which turns into Foster Point Road. The sanctuary is four miles from Route 1, three miles from the beginning of Foster Point Road.

---

22 Thorne Head Preserve is protected by the Kennebec Estuary Land Trust. Tall pines that grew here in the colonial era were used for masts in the King's navy. After extensive logging, the area became pasture land. Stone walls still wind through the woods. Today, the re-generated forest consists of white pine, hemlock, and oak, interspersed by vernal pools and freshwater marshes. The preserve provides a short pleasant hike for canopy warblers and vireos, especially Blackburnian Warblers.

Directions: from downtown Bath, follow High Street north 2 miles to the end.

---

23 Popham Beach State Park is remarkable year round, though the park is popular in summer. The best birding is at low tide. (Reid State Park across the river is best at high tide.) At low tide, it is possible to walk across the exposed sand bar to Fox Island. From this vantage point, it is easier to scan the deep waters for diving ducks. This may be the best spot in Maine to see Red-throated Loons. Common Loons and Eiders, Horned and Red-necked Grebes, at least two species of scoter, Black Guillemots, Red-breasted Mergansers, Buffleheads, and Long-tailed Ducks are typical sightings in colder months. Be aware that the incoming tide swallows the sand bar quickly. The inattentive risk a cold, wet return. Low tide exposes a large amount of sand where sandpipers and plovers stop to feed during migration. Piping Plovers sometimes

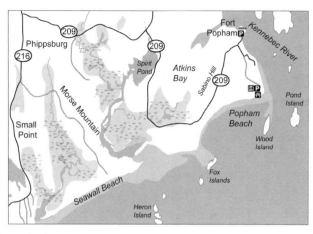

nest on the beach, though they usually breed in a conservation area separated from the park by the Morse River inlet. Least Terns nest near Piping Plovers and their smaller size helps distinguish them from the Common, Arctic, and Roseate Terns that fish these waters in summer. The most productive beach area is at the tidal flats of the Morse River inlet, so if the plovers and terns are not on the main beach, look for them across the inlet.

The salt marsh behind the beach and along Route 209 is habitat for Great Blue Herons and Snowy Egrets. American Bitterns, Green Herons, Black-crowned Night-Herons, and Great Egrets also turn up regularly. Pine Warblers breed among the pitch pines, while Yellow Warblers and Common Yellowthroats are often seen in the open shrubbery. Song and Swamp Sparrows are common, and when a Sharp-tailed Sparrow is encountered, take care to differentiate between Sharp-tailed and Nelson's. Both species are possible. In migration, a variety of hawks pass the beach. In cold months, Horned Larks and Snow Buntings may forage on the beach and dunes. Northern Shrikes occasionally perch on open snags. Red and White-winged Crossbills have turned up in the pitch pines.

Before leaving the area, continue on Route 209 to the end. Fort Popham is a well-preserved fortress that has guarded the strategically critical entrance to the Kennebec River since the Civil War. It provides another sheltered spot to scan for Long-tailed Ducks, Buffleheads, and Goldeneyes, and it produces closer tern sightings than the beach.

Directions: from Bath, proceed south on Route 209 toward Phippsburg. After 11 miles, turn left and continue following Route 209 to the park entrance at 15 miles.

24 Reid State Park,
like Popham Beach State
Park to the southwest, is
often crowded in sum-
mer. It is best birded in
the off-season at high
tide. The water is deep
close to shore, so div-
ing ducks approach the
beach for easy viewing.
Reid State Park is an
ideal spot to watch for
grebes in the winter.
Large rafts of Red-
necked Grebes often
float together, while
more solitary Horned

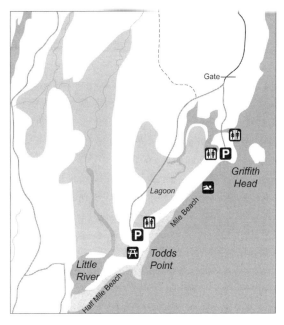

Grebes are peppered throughout the ocean. Long-tailed Ducks also
draw close to shore. Rafts of Common Eiders sometimes harbor a King
Eider. Like most of Maine's sandy beaches, a southeastern exposure
allows the shoreline to escape the punishing erosion of prevailing winds
and major storms, and it creates a warmer microclimate. Sanderlings
may be found even in January. Wintering Purple Sandpipers are common on the rocks at both ends of the beach and sometimes forage there
like Sanderlings, an unusual behavior for this species.

Surf Scoters are the most commonly sighted, but Black and White-
winged Scoters may also be present. Red-breasted Mergansers and
Black Guillemots are usually around. This is the northernmost large
sand beach along the Maine coast and the last protected breeding area
for endangered Piping Plovers and Least Terns.

A typical outing begins with a quick peek into the tidal lagoon
where the entry bridge crosses into the parking lot. Look for American
Black Ducks at any time and other ducks in migration. Smaller diving
ducks, such as Buffleheads and Red-breasted Mergansers, regularly
feed in the lagoon's shelter. Next, ascend Griffith Head. The entire
expanse of Mile Beach and ocean is visible from here. Stroll the beach
at least as far as Todds Point on the opposite end. There is a picnic area
atop Todds Point and the road that serves it is squeezed between the

tidal lagoon and wetlands. This access road is frequently used to make a loop out of the beach trip, returning to the entrance gate through an area that is good for songbirds. Horned Larks, Snow Buntings, and the occasional Lapland Longspur are possible from late September through March around the dunes and beach edges. A few hardy Yellow-rumped Warblers may linger in milder winters. When present, Northern Shrikes are easy to spot, perching high on the spindly tops of shrubs and trees. In summer, Nelson's Sharp-tailed Sparrows nest in small numbers in the salt marsh fed by the Little River. Look carefully for any dabbling ducks in the river on the far side of the service road. Canada Geese are usually present if the water isn't frozen. Where the service road passes through woods, as it does just after the entrance gate and before Todds Point, the habitat is significantly coniferous. Golden-crowned Kinglets are always present. Ruby-crowned Kinglets are common in summer. Brown Creepers are likely in any season, and crossbills are possible in heavy cone years.

Directions: from Woolwich (on the east side of the Kennebec River from Bath) take Route 127 south through Arrowsic and Georgetown 10.7 miles to the right turn toward the park. Follow to the gate.

Additional Sites:

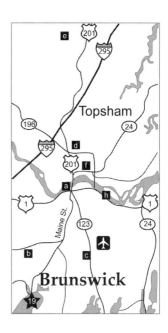

a **Downtown Brunswick** should be checked for Fish Crows, an uncommon species in Maine. Look and listen near the Hannaford supermarket on Elm Street, just behind the downtown intersection of Maine and Pleasant Streets. Also try the tall pines of Bowdoin College, accessible from a short nature trail behind the Cram Alumni House at 83 Federal Street.

In May or June, it's worth a stop at the fish ladder behind Fort Andros on the Androscoggin River, open to the public Wednesday–Sunday from 1 to 5pm. Every year, over 100,000 alewives struggle upstream past this point. These anadromous fish spawn in Maine's freshwater rivers but spend their lives at sea. Just beyond, on the Topsham side of the river, there is a pleasant walking path along Summer Street that offers a peek at gulls, Double-crested Cormorants, and Common Mergansers as they take advantage of the moveable feast. Baltimore Orioles and Carolina Wrens are sometimes encountered along this short trail.

Directions: Fort Andros is in the center of town at the intersections of Route 1 and Maine Street. The fish ladder is in the dam behind a large shopping complex that has been converted from an old mill. There is limited parking. The walking path is immediately across the river in Topsham, along Summer Street.

b **Crystal Spring Farm** has been restored by the Brunswick-Topsham Land Trust. It is now a community-supported organic farm that provides fresh produce to members and hosts Brunswick's Saturday morning farmers market. The farm also supports several miles of trails through fields, woods, and blueberry barrens. Common warblers such as Black-throated Green, Northern Parula, and Black-and-white are present throughout the wooded parcels. Eastern Meadowlarks nest in the grassland, and Field Sparrows and Eastern Towhees are possible on the field edges. Cliff Swallows nest on one of the farm buildings.

Directions: proceed south on Maine Street in Brunswick. After passing Parkview Memorial Hospital, turn right onto Pleasant Hill Road. The farm is about a mile beyond the intersection. The farm can also be reached from Freeport. Take Bow Street to Mast Landing Road, turn left onto Pleasant Hill Road, and proceed five miles past the intersection with Woodside Road.

c **Brunswick Town Commons** is another pleasant stroll. It is the remainder of a thousand acre "commonage" granted by its colonial owners in 1719. A large stand of pines shelters the entrance and picnic area, and the trails traverse wetlands, a peat heath, remnants of blueberry fields, and an uncommon pitch pine barren. The understory is sparse and it is unusually easy to spy common warblers, vireos, and flycatchers along these paths.

Directions: from the intersection of Routes 24 and 123 in downtown Brunswick, take Route 123 south toward Harpswell 1.6 miles. Look for the parking lot on the right.

d **Mt. Ararat** in Topsham is neither tall nor isolated, but its location marks a transition zone. Many of the bird species found here are reminiscent of habitats farther south. Prairie Warblers, Field Sparrows, Eastern Towhees, Indigo Buntings, and Brown Thrashers breed along the fields and power lines that border the mountain. Common warblers such as Black-throated Green and Northern Parula work the forest edges. On Route 201 adjacent to Mt. Ararat High School, probe the trails under the power lines on both sides of the road. There is parking on the west side of Route 201 under the power lines, and additional parking is available under the power lines on the access drive to the high school. There are no facilities.

Directions: Mt. Ararat High School and the power lines are on Route 201 in Topsham, just over a mile north of the Androscoggin River.

e The 230-acre **Cathance River Nature Preserve** is reached from the Highland Green development. Public hiking and cross-country ski trails connect the development and its golf course with the Cathance River, passing quarries and a heath sanctuary. The preserve slopes to the river through fields and forest, then runs along 1.5 miles of the Cathance River shoreline. The heath sanctuary has a trail around its perimeter and is connected with the remainder of the preserve through a narrow corridor. Five interconnected loop trails are marked with different color blazes for easy navigation. Though the surrounding area has become quite developed, the preserve is an oasis for attracting songbirds, particularly those in migration.

Directions: the Cathance River Nature Preserve is located in the Highland Green development off the Route 196 bypass around Topsham. From the intersection of Routes 201 and 196 in Topsham, take Route 196 east for 0.5 mile toward Brunswick and Route 1 North. At the first stoplight, turn left onto Village Road. From the intersection of Routes 24 and 196, take Route 196 west for 0.8 mile, and at the stoplight turn right onto Village Road. Follow Village Road 0.8 mile and then turn right onto Evergreen Circle. Parking is available in a small lot on the left, across from the outlet of Redpoll Drive. Maps are available at the Highland Green sales office, off Village Road beyond Evergreen Circle.

f **Bradley Pond Farm Preserve** was created in 1991 when Frederick and Florence Call granted a conservation easement on their 163 acres of farmland to the Brunswick-Topsham Land Trust. A 2.5-mile network of trails surrounds the property. The property is still a work- ing farm with a private residence, so you should stay on the trails. No dogs are allowed. The trails traverse hardwood and softwood forests and provide views of Bradley Pond, the Cathance River, and the sur- rounding wetlands. Black-throated Green Warblers, Rose-breasted Grosbeaks, Red-eyed and Blue-headed Vireos are typical. Hermit and Wood Thrushes breed on the preserve and are often heard at dawn and dusk. Northern Waterthrush can be found in the wetlands and Bank Swallows breed in the quarry.

Directions: proceed north on Route 201 five miles from the Androscoggin River and look for the entrance on the left. It is another 0.75 mile along the access road to the limited parking area.

g **Bailey Island** is known more for its scenery than birding. The ocean views are spectacular. Common Eiders, Buffleheads, Long-tailed Ducks, Red-breasted Mergansers, and any of the scoters are probable. In winter, look for Purple Sandpipers along the mainland shore and on the nearby islands and ledges.

Directions: from Cook's Corner in Brunswick, follow Route 24 south to the end.

h **The Brunswick Bike Path** runs along one of the prettiest sections of the Androscoggin River, opposite Cow Island, and it's a good place to scan for Common Goldeneyes, Mergansers, and Loons, as well as Ring-necked Ducks and other divers. The path is shared with bikers, joggers, rollerbladers, and baby strollers. Highway noise obscures bird songs, but it is still possible to turn up open-area birds such as Balti- more Orioles, Yellow Warblers, and American Redstarts.

Directions: the path begins along the river on Water Street in Brunswick and terminates at Cook's Corner.

i **The Abbagadasset River** joins the Kennebec River just east of Bowdoinham on the north end of Merrymeeting Bay. Wild rice grows throughout the bay, attracting great quantities of waterfowl in migra- tion. However, there are few places where the birds can be seen easily from shore. The "Mouth of the Abby" is an exception. For a couple weeks in April, after ice-out, thousands of ducks congregate in this spot. Average numbers are lower during the extended fall migration, but shorebirds periodically take over the spotlight during this time, with good numbers of yellowlegs and a variety of peeps.

Directions: from I-295, take the Bowdoinham exit and follow Route 138 east toward Bowdoinham, where it becomes Main Street. From Route 138, turn left onto Route 24 and follow north less than a mile to a right turn onto the Brown Point Road. Proceed 1.7 miles, cross the one-lane bridge, and park under the power line. Be careful not to disturb the birds, which are sometimes quite close.

j **Bay Bridge Park** is a secluded spot to scan part of Merrymeeting Bay for waterfowl. Named for a former bridge across the Androscoggin River, it is located on the back road between Brunswick and Bath. The landing extends into the river and affords views up- and downstream. Marshy wetlands border both sides of the landing, and dabbling ducks compete for attention with the diving ducks in midstream. For many years, Bald Eagles have returned faithfully to a nest on Freyee Island, about a third of a mile downstream, easily visible through binoculars. The brush and stunted secondary growth along the riverbank are prime habitats for Common Yellowthroats, American Redstarts, and Yellow and Chestnut-sided Warblers. Song and Swamp Sparrows are also present. There are no facilities here.

Directions: from Route 1, exit at Cook's Corner/Route 24. Turn left onto the Brunswick-Bath Road. Go east for 0.4 mile, then turn left at the second light onto Old Bath Road and follow 2 miles. Go left at the sign for Bay Bridge Estates (a mobile home park) on Driscoll Street. Turn left at the stop sign and continue straight ahead to the community buildings at the end. The landing is to the right, on the river.

k **Butler Head Preserve** extends into Merrymeeting Bay. As winter changes to spring, Common Goldeneyes and Common Mergansers are joined by Ring-necked Ducks. The diverse habitat features taller stands of white pine, red maple, beech, red oak, two species of aspen, and four species of birch. Black cherry, balsam fir, white oak, and witch hazel are characteristic of the emerging understory. Marsh, field, and shoreland make up the remainder. Wild rice proliferates on the southern edge of the preserve and in Butler Cove, which attracts waterfowl. Rare divers have included Canvasbacks and Redheads. The transitions between the taller trees, shrubs, and marsh provide habitat for Common Yellowthroats, Yellow, Chestnut-sided, Blackburnian, Black-and-White, and Black-throated Green Warblers. Song, Swamp, and White-throated Sparrows are often encountered. Sandpipers have included Semipalmated, Least, Spotted, Pectoral, and Solitary, as well as Greater and Lesser Yellowlegs.

Directions: from High Street in Bath, proceed west on Whiskeag Road 1.1 miles. Turn right onto North Bath Road and go 1.5 miles. Turn right onto Varney Mill Road. Look for the second left in 0.6 mile and take this road to the preserve.

l **The town boat landing in Bath** is best for birding in the colder months. When the Kennebec River is not choked with ice, Common Mergansers raft between here and the bridge. Red-breasted Mergansers also appear and even Hooded Mergansers are possible. Both Common and Barrow's Goldeneyes regularly join the mergansers. Bald Eagles are seen along this stretch of river in all seasons and perch on backyard trees. There are no facilities here.

Directions: from the center of downtown Bath, follow Front Street north along the river to the end. Caution: the town boat landing may not be plowed in winter.

m **The Basin** represents 1,910 acres of prime land given to The Nature Conservancy by an anonymous donor in 2006, one of the most generous gifts ever received by the Conservancy. The preserve protects four miles of shoreline in an area important to migrating and wintering waterfowl. The unbroken forest supports large populations of songbirds, particularly Hermit Thrushes, Veeries, Ovenbirds, and Black-throated Green Warblers. There are good numbers of Black-and-white and Yellow-rumped Warblers in the deep woods, while Chestnut-sided and Yellow Warblers abound in the secondary growth near the basin itself. Ospreys and Bald Eagles are also common around the basin. There are several snowmobile trails through the woods, and foot trails are planned. Traffic is light and the preserve can be birded from the road. Much of the birding is concentrated around the basin, where Tufted Titmice add to the din.

Directions: while on Route 209 passing Center Pond, look for Basin Road opposite the pond's midpoint. Basin Road turns to dirt after 0.4 miles and continues completely through the preserve. One spur brushes the basin.

n **Center Pond Preserve** is a Phippsburg Land Trust property protecting 253 acres of old-growth forest. Pine, Yellow-rumped, and Black-throated Green Warblers are most prevalent in the canopy, but Blackburnian Warblers, Red-eyed Vireos, Eastern Wood-Pewees, and Scarlet Tanagers also sing from the treetops. Closer to earth, Brown Creepers, Ovenbirds, and Hermit Thrushes are easier to see, and finding a Tufted Titmouse is almost inevitable. Broad-winged Hawks nest on this tract and are often heard. There is a sizeable beaver pond in the middle of the preserve that should always be checked for waterfowl. The Drummond Loop that circumnavigates this pond is relatively short and easy to walk. A longer perimeter trail that follows the shoreline of Center Pond makes this preserve particularly good for hiking. There are no facilities.

Directions: from Route 209 turn onto Parker Head Road. The parking lot and trailhead are a half mile ahead on the right.

o **Sprague Pond Preserve** is a 114-acre property of the Phippsburg Land Trust. The trail passes a beaver pond near the trailhead, crosses a planked boardwalk by the dam, extends less than half a mile through hardwood forest, and then skirts the length of a larger pond just beyond. The wetland of the first pond has plenty of Common Yellowthroats and Yellow Warblers. Swamp and Song Sparrows are numerous. Both Alder and Willow Flycatchers may be present; they can only be separated in the field by voice. From the first pond, the trail ascends through hardwoods that contain Ovenbirds and Hermit Thrushes, plus Black-throated Green, Black-and-white, and Yellow-rumped Warblers. Sprague Pond is a cold, spring-fed pond stocked with trout, and it draws a good number of Great Blue Herons and Ospreys. The trail hugs the pond on the west side but it does not loop.

Directions: the trail begins at the small parking lot on the west side of Route 209, 1.9 miles south of the Phippsburg Town Hall.

p **Bates-Morse Mountain Conservation Area** requires special sensitivity when visiting its nearly 600 acres. It is a private research conservation area managed by Bates College. Its unusual birds and plants are vulnerable to disturbance. Stay on roads and hard beach surfaces, and stay distant from birds on the beach. Respect the adjacent private property and do not go past the red pole on the beach, a half-mile west of the trail entrance.

A paved access road serves as a self-guiding nature trail, with maps and brochures at the gate. The trail starts on Route 216 and winds through several different habitats, beginning with a mature oak/fir forest that is home to many Black-throated Green and Blackburnian Warblers. Yellow-rumped Warblers, Brown Creepers, and Golden-crowned Kinglets are also plentiful. Early in the walk, a portion of the Sprague River salt marsh intrudes into the forest. This should be checked carefully for wading birds such as Glossy Ibis and Snowy Egrets early in summer, and shorebirds later in the season. Both Nelson's and Salt-marsh Sharp-tailed Sparrows are possible.

Upon re-entering the woods, the path leads gently uphill where there is a side trail to the summit of Morse Mountain. Although it is only 180 feet above sea level, it offers impressive views and an opportunity for hawk-watching in September. Pitch pines take over the forest from the summit to the beach, and the thinner canopy improves the chances of spying American Redstarts. Seawall Beach extends over a mile from the Small Point Association property on the west to the Morse River on the east. Popham Beach State Park lies beyond the river. At low tide, there is an enormous expanse of sand on both beaches. Piping Plovers and Least Terns nest above the high tide line in some years. Watch your step and stay clear of all fencing. From August through September, other shorebirds may forage on the beach, particularly Sanderlings. Throughout summer, Common Terns are seen from the beach and large numbers concentrate around the offshore islands.

Directions: from Bath, go south on Route 209 towards Phippsburg. Proceed for 11.6 miles. Where Route 209 turns left to Popham Beach, continue straight ahead on Route 216 for 0.4 of a mile. Turn left on Morse Mountain Road. There is a summer gatekeeper and when the lot is full, no more vehicles will be permitted to enter.

q **Josephine Newman Sanctuary** is under the stewardship of Maine Audubon. It is sandwiched between two branches of Robinson Cove, on mature forested upland. There are three blazed trails that total 2.5 miles of hiking. The shortest is a blue blazed, self-guided, geology trail. Though only 0.6 mile, the terrain is steep and varied. This trail traverses mostly mature pines and hemlocks, and is home to Black-capped Chickadees, Red-breasted Nuthatches, Hermit Thrushes, and common woodpeckers. Pine and Blackburnian Warblers are typically spotted.

The Rocky End Trail is blazed in red and branches off the Geology Trail near the cattail marsh. This trail is 1.25 miles and ascends through deciduous forest to the highest point on the preserve. Warblers include Black-throated Green, Northern Parula, Black-and-white, and Ovenbird, as well as Red-eyed and Blue-headed Vireo. The easiest hike is the orange-blazed Horseshoe Trail, which is only 0.75 mile.

Indian River in Georgetown is sometimes a hiding place for waterfowl. On the way to Reid State Park, it's worth a quick peek. Just to the east of Josephine Newman Sanctuary, look for a small, easily overlooked road that leads to Indian Point. The small pond that abuts the entrance to this road merits a scan, especially for Hooded Mergansers. The next pond is even more likely to contain them, usually in the off-season.

Directions: from the junction of U.S. Route 1 and Route 127 in Woolwich, just east of the Woolwich-Bath bridge, head south on 127 for 9.1 miles to Georgetown. Turn right at the sanctuary sign and follow the entrance road to the parking area.

➤━◆━◄

Official Maine Birding Trail Sites

Lincoln County

★ **25 Lobster Cove Meadow** in Boothbay is the most productive of several properties owned by the Boothbay Region Land Trust. Though only 46 acres, it makes up in variety what it lacks in size. The combination of ATV trails and footpaths winds through a mature softwood forest of white pine and spruce, following the slope

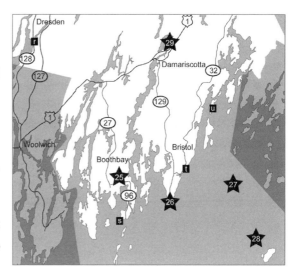

downward through an open, grassy meadow dotted with ancient apple trees, until reaching an extensive marsh. The combination has produced sightings of virtually every thrush, including a Gray-cheeked in migration, and eight of Maine's nine flycatchers. Twenty-one warbler species have been observed on the property. Green Herons, Least Bitterns, Virginia Rails, and Sora have been found in the marsh. There are no facilities.

Directions: from the intersection of Routes 27 and 96 in Boothbay Harbor, take Route 96 for 0.4 mile. Turn right onto Eastern Avenue for 0.1 mile. Look for a small parking lot on the left at the trail entrance. The trail begins to the left of a private residence.

26 Pemaquid Point is one of many places where alcids, pelagic species, and migrant songbirds are regularly spotted. From the lighthouse, Common Eiders and Black Guillemots are usually observable. Common Loons, Red-necked and Horned Grebes, and scoters are regularly spotted in winter and a King Eider is possible. Besides the normal gull species, Bonaparte's and Laughing Gulls may be present and Black-legged Kittiwakes are seen occasionally. Eastern Egg Rock is six miles to the east, so its breeders may forage close to shore here: Atlantic Puffins and Common, Arctic, and Roseate Terns. Razorbills, and Common and Thick-billed Murres are infrequent sightings. Greater, Sooty, and Manx Shearwaters sometimes approach land from June through September.

In migration season, this is a coastal site to observe Northern Gannets. Parasitic and Pomarine Jaegers are seen annually. Check both the fields and the surrounding trees for unusual migrants, especially in fall. Nocturnal migrants "fall out" on Pemaquid with some frequency. Using best birding etiquette, poke around the trees and lawns of the Pemaquid Hotel complex for migrants. Opposite the hotel, drive or walk the small loop road that wraps around the west side of the peninsula. The trees of the loop road are especially good for migrant warblers and finches. Common Ravens thrive in this area. Crossbills have nested here.

Directions: from Route 1, there are two roads that lead to Pemaquid Point. From the south, the more direct choice is Route 129 from Damariscotta, bearing right onto Route 130 through Bristol, on through New Harbor and Pemaquid. From this direction, it is just shy of 12 miles to Pemaquid from Route 1A. From the north, take Route 32 south from Waldoboro. At the end of 19.7 miles, it will intersect with Route 130 in New Harbor and the total distance to Pemaquid will be 22.6 miles.

27 **Eastern Egg Rock** is the southernmost breeding colony of Atlantic Puffins in the world. From mid-May through mid-August, the Hardy Boat departs from New Harbor on daily boat trips around the island. Landing is not permitted, but Captain Crocetti is able to edge his cruise vessel close to shore for excellent views of the puffins, as well as the Common, Arctic, and Roseate Terns that breed here. Razorbills, Common Murres, Northern Gannets, and Wilson's Storm-petrels are sometimes encountered. This company also offers other local cruises, private charters, and service to Monhegan Island. Call 1-800-2-Puffin or visit www.hardyboat.com. Less frequently, Cap'n Fish conducts puffin trips from Boothbay Harbor. Check the schedule at 800-636-3244 or www.puffins.capnfishs.com. Maine Audubon also schedules trips to Eastern Egg Rock. Check the calendar at 207-781-2330 or www. maineaudubon.org.

Directions: New Harbor is on Route 32, 19 miles from its intersection with Route 1. Meet the boat at Shaw's Fish & Lobster Wharf.

---

28 **Monhegan Island** is the destination for many commercial tour companies. It is a famous migrant trap, as the birds often descend into the trees and shrubs of the village itself, feeding voraciously and ignoring the closest observers. The village is confined to the western side of the island. The eastern side is a dramatic series of cliffs and coves. Though the island is only one square mile in size, 17 miles of interwoven trails crisscross

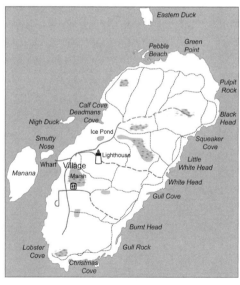

it. It is possible to sit on any of the cliffs and scan for passing Northern Gannets, and perhaps Parasitic or Pomarine Jaegers. Breeding Common Eiders and Black Guillemots surround the island. Laughing Gulls mix with the Herring and Great Black-backed Gulls. Peak birding occurs during the last three weeks of May and from late August through early October. Summer breeders include Blackpolls, Black-throated Green Warblers, and Northern Parulas.

At peak migration, a morning of birding might turn up twenty different species of warbler. Sharp-shinned Hawks, American Kestrels, Merlins, and Peregrine Falcons follow coastal migration routes and often touch down on the island. Out-of-range species are a common occurrence. Before heading for the cliffs, spend plenty of time in the village. Venture down to Lobster Cove, a particularly good place to watch Northern Gannets, Peregrine Falcons, and storm-tossed pelagic species. Stroll back through the village to the area around the old ice pond, which is good for warblers, vireos, waterfowl, and waders. The tall spruces around the pond are a common place to find roosting raptors. Nearby, behind the lighthouse, an old ball field is a fine site to find woodpeckers and cuckoos. The wet meadow behind town harbors rails, bobolinks, and ducks. Burnt Head is the easiest cliff hike. Trails to the other heads can be more challenging to anyone with limited mobility, but all offer spectacular views.

In addition to great birding, the island has other charms. Located 10 miles offshore, it is accessible only by boat and there are no paved roads on the island. For over a century, Monhegan has been the summer home of a well-established artist colony. Galleries, craft outlets, and gift shops are pervasive. Day trips to Monhegan are enjoyable, but the true magic of birding the island happens early in the morning after a good overnight fall-out of migrants. Make SURE to reserve accommodations ahead of time because space is very limited and no overnight camping is allowed on the island.

Three boats provide ferry service to the island. The Monhegan Boat Line (www.monheganboat.com) departs from Port Clyde and provides three daily trips in summer, two daily in spring and fall, and three trips a week in winter. Charters and puffin trips are also available. Call 207-372-8848. Hardy Boat Cruises leaves twice a day in summer, and once a day in spring, departing from New Harbor. It operates mid-May through Columbus Day (see previous entry for additional information). The Balmy Days II (www.balmydayscruises.com) makes daily round trips from Boothbay Harbor, and also offers an additional cruise around the island in the afternoon. Call 207-633-2284 or 800-298-2284. All three boats pass close enough to nesting islands to make sightings of terns possible. Wilson's Storm-petrels move into the waters in June. Greater and Sooty Shearwaters are also encountered, especially when northerly breezes prevail.

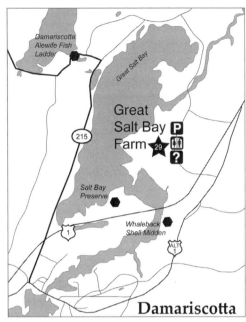

29 Great Salt Bay Farm is one of more than twenty preserves owned by the Damariscotta River Association. The association's headquarters, an 18th-century farmhouse, sits atop 115 acres of former farmland overlooking the river. A restored marsh has succeeded in luring American Black Ducks, Wood Ducks, and Hooded Mergansers as breeders, and numerous other species in migration. Great Blue Herons, Green Herons, and American Bitterns are typically observable. Secretive Virginia Rails announce their presence at dawn and dusk, while chattering Marsh Wrens may be heard at any time through early summer. A mowed path around the marsh facilitates viewing from all angles. Bobolinks and Savannah Sparrows are common through the fields. Pine Warblers are audible from the tall pines bordering the right side of the field. Yellow and Chestnut-sided Warblers and Common Yellowthroats are regularly spotted in the brushy growth along the left side. Ospreys and Bald Eagles are common sights over the nearby river.

There are three other DRA-affiliated preserves nearby. The Whaleback Shell Midden State Historic Site, owned by the Bureau of Parks and Lands, contains the remnants of prehistoric piles of oyster shells and artifacts left by Native Americans several thousand years ago, and affords a clear view of the Glidden Midden, one of the larger extant oyster shell heaps on the east coast. As sea levels rose, the oysters disappeared around a thousand years ago, but the rubbish piles remained until the turn of the last century, when the majority of the shells of Whaleback Midden were processed into a chicken feed additive. Glidden Midden, on the other hand, remains, still some 30 feet deep in places. The Salt Bay Heritage Trail lies at the south end of Great Salt Bay and offers a pleasant 3-mile footpath. Most of the path offers open views of diving ducks, Ospreys, and Bald Eagles, but the first half mile crosses a small salt marsh where shorebirds, dabblers, and Horseshoe Crabs may be hiding. The Damariscotta Mills Alewife Fish Ladder can be spectacular when the alewives are running in May and June. Ospreys and Bald Eagles often congregate around the ladder, gorging themselves on the jumping fish. The ladder ascends 42 feet to Damariscotta Lake and is a remarkable curiosity even when the fish aren't running. Pick up more information and directions to these three sites at the Great Salt Bay Farm headquarters.

Directions: Great Salt Bay Farm is located on Belvedere Road off Route 1 (the blinking yellow light about 1 mile north of the Damariscotta exit).

⟫──◈──⟪

Additional Sites:

r **Green Point Farm Wildlife Management Area** in Dresden is a combination of fields, old orchards, and wooded wetlands. The state maintains the site as grassy meadow, which produces a wealth of nesting sparrows, mostly Song and Savannah. Shrubs bordering the field provide nesting for Yellow and Chestnut-sided Warblers. The sparrow numbers swell in fall migration, which is also a good time to look for Horned Larks, Snow Buntings, and American Golden Plovers. Waterproof footwear is recommended in wet seasons and on dewy mornings. The site borders the confluence of the Kennebec and Eastern Rivers in a shallow area full of wild rice. Large numbers of ducks are sometimes found during the migration periods in April and late autumn.

Directions: from Route 1 in Woolwich take Route 127 north. Go 1.8 miles; turn left onto Route 128, then north on 128 to the Eastern River Bridge. Park at the large green shed on the west side of the road, 0.3 mile north of the bridge.

s **Ocean Point** lies at the end of Route 96 in Boothbay. The point overlooks several islands and lighthouses. It is a place where sea ducks and seals frolic. In summer, Common Eiders, Common Loons, Black Guillemots, and Double-crested Cormorants are normally within view. There is a small walking path on the left that enables more exploration of the point. In winter, scoters, grebes, and occasional alcids join the resident eiders. Ocean Point has been a promising place to spot a King Eider in winter for many years, and has produced more than its share of Rough-legged Hawk and Snowy Owl sightings. Expect to share the point with tourists, due to the extraordinary scenery. Parking is limited and private property must be respected. There are no facilities.

Directions: follow Route 96 to the end. Though the point marks the end of the route, the streets around the west side of the point rejoin Route 96 in a loop. Park only where permitted.

t **The Rachel Carson Salt Pond Preserve** was brought under the protection of The Nature Conservancy in 1966 and dedicated to her legacy in 1970. In 1962 Rachel Carson wrote *Silent Spring*, a watershed in the world's understanding of pesticide misuse and its role in songbird extinction. The preserve encompasses 78 acres, including forested upland trails, but the main attraction is the one-quarter acre tidal salt pond itself.

Directions: proceed south on Route 32, 18.6 miles from its intersection with Route 1. In the off-season, there may not be signs identifying the preserve, but the tidal pool is large and obvious on the left.

u **Hog Island** has been an Audubon educational camp since 1936. Roger Tory Peterson was Audubon's first teacher on the island, shortly thereafter joined by another of America's most famous ornithologists, Allan D. Cruickshank. The camp operates as a staging facility for the Audubon Seabird Program, more commonly known as the Puffin Project. Hog Island is offshore and makes up 330 acres of the 365-acre Todd Wildlife Sanctuary. Back on the mainland, the remaining 35 acres contain a seasonally operated visitor center, workshop, and nature store. A one-mile, self-guided trail called the Hockomock Nature Trail begins on the right side of the road beyond the nature center. It traverses a variety of habitats, with views of the Medomak River and Muscongus Bay, beginning in open meadow, passing into the forest, brushing the shoreline, and rising over a bit of elevation. The sanctuary is not known for specialty birds, but it can be an enjoyable place to observe some of Maine's common woodland species.

Directions: 8.3 miles south of the intersection of Routes 1 and 32, look for a left turn onto Keene Neck Road. Follow Keene Neck Road 1.5 miles to the Audubon Center.

Official Maine Birding Trail Sites

Knox and Waldo Counties

30 **Weskeag Marsh** in South Thomaston is one of Maine's best birding marshes. The marsh is a mix of salt, brackish, and fresh-water habitat. It is also a mix of cattails and grass, of potholes and mud flats, and of brook, stream, and river all bordered by forest, scrubland, and hayfields. In short, it contains a good variety of habitats in an area of less than a thousand acres. The state man-

ages 537 of these acres as the R. Waldo Tyler Wildlife Management Area. Weskeag Marsh is noted for waders, waterfowl, and shorebirds, primarily from ice-out in late March through October. It is the northernmost site where the breeding ranges of Nelson's and Saltmarsh Sharp-tailed Sparrows overlap, though the former is seen more often.

A general view of the marsh can be enjoyed from the small parking area where Buttermilk Lane crosses the Weskeag flowage. The marsh suffers from excess visitation, and birders should avoid tramping into the wetland areas. It is usually possible to locate the Nelson's Sharp-tailed Sparrows where the stream crosses under the main road. The adjacent slopes of the hayfield provide good views. A short distance farther south on Buttermilk Road—just up the hill, by a copse of trees and old foundation—there is another distant overlook to the marsh. Egrets and herons are often in the back of the marsh and can be seen more readily from here. There are no facilities.

Directions: from Route 1 in Thomaston, turn onto Buttermilk Road and in 0.8 mile look for the parking turnout at the marsh.

31 **Beech Hill Preserve** is a 295-acre property owned by the Coastal Mountains Land Trust. It conserves the only bald hilltop in the area, including an old stone building at the summit that is on the National Register of Historic Places. Named Beech Nut, the views from the porch of this sod-roofed cabin are panoramic, overlooking the blueberry barrens and grasslands to the ocean beyond. The preferred trail begins in mature woods among Hermit Thrushes and Ovenbirds. Soon, it traverses a large area of regenerating forest that provides habitat for perhaps the biggest concentration of Eastern Towhees in Maine. Catbirds and Song Sparrows are also abundant until the trail breaks out of the trees and onto the grasslands. Here, Field and Savannah Sparrows are known nesters. Yellow, Chestnut-sided and Prairie Warbler sightings are possible. The trail is well maintained and well used in all months, and Snowy and Short-eared Owls have been noted around the summit in the off season. Snow Buntings are possible from early autumn through winter.

Directions: From southbound on Route 1, pass Route 90 in Rockport and turn right just beyond Fresh Off The Farm onto Rockville Street. Turn right again, following Rockville Street 0.75 mile to the trailhead parking lot. From northbound on Route 1, turn left onto South Street and follow 1.3 miles to Rockville Street. Turn right onto Rockville Street and look for the parking lot ahead on the left.

---

32 Camden Hills State Park doesn't usually offer rarities, but it does provide most of Maine's common species in a splendid hiking environment. Over 25 miles of trail cross a series of peaks, marching through mixed forest. Views of Penobscot Bay are stunning. Park residents include such normal warblers as Black-throated Green, Black-throated Blue, Northern Parula, Magnolia, Black-and-white, Nashville, Chestnut-sided, Yellow-rumped, Blackburnian, Ovenbird, and Common Yellowthroat. Veery, Wood,

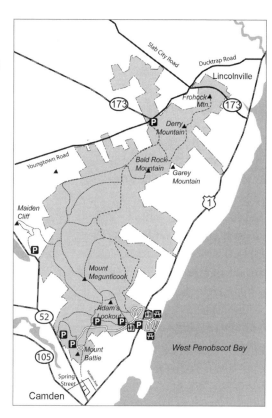

and Hermit Thrushes are all found in the park. Least and Great-crested Flycatchers are common. Pileated, Downy, and Hairy Woodpeckers, Yellow-bellied Sapsuckers, and Northern Flickers are plentiful. Turkey Vultures, Scarlet Tanagers, Rose-breasted Grosbeaks, and Eastern Towhees are summer residents, while Ruffed Grouse may be found in any season. The summits of Mount Megunticook and Mount Battie are fruitful during hawk migration, and any of the eastern species may be encountered. Sharp-shinned, American Kestrel, and Broad-winged Hawks are the most common, but Cooper's Hawks, Northern Harriers, Merlins, Peregrines, Ospreys, and Bald Eagles pass by regularly. Although Mount Battie is only half the height of Mount Megunticook, the auto road to the tower at the summit makes it more convenient. The tower was constructed in 1921 as a World War I monument. It stands upon the former site of a summit hotel that existed from 1898 to 1920. There is a small entrance fee to use the auto road.

Directions: the entrance is prominently marked on Route 1 north of Camden. Two other entrances to the back side of Camden Hills State Park are found on Route 52, just west of town and adjacent to Megunticook Lake. Another entrance that is popular with birders — because it is wide, less crowded, and moderately more birdy — is found in Lincolnville at the intersection of Route 173 and the Youngtown Road.

—————»•○•«—————

33 The Sheepscot Wellspring Land Alliance has made great strides in conserving an undeveloped section of Waldo County in Montville. The forest is an almost equal mix of maple, oak, birch, pine, spruce, and balsam fir, making it possible to find balanced numbers of Wood and Hermit Thrushes, Red-eyed and Blue-headed Vireos, and Black-throated Blue and

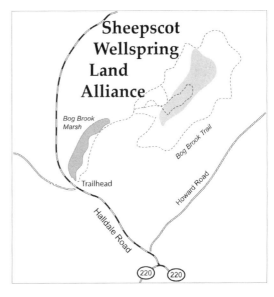

Green Warblers. A good morning should produce Blackburnian, Chestnut-sided, Nashville, Yellow-rumped, Yellow, Magnolia and Canada Warblers, as well as Northern Parula, Common Yellowthroat, American Redstart, Ovenbird, and Northern Waterthrush. Ruby-crowned Kinglets are summer residents; Golden-crowned Kinglets occur year-round. Eight species of flycatcher have been seen here, including Olive-sided, Eastern Wood-Pewee, Alder, and Willow. There are no facilities.

Directions: all trails are on Hall-Dale Road. The main trail enters the woods just before a pond, located a half mile west of the intersection with Route 220 (South Mountain Valley Road). Park on the shoulder. The trail loops around the pond and a more distant marsh, returning to Hall-Dale Road a quarter-mile west of the entrance.

———✺———

34 **Belfast Harbor** is one of the prime spots in Maine to look for wintering Iceland and Glaucous gulls. It's also exceptional for Barrow's Goldeneyes. Start at the town pier. Check the gulls that hang out on the light poles and roofs. Then scan the harbor. Common Loons, Common Goldeneyes, Buffleheads, and Red-breasted Mergansers ought to be evident. Next, focus northward and examine the waters under the bridge that spans the mouth of the Passagassawaukeag River. Depending on the tide, this is the likely spot for Barrow's Goldeneyes. If the tide is high, they may be in the tidal basin beyond the bridge. At low tide, they are pushed closer to the pier.

Upon leaving the pier, turn right onto Front Street and then onto Water Street. There is also a historic footbridge that offers another good opportunity to scan. Roosting gulls tend to congregate at scope range on ice flows or exposed mud flats in the river under and beyond the bridge, intermingling with American Black Ducks and Mallards.

Directions: Route 1 skirts Belfast. From the south, exit onto Northport Avenue and follow into town where it becomes High Street. In the center of town, turn right onto Main Street and the town pier is at the bottom of the street. From the north, exit onto Route 137 after crossing the Passagassawaukeag Bridge, turn left onto High Street, and left again onto Main Street, following to the end.

35 **Sears Island** is one of the largest undeveloped islands on the coast. In the mid-1980s a controversial cargo port was proposed for the 940-acre island, but in 1996 the State of Maine abandoned the project. The site remains a candidate for limited commercial development, but much of the island is expected to remain in conservation to preserve this ideal spot for strolling and birding. Just north of Searsport, turn east onto Sears Island Road. Check for gulls along the causeway, particularly Bonaparte's Gulls from late summer through October. Common Loons, Eiders, and Goldeneyes are regular in the off-season. Scoters, Red-breasted Mergansers, Buffleheads, Horned Grebes, and Black Guillemots are present in winter. Mallards and American Black Ducks are prevalent in the sheltered, shallow areas. Check for shorebirds from mid-August through September.

A paved road runs up the spine of the island, but there are also several hiking paths that are the remnants of the old farm roads that once crisscrossed the island. There are no longer any buildings on the island, but stone walls and old apple trees give clues to its agricultural heritage. Low brush near the gate soon gives way to mixed hardwood, spruce, and white pine. Expect a variety of warblers and sparrows, plus Golden-crowned and Ruby-crowned Kinglets. Expect to share the trails with dog-walkers. There are no facilities.

Directions: from Route 1, turn onto Sears Island Road 2 miles north of Searsport. Follow a short distance to the gate.

---

36 **Cape Jellison** is one peninsula north of Sears Island. The cape extends from the village of Stockton Springs into the outflow of the Penobscot River where it enters Penobscot Bay. From the south, follow the right-hand split of Route 1 into Stockton Springs. It is 0.6 mile from this split to a right turn onto Cape Jellison Road. From the north, it's only a half-mile from the left-hand fork off

Route 1 onto Cape Jellison Road. Follow this road for 1.9 miles (bearing left at an intersection) to a good viewing spot of Fort Point Cove, also sometimes referred to as Grants Cove. Just beyond the boat landing there is a convenient pull-off to scan the bay. Ruddy Ducks often gather here in winter, though ice and tide may push the birds to the limit of binocular range. Scoters, Red-breasted Mergansers, and Buffleheads are also seen regularly.

Fort Point State Park is just ahead at 3.1 miles. Like most parks, it is gated during the off-season, but visitors can park near the gate and hike the mile-long entrance road—or cross-country ski in winter.

The park is home to an early colonial fort established to protect the vital entrance to the Penobscot River, and the earthworks and gun emplacements are still visible. The nearby lighthouse was built in 1836 and the trees near this prominent spot attract Bald Eagles. The park can also be entered from Lighthouse Road, just beyond the park access road. Drive past the private residences and park in the state lot. There is a small park entrance fee.

Directions: see above.

―――――

Additional Sites:

V Twenty-three miles offshore, **Matinicus Island** is more remote, rustic, and inaccessible than Monhegan. It is slightly larger, but with a year-round population of only about 65 people. It, too, deserves its reputation as a migrant trap and birders are likely to see many of the same species as on Monhegan. Though it lacks most of the tourist amenities of Monhegan, this is exactly the rustic charm that some visitors relish. Again, the best birding seasons are mid- to late May and late August through early October.

There are several rental cottages and one B&B on the island. Transportation is by boat or plane. The Maine State Ferry Service makes several trips a month. Call 207-596-2202. Also try Penobscot Ferry and Transport (www.penferry.com) at 207-691-6030 and Matinicus Excursions (www.matinicusexcursions.com) at 207-691-9030, offering runs by reservation on a limited schedule. To fly, contact Penobscot Island Air (www.penobscotislandair.com) at 207-596-7500.

Matinicus Rock rises 60 feet out of the Atlantic five miles south of Matinicus Island. Famous as an Atlantic Puffin nesting colony, it is also home to nesting Razorbills, Black Guillemots, and Arctic and Common Terns. Leach's Storm-petrels spend the day in their nesting burrows, emerging at night to feed. Scan the Double-crested Cormorants for the few Great Cormorants that are usually around, and also watch for a handful of Common Murres. Maine Audubon runs occasional pelagic trips to the island. Check the trip schedule at www.maineaudubon.org.

W **The Nelson Preserve** in Friendship is a secluded property managed by the Midcoast Chapter of Maine Audubon. The trails loop through mixed woodland, descending into a forested wetland. The small changes in habitat produce a good avian variety, but the trails are lightly used and footing can be uneven. There are no facilities.

Directions: The preserve is on Route 97 (Cushing Road) exactly 8 miles south of the intersection with Route 1. The entrance to the trailhead parking lot is narrow and hard to spot.

X **Rockland** has a lot of gulls. Herring, Great Black-backed, and Ring-billed Gulls are numerous. A few Laughing Gulls are usually present. Bonaparte's Gulls are found year-round, though they are much more common in spring and from mid-July through autumn. A few Common Black-headed Gulls turn up every year, as noted on Christmas Bird Counts. In winter, scan for Common and Red-throated Loons, Horned and Red-necked Grebes, Red-breasted Mergansers, Long-tailed Ducks, Buffleheads, Great Cormorants, Canada Geese, Mallards, and American Black Ducks. White-winged Scoters are the most commonly seen of the scoters. Greater Scaups occur irregularly. There are several access points described in the directions below. In particular, the breakwater is an inviting place to bird in winter if temperature and wind cooperate. It's a great spot for Purple Sandpipers and one of the better locations to check for Common Black-headed Gulls and Great Cormorants. King Eiders are occasional visitors. Scan for grebes and loons.

Rockland, Rockport, and Camden are home ports for much of Maine's windjammer fleet. These sailing vessels offer a range of trips, from day sailing to overnight. Because Maine's coastal scenery involves bays, coves, and inner islands, most vessels stay relatively close to land. Common Eiders, Black Guillemots, Northern Gannets, and Wilson's Storm-petrels are often seen on day trips. Overnight trips are more likely to venture out to pelagic waters where shearwaters, jaegers, fulmars, and alcids forage.

In September 2005, Maine Audubon opened a new Project Puffin Visitor Center at 311 Main Street near the Maine Lighthouse Museum. Visitors can watch live streaming video of breeding Atlantic Puffins from Matinicus Rock, a 15-minute educational film, and interactive maps and exhibits about seabird restoration on many of Maine's offshore islands. It also includes an art gallery and gift shop.

Directions to harbor access in Rockland: The downtown area is anchored on the south end by the police station, Landings Restaurant, and the fish pier. The Community Building and the Maine Lighthouse Museum are here. Check the gulls on the roofs of the wharf buildings, but take care not to get in the way of operations. The wharf at the end of Tillson Avenue is home to the Coast Guard, a few commercial establishments, and a windjammer pier. Immediately south of the downtown area, Atlantic Point contains modern office buildings and a pier that offers good views. From the bend at Route 1 downtown, follow the signs to Owls Head, then follow Water Street to Ocean Street. In midtown, the Maine State Ferry Service pier has plenty of parking and viewing for the inner harbor. Just north, a small, seasonal pier used by Atlantic Challenge lies opposite the Knox County Federal Credit Union between James Street and Rockland Street. The breakwater is reached via Waldo Avenue. Proceed half a mile and turn down Samoset Road.

Y **Owls Head Light State Park** is home to a lighthouse that overlooks the southwestern entrance to Penobscot Bay. The park is small and it can be birded easily in a short time. Scan from the lighthouse and from the picnic area reached by trail from the parking lot. Because the site is a prominent extension into the bay, it gets more than its share of warblers in migration. The forest is mixed hardwood and spruce, attractive to an assortment of migrants, including spruce-loving Blackpolls and Bay-breasted Warblers. Thrushes include Veery, Hermit, and Swainson's. In summer, the birding is pleasant but average. In winter, bring a spotting scope up to the lighthouse boardwalk and scan for seaducks, particularly grebes.

Directions: from Route 1 in downtown Rockland, take Route 73 south toward Owls Head, following the signs to the park. Follow 1.9 miles to a left turn onto South Shore Drive, follow 2.6 miles to the small town center, and turn left onto Main Street. Proceed to Lighthouse Road and follow the signs to the park.

z **Merryspring Nature Center** straddles the Rockport/Camden line and is prone to good warbler fallouts in May. For the rest of the summer, it is a pleasant stroll over 66 acres. The gardens around the gazebo are attractive to hummingbirds and photographers. Walking trails wind through mixed forest and fields. Song, Chipping, and White-throated Sparrows work the margins of the fields, as do Common Yellowthroats, American Redstarts, Chestnut-sided, Yellow, Nashville, and Magnolia Warblers. Pine Warblers are present in the thick stands of pine. A Tufted Titmouse is possible around the parking lot. The Kitty Todd Arboretum in the back of the park shelters Ovenbirds and American Woodcocks. Dog-walking is very popular on the footpaths and they are allowed off leash in the North Meadow. Birders should be prepared for canine encounters. Maps and brochures are available at the Nature Center office.

Directions: from Route 1 on the southern edge of Camden, turn west onto Conway Road (next to a Subway sandwich shop). It is 0.3 mile to the park.

aa **Clarry Hill** is a well-known site among Maine birders. With support from the Land for Maine's Future Program, the Medomak Valley Land Trust has secured easements to protect some of these important blueberry fields and grasslands. Birders are drawn by the Upland Sandpipers and Vesper Sparrows that breed here. Song, Savannah, and Chipping Sparrows are also common. During fall migration, this is a site for hawk watching. Later in autumn, it is the type of field that lures Snow Buntings, Horned Larks, and prowling Northern Shrikes. Because the blueberries are a commercial agricultural crop, it is imperative that people and pets stay on the road. There is a road to the summit, but it is private and its use is subject to change without notice. Check for signs for landowner instructions.

Directions: from Route 1, turn onto Route 235 and follow 5.2 miles to a left turn onto Clarry Hill Road. Continue 2.5 miles and look for the dirt road on the left, located at a sharp bend in the road. From Route 17 in Union, turn south onto Clarry Hill Road and proceed 1.9 miles to the sharp bend.

bb **Morgan's Mill** in East Union is a "stop & peek" site for waterfowl in spring. As soon as the ice is gone, migrating ducks collect for easy viewing near the road. Later in the year, exploration by canoe can be rewarding.

Directions: from Route 17, turn north on Route 235 in East Union. The site is only a quarter mile ahead, just beyond an intersection.

cc **Norton Pond** in Lincolnville is another good "stop & peek" site for waterfowl in spring. Ducks of all kinds may be spied on both sides of the road in April.

Directions: from Camden, go north on Route 52 six miles to the intersection with Route 173. Turn left and follow 0.2 mile ahead to the site. From Lincolnville, take Route 173 five miles to the intersection with Route 52, turn right and follow 0.2 mile to the site.

dd **Tanglewood 4-H Camp** lies in the woods along the Ducktrap River, within the boundaries of Camden Hills State Park. It is a summer camp for children, but the trail system leaves from the parking lot and there is no need to go near

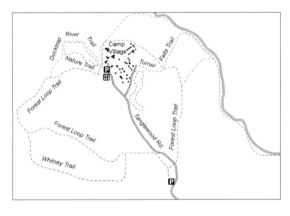

camp operations. Responsible hikers and birders are welcome. The forest floor is mossy damp and the canopy is of mixed species, height, and maturity. The unevenness of the treetops provides habitat for virtually all of Maine's common warblers, Blackburnians and Northern Parula preferring the taller stands, Nashville, Magnolia, and American Redstart opting for the lower. Black-throated Green Warblers gravitate toward oak and maple, while Black-throated Blue choose birch and beech. Pine Warblers command the pines. Red-eyed Vireos prefer hardwoods, while Blue-headed choose the softwoods. Ovenbirds, Veeries, and Hermit Thrushes inhabit the understory. Otters are seen occasionally in the river.

Directions: from Route 1 in Lincolnville, look for the sign and turn onto Ducktrap Road. Travel 0.8 mile and turn right onto Tanglewood Road, following the sign. Proceed 1 mile to the gate area and 1.8 miles to the main parking lot, where the trail begins.

ee **Ducktrap Harbor**, where the river meets the sea, can be interesting any time of year but particularly in winter. It is usually ice free and it can be scanned from a warm car on a cold day. Cormorants, Red-breasted Mergansers, Common Goldeneyes, and Buffleheads often sneak into its sheltered calm. In migration, other waterfowl provide a steady stream of surprises.

Directions: the small harbor is obvious from Route 1 just north of Lincoln-ville. Turn down Howe Point Road and park in the small lot.

ff **Ruffingham Meadows** is a Wildlife Management Area on Route 3 in North Searsmont. Though best explored by canoe, most of its expanse can be scanned from the parking lot at the outlet dam. "Stop & peek" for the migrating waterfowl that gather in the back of the pond soon after ice-out in April, and again as winter draws near in the fall. Common Loons may be found throughout summer.

Directions: the site is obvious on Route 3 in North Searsmont, just over 30 miles east of Augusta or 10 miles west of Belfast.

gg **Moose Point State Park**, just north of Belfast, is a 183-acre state park offering oceanside picnic tables and open fields. In summer, it's seldom worth a stop for birding. In winter, it is possible to park by the gate and walk to the shoreline, carefully as the road may be icy. The view of Penobscot Bay is expansive, though best scanned in calm conditions. There is also a short hiking trail southward to Moose Point that gives a view southward toward Belfast. Like all gated parks and beaches along the coast in winter, it is a favored spot for local dog owners. Watch your step. Pit toilets are available year-round.

Directions: located directly on Route 1 between Belfast and Searsport.

hh **Sandy Point Wildlife Management Area** in Stockton Springs is a mile-long wetland that is hard to bird by land. From the short access road at the outlet dam, strong binoculars or a spotting scope will provide distant sightings, but this is a place best enjoyed by canoe. Breeding waterfowl include Pied-billed Grebe, Ring-necked Duck, Hooded Merganser, and

Common Loon. Mallards, American Black Ducks, Wood Ducks, and Canada Geese are likely. Sora and Virginia Rails are common. Marsh Wrens are abundant. American Bitterns are regular, while Least Bitterns and Green Herons are resident but more reclusive. A nearby sand pit provides the nesting area for Bank Swallows and it is not unusual to spot them amidst the many Tree and Barn Swallows that hawk over the marsh. There are no facilities.

Directions: turn onto Muskrat Farm Road in Stockton Springs and look for the first right onto a dirt road to the dam outlet. Muskrat Farm Road is 3 miles north of the Route 1 and 1A junction in Stockton Springs or 3 miles south of the Verona Island bridge on Route 1 near Bucksport.

ⅱ **Frankfort Marsh** is one of the best sites to find Nelson's Sharptailed Sparrows. Also watch for Northern Harriers and waterfowl. The marsh runs along Route 1A from the village of Frankfort to the intersection with Route 174 in Prospect. It includes 370 acres managed by the state as the Howard L. Mendall (Marsh Stream) Wildlife Management Area. The best spot for sparrows is at the bridge on Route 174 just east of the intersection. Listen for their unusual song and watch for them flitting throughout the meadow. They typically arrive in early June and sing through July and into August. Park carefully at this location, because space is limited and traffic is fast. There are no facilities.

Directions: from Bangor, follow Route 1A south through Winterport, Prospect, and Frankfort. Turn right onto Route 174, cross train tracks, and park safely near bridge. From coastal Route 1, turn onto Route 174 near Fort Knox in Prospect. Follow to marsh.

ⱼⱼ **Carlton Pond Waterfowl Production Area** in Troy is well hidden. It is supervised as a separate unit of the Sunkhaze Meadows National Wildlife Refuge. In spring, it entices a large number of northbound waterfowl. In summer, it supports a sizeable population of nesting Black Terns. Nearly all of the wetland is invisible from the road, and even from neighboring homes. It is best enjoyed by canoe, though foraging terns come close enough to the road for observation. When paddling, it is important to stay well away from tern activity. Tern chicks react to human encroachment by scattering rather than hiding. This makes them vulnerable to their real predators: Snapping Turtles, American Bitterns, Northern Harriers, and an assortment of mammals. Bald Eagles, Ospreys, and several species of swallow are commonly seen over the pond. There are no foot trails around the pond and no facilities.

Directions: from Route 202/9 in Troy, turn north onto Route 220. Follow 3.25 miles and look for Bog Road on the right. Follow this small, dirt road a third of a mile to the outlet stream. From I-95, exit to Pittsfield. From downtown Pittsfield, follow Route 69 toward Detroit. At 5 miles, turn onto Route 220 and follow 7 miles to the entrance to Bog Road on the left. From Newport, follow Routes 11/100 south for 2.25 miles, turn left toward Detroit, turn onto Route 220 and follow 7 miles to Bog Road as above.

DOWN EAST & ACADIA

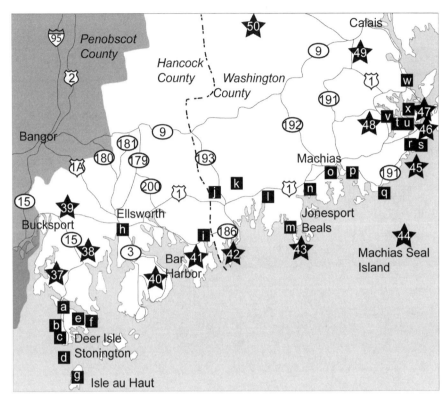

This is a big geographic area. Hancock County is larger than Rhode Island, and Washington County is larger than Delaware. The character of the coast changes in Ellsworth. To the south, coastal towns foster a thriving tourism industry with many services and amenities. To the north, the coast is less developed, while still offering pockets of cultural attractions and serene villages. The best of both worlds is found around Acadia National Park.

Hancock County contains three major peninsulas, two of which enclose Acadia National Park. There are several preserves that receive light traffic and provide good birding. Deer Isle and Stonington essentially mark the southern limit for Boreal Chickadees and Spruce Grouse.

The middle peninsula extends onto Mount Desert Island, where the bulk of Acadia National Park is located. Access to the area from Route 1 is through Ellsworth along Route 3 to Bar Harbor. The town bustles with shoppers and sightseers from late April through October. When these opportunities are combined with the spectacular beauty of the park, the Acadia area is justly regarded as an ideal place to bird with families. Walking the rugged coast, biking the carriage trails, or venturing offshore for whales allows all family members to experience the beauty and wildlife of Maine in their own ways. While Bar Harbor is notoriously busy in summer, the other side of the island is locally known as The Quiet Side. A gentler pace persists in Northeast Harbor, Southwest Harbor, and the nearby villages. Some of the habitat on Mount Desert Island is still influenced by a devastating fire that devoured the island in 1947, and took 10 days to control. Dense stands of tall trees are missing from much of the island, replaced by birches, aspens, and white pines.

The northernmost peninsula, Schoodic, lies north across Frenchman Bay and contains a non-contiguous part of Acadia National Park. The loop road runs closer to the water than the road on Mount Desert Island, making it easier to view sea ducks from the car. Schoodic Point projects so far into the ocean that it's a terrific place to scan for ocean birds. The pounding surf must sound inviting to Harlequin Ducks, because a few turn up here every winter. Indeed, storm surges are so powerful that the roiling ocean can throw bowling-ball sized rocks across the road. Viewing such a spectacle can be irresistible, but people have been swept out to sea and drowned here. ALWAYS stay well out of reach of any surf!

Washington County has everything except crowds. It would be one of the most heavily birded areas in America, if America's birders only knew about it. The region has every northern forest habitat: mature hardwood, mixed growth, and thick stands of boreal softwood. It has fast and slow rivers, marsh and bog wetlands, rocky coasts and mud flats, grasslands and blueberry barrens. It has two national wildlife refuges and one of the best offshore nesting islands on the east coast. All of Maine's most highly sought-after species are found here, sometimes in abundance.

Winter holds pleasant surprises. The population of sea ducks triples in winter. Bald Eagles are seen everywhere. In some winters, flocks of American Robins gather by the hundreds to eat the berries near Quoddy Head State Park in subzero temperatures. It is the first place to be invaded by redpolls, Northern Shrikes, and crossbills each December.

Few of the recommended trails and sites have facilities, so never waste an opportunity to stop in one of the coastal communities and fishing villages. This is an area of stark beauty and simple living. Lodging and dining opportunities are plentiful but not extravagant. Chain restaurants are few and far between. You won't miss them.

Trip planning: www.DownEastAcadia.com or 888-665-3278

━━━➤━०━◄━━━

Official Maine Birding Trail Sites

Hancock County

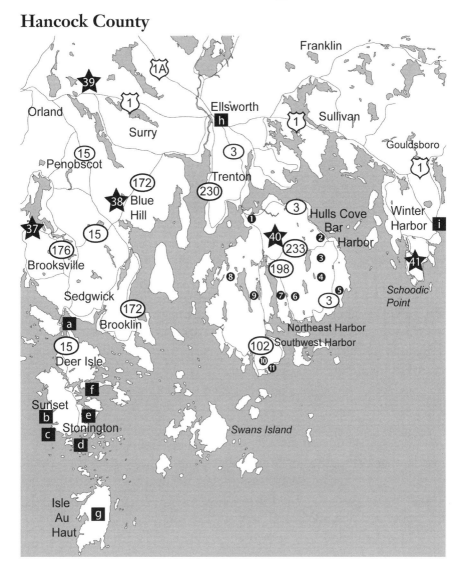

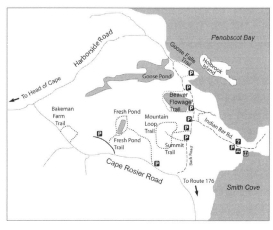

37 Holbrook Island Sanctuary State Park is unique in Maine. Technically, it is a state park. But when Anita Harris donated 1,230 acres to the state in 1971, her vision of a sanctuary unaltered by modern park facilities was honored. The network of old roads, paths, and animal trails is good for birding. The variety of ponds, marshes, forests, and shoreline can take a full day to explore.

To save time, stop at the visitor's center, where maps and a local bird checklist are available. A pair of pit toilets represents the only restroom facilities in the park. From Cape Rosier Road watch for the signs and turn right onto Back Road, then right again onto Indian Bar Road. Check Smith Cove for Bald Eagles, Ospreys, Great Blue Herons, and bay ducks. The fringes of the parking lot and grassy margins should offer such warblers as American Redstarts, Chestnut-sided, Northern Parula, and Black-throated Green. Backshore Trail near the beginning of Indian Bar Road leads through old fields to another section of the shoreline on Penobscot Bay.

The quick hike to the summit of Backwoods Mountain passes through wooded uplands filled with woodland warblers, thrushes, woodpeckers, and Ruffed Grouse. The Mountain Loop trail that circumnavigates the slopes is relatively easy and provides many of the same birding experiences. Panoramic views wait at the top.

The Beaver Flowage Trail is easy but often wet. There are small parking areas on the north and south sides of the flowage. American Redstarts and Chestnut-sided Warblers work the secondary growth. Yellow Warblers inhabit the open areas. Yellow-rumped, Northern Parula, Black-throated Green, and Black-and-white warblers occupy the forest edge. Canada Warblers nest in the low thickets bordering the wet areas. Song Sparrows in the dry grass yield to Swamp Sparrows in the wet grass. Marsh Wrens nest in the cattails. American Black Ducks, Wood Ducks, and teal are sometimes visible in the open water areas.

The Goose Pond Estuary contains a salt marsh that is home to Common Goldeneyes and Belted Kingfishers. The natural ledges are made of volcanic ash rock, but the "mountain" was created by a copper mine that used to operate here. In season, note the abundance of sea lavender.

There are two trails that lead to Fresh Pond, of which the Aaron Trail is the more strenuous. Explore the woods and old homestead fields before checking the pond for waterfowl. Canada Warblers may be found in thickets near wet areas. Blackburnian Warblers prefer the mature tree stands.

Directions: from Route 176 in Brooksville, turn north onto Cape Rosier Road. Proceed 1.5 miles and watch for a small sign that indicates the right turn onto Back Road. Continue less than a mile and turn right again onto Indian Bar Road.

38 **Blue Hill Mountain** is the prominent peak that gives the town of Blue Hill its name. It is a hill of multiple uses, all of which improve the birding. Much of the hill is maintained for blueberries and open grassland, making it one of the best places to find Field Sparrows, Eastern Towhees, Indigo Buntings, and Brown Thrashers this far north along the coast. Blackburnian and Black-throated Blue warblers are

among the dozen regular warblers to be found in the mature forested areas. Golden-crowned Kinglets and Winter Wrens are common in the scrubby, evergreen areas. In autumn, migrating raptors make a beeline for Blue Hill, crossing Blue Hill Bay from the peaks of Acadia National Park.

There are three trails. The most commonly used trail through the old Morse Farm property ascends the summit from Mountain Road, and a parking lot is available at the trailhead. The Osgood Trail rises through Blue Hill Heritage Trust land from a trailhead on Route 15. A 4-wheel-drive utility road serves the communication towers from the east side.

Directions: look for Mountain Road stretching between Routes 15 and 172 just north of Blue Hill Village.

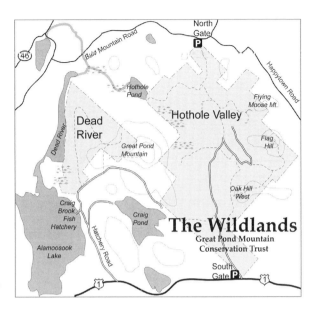

39 The Wildlands were once targeted for subdivision, until the Great Pond Mountain Conservation Trust rescued 4,300 acres in one of the state's largest acquisitions ever made by a local land trust. The result is a sizeable, multi-use tract that is ideal for biking, horseback riding, cross-country skiing, and birding. Surveys have turned up Whip-poor-will, Northern Saw-whet Owl, Ruffed Grouse, American Woodcock, and plenty of songbirds. Much of the timber was removed before acquisition, so the viewshed is extensive and the regrowth areas are productive and varied. This is a parcel that invites long bird walks to places with intriguing names like Flying Moose Mountain and Hothole Pond.

There are two sections. Hothole Valley is the larger section, at 3,420 acres. From the trailhead on Route 1, a number of foot trails lead from a gravel road that runs through the center. The Dead River section is 875 wooded acres sandwiched between Great Pond Mountain and the Dead River flowage. Choose the former for upland birds in dry habitat. Choose the latter for wetland birds, including those to be found in Hellbottom Swamp. Otters and beavers are among the possible sightings there, and moose may be encountered in either area.

Directions: from Route 1, access the Dead River section via the boat launch at Craig Brook National Fish Hatchery on Alamoosook Lake; or on foot from Don Fish Trail, 0.5 mile past the Hatchery. The parking lot and trailhead for the Hothole Valley section is on Route 1, just west of the intersection with Route 176. There is also a north gate on Bald Mountain Road in Dedham.

40 **Acadia National Park** on Mount Desert Island (MDI) was the first national park east of the Mississippi River. It is a park that was more assembled than created, weaving its way through and around communities and private properties as parcels were donated and purchased over time. Thus, the towns and villages are as much a part of the Acadia experience as the park itself. This guide describes MDI as a whole.

1 **Thompson Island:** In Ellsworth, Route 1 takes a sharp turn northward, heading along the coast toward Canada. Meanwhile, Route 3 diverges and runs due south to Mount Desert Island. The 15-minute drive between Ellsworth and MDI is scenic, with salt marshes and ponds that contain Mallards, American Black Ducks, and occasionally Hooded Mergansers. This section of road is most notable for its lobster pounds, particularly the Trenton Bridge Lobster Pound, which has been run by the same Maine family since 1956 who ships their lobsters around the world. Not only is it the quintessential Maine lobster pound experience, it is also located at the causeway entrance to Mount Desert Island, which provides the first true Acadia National Park birding experience: Thompson Island. Route 3 exits the mainland over a bridge at Mount Desert Narrows. There is a Chamber of Commerce visitor's center on the right and a picnic area entrance on the left. This spot provides excellent access for viewing the channel. The lot may be gated in winter, but visitors may park across the street in the visitor's center lot and walk in.

As is typical of the Maine coast, there are more interesting waterfowl in winter. From October to May, Thompson Island is a good place to look for Common Goldeneyes, Greater Scaup, Common Loons, Double-crested Cormorants, and Red-breasted Mergansers. Laughing Gulls and Bonaparte's Gulls visit the channel infrequently in summer. On Route 3, just beyond the parking lot, there are a couple of places where the ocean approaches the road. Greater and Lesser Yellowlegs are sometimes present in these shallows in the spring and fall.

Directions: just beyond Thompson Island, the road splits. Bearing left on Route 3 leads to Bar Harbor. Not only is this the more touristy side of the island, the bulk of Acadia National Park's visitor infrastructure is on this side. Proceeding straight along Routes 102 and 198 leads to the part of the island that natives refer to as The Quiet Side.

2 The drive along Route 3 to Bar Harbor is scenic and pleasant.
About 7.5 miles after the split at Thompson Island, **Hull's Cove** appears on the left. This is the first close encounter with open ocean and
a good crack at viewing seabirds. At high tide, Buffleheads, Long-tailed
Ducks, Surf and White-winged Scoters, and Black Guillemots are often
present during the winter season. Common Goldeneyes and Greater
Scaup may be observable and Common Eiders are usually abundant.

After Hull's Cove, the Acadia National Park Visitor Center is a
half-mile ahead on the right. This is the summer opportunity to get
acquainted officially with the park. The first entry to the Park Loop
Road exits from the back of the parking lot, so many tourists enter the
loop here. In winter, this part of the loop, as well as the visitor center,
is closed.

On the approach to Bar Harbor, the Marine Terminal for the ferry
to Nova Scotia is on the left. For many years, the M.V. *Bluenose* made
daily runs to Yarmouth, Nova Scotia. In 1998 a high-speed catamaran
named *The Cat* replaced the *Bluenose*. A crossing that used to take 6
hours now takes only 2 hours and 45 minutes. Daytrippers sometimes
use *The Cat* for a pelagic trip to Nova Scotia. Call 1-877-359-3760 or
visit www.catferry.com.

The Bar Harbor Sand Bar sometimes shelters thousands of sea
ducks in the lee behind Bar Island during high tide, when the bar is
covered by six feet of water. Common Eiders gather, joined by Common Goldeneyes, American Black Ducks, Mallards, and occasional
Greater Scaup. Surf Scoters, Common Loons, Red-breasted Mergansers, Long-tailed Ducks, and Buffleheads should also be observable.
Scan the eiders carefully for a King Eider. Before leaving, swing a spotting scope onto the islands for Bald Eagles.

*Directions: from Route 3, turn onto West Street 2.1 miles past the visitor
center. Turn left onto Bridge Street and proceed to the dead end at the bar.
The nearby resort has been renovated in recent years and ongoing expansion is
likely. Steer clear of construction activities. In winter, the last few feet of road
before the bar tends to be exceedingly icy.*

The Bar Harbor Town Pier is always worth a scan. Black Guillemots and Common Loons are always close, accompanied by Long-
tailed Ducks in winter. In summer, this is also the place to sign up for a
whale-watching trip.

Whale-watching provides some of the best pelagic birding in the state. Finback and Humpback Whales are the main quarry for these boats, though the endangered Right Whale is a possibility and the smaller Minke Whales are relatively common. Harbor Porpoises are almost a certainty on any trip. Sea birds are drawn to the same food sources as the whales, so expect to encounter Greater and Sooty Shearwaters, especially later in the summer. Manx Shearwaters are less common but show up regularly. Cory's Shearwaters are a remote possibility, though they prefer the warmer Gulf Stream well offshore. Wilson Storm-petrels are likely from mid-June until September, sometimes joined by Leach's Storm-petrels. Tens of thousands of Leach's Storm-petrels nest on nearby islands but their nocturnal behavior makes sightings an uncommon treat. Northern Gannets are inevitable. Parasitic and Pomarine Jaegers are possible, especially later in the season. Northern Fulmars arrive still later. For more information on whale-watching, contact the Bar Harbor Whale Watch Company, which has a fleet of boats: 207-288-2386. www.barharborwhales.com.

❸ Sieur de Monts Spring is the best warbler-watching spot on the island. The mountain spring alone would be enough to attract birds, but this is also home to the Wild Gardens of Acadia. Mature deciduous trees — mostly oak, sugar maple, hawthorn, and beech — predominate around the spring. The garden is divided into 12 sections, each an example of the different habitat types found in Acadia. Thus, it is a wild garden, not a typical suburban flowering garden. The Bird Thicket provides plants that are attractive to fruit and seed eaters. Red-eyed Vireos are very common, while the most frequently occurring warblers are Yellow, Black-throated Green, Common Yellowthroat, American Redstart, and Ovenbirds. Also look for Black-and-white, Northern Parula, Chestnut-sided, and Yellow-rumped Warblers around the parking lot. Common flycatchers include Eastern Phoebes near the buildings, Eastern Wood Pewees in the mature trees beyond the Abbe Museum, and Alder Flycatchers in the brushy fields on the outskirts of the site. Woodpeckers are abundant in the area. Hairy, Downy, and Pileated Woodpeckers, Yellow-bellied Sapsuckers, and Northern Flickers are seen regularly.

There are several walking paths available, but the most productive trail exits the parking lot on the right side of the Wild Gardens. At the outset, the small trees are handy for American Redstarts and Chestnut-sided Warblers. As the path leaves the saplings and enters the grove of

mature hemlocks, Blackburnian Warblers, Scarlet Tanagers, Hermit
Thrushes, and Ovenbirds are a good bet. Beyond the grove, the trail
circles a damp, open area that is promising for Nashville Warblers,
Swamp Sparrows and Alder Flycatchers. Other enjoyable paths lead
southward from the parking lot, past the Abbe Museum, and on to a
small pond called The Tarn. Check the pond carefully because there
are always ducks hidden in the reeds. Black-throated Blue Warblers
are usually heard singing from the extensive stands of birches on the
mountainside beyond the pond.

*Directions: from Route 3 south of Bar Harbor or from the Park Loop
Road, follow the signs to the spring. Deciduous trees predominate here, unlike
the spruce/fir mix that prevails along the ocean edge.*

❹ **Cadillac Mountain** receives the first ray of sunshine in the
U.S. each morning. Drive up if only for the view. Expect it to be cool
and breezy. The birding is ordinary, except in September when it is
one of the two best places in the park for hawk watching. (The other
is Beech Mountain.) During hawk migration, naturalists staff a daily
hawk-watch and encourage participation. On a good day—typically
a day when northwest breezes follow a cold front—American Kestrels and Sharp-shinned Hawks pass closely, joined by a few Cooper's
Hawks, Broad-winged Hawks, Ospreys, Turkey Vultures, Peregrine
Falcons, Merlins, and Bald Eagles. Interestingly, Eastern Towhees
nest on the mountaintop, though they are uncommon outside of
southern Maine. Dark-eyed Juncos and Yellow-rumped Warblers can
also be expected around the summit.

❺ **The Park Loop Road** navigates the park's features. The Preci-
pice Trail is a highlight. Peregrine Falcons have nested here since 1991.
Several pair nest in the park, but these are usually the most visible.
Rangers and docents are stationed below the peak to point out the
locations of the falcons. During the nesting season, the trail is closed.
When the trail reopens in mid-August, it offers a spectacular climb
to the summit of Champlain Mountain. In several places, iron ladders
hammered into the cliff assist the hiker over vertical passes. Though
this sounds challenging, kids and adults alike enjoy the climb. The
ascent takes most people about an hour and the view from the top is
spectacular.

In summer or winter, strolling Sand Beach is enjoyable. Its pure southern exposure has created a small sand beach that is rare north of Portland. Sheltered from prevailing breezes and facing into the sunlight makes sitting in the sand pleasant even in January. Common Eiders, Common Loons, Red-breasted Mergansers, Buffleheads, and Horned Grebes should be present in winter. The loons especially favor the left shoreline. Red-throated Loons and Harlequin Ducks have appeared here occasionally.

The walking path from Sand Beach to Thunder Hole and on to Otter Cliffs showcases Black-capped Chickadees and Golden-crowned Kinglets in any season. Common Eiders are present year-round, though their numbers triple in winter. A scan of the water in winter usually reveals Black Guillemots, Red-breasted Mergansers, Horned Grebes and possibly Red-necked

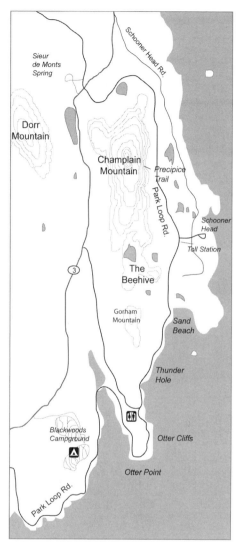

Grebes. In winter, Great Cormorants replace Double-crested Cormorants and their white faces and wing patches should be evident as they fly by. From late summer well into December, Northern Gannets can often be seen in the distance. The rocks along this section of the coast are an excellent place to look for Purple Sandpipers in winter. Peeps on the wing in winter are almost certainly from these. However, when they are roosting motionless on rocks, or feeding quietly, they are surprisingly easy to overlook. Their coloration blends with the quartz-laden granite, making them appear as innocuous bumps or vegetation on the rocks.

Thunder Hole is one of Acadia's top attractions. At times, the surf crashes into the natural grotto with explosive force. However, it requires the right combination of tide and wind to get the full effect. It's a great place to scan for sea ducks and harbor seals.

Otter Cliff lies just beyond a gate that is closed in winter. In the off-season, it is an excellent spot for irruptive crossbills, especially White-winged. In some years they may be found anywhere among the cone-bearing trees along the Park Loop Road. The cliff is panoramic but, despite the name, there are no otters. A bell buoy offshore marks a rock reef that is visible at low tide. In winter, Great Cormorants are a good bet, sometimes roosting on the bell.

Continue around the bend and down to Otter Point. The woods in this area are full of Golden-crowned Kinglets, Black-capped Chickadees, and Red-breasted Nuthatches. A short path leads to Otter Point and it's worth another scan, especially along the rocks for wintering Purple Sandpipers. Continue around the corner and downhill to the Fabri Picnic Area. This was the site of an early World War I radio communications facility that was, at the time, the most advanced in the world. Scan the inlet from this vantage point for more Common Loons and Red-breasted Mergansers. In breeding season, this is a particularly good spot to see a variety of warblers.

At the bottom of the inlet, the Park Loop Road makes a deep U-turn over a causeway that carries water in and out of a tidal pond. Buffleheads and American Black Ducks are likely. Continuing back up the hill on the far side of the cove, there are more scenic overlooks. It is not marked, but Acadia's Blackwoods Campground is in the woods behind the loop road here. Though there are no services in winter, this campground is accessible and is enjoyed by hearty snowmobilers and cross-country skiers. Within another mile, the road turns away from the ocean and reenters woods that are normally noisy with Black-capped Chickadees, Red-breasted Nuthatches, Golden-crowned Kinglets and Brown Creepers.

Most of the Park Loop Road is closed and unplowed in the winter, to the benefit of snowmobilers and cross-country skiers. However, the most popular 2-mile section from the Entrance Station to Otter Cliffs is open and accessible from a winter entrance.

Directions: heading south from Bar Harbor on Route 3, note the ball fields on the right. In about 0.7 mile, the road forks in front of the Ocean Drive

Dairy Bar. Bearing left leads to the winter entrance, marked by a small sign. For 2.5 miles the road advances through birch and aspen groves, and frozen marshes impounded by beavers. At the T intersection, a left turn leads to a scenic overlook parking lot. The trail to the seaside is paved but it is often icy in winter. A right turn leads to the Entrance Station. There is no entry fee from November through April. The winter exit from the Park Loop Road bears right just before Otter Cliff and returns to Route 3.

❻ Jordan Pond House, like Sieur de Monts Spring, features mature stands of deciduous trees and supports a greater concentration of warblers and other neo-tropical migrants. It gets crowded around the restaurant in summer, especially during lunch when diners enjoy the popovers that have been the kitchen's claim to fame for more than a century.

The Bubbles are two scenic knobs that tower above a section of the Park Loop Road just beyond Jordan Pond. It is a favorite hiking place in the park, and is dominated by mixed and open foliage, making it favorable for warblers.

The Carriage Roads around the Jordan Pond House and Wildwood Stables once belonged to the summering wealthy. Some of them go for miles, providing general birding at its best. Hikers, bikers, equestrians, and birders use this network of carriage trails in the park for their adventures. There are no particular hot spots but any of the passerines typically found in Acadia may be encountered while traversing these trails. The width of the trails is an advantage because they usually offer good birding visibility. During the summer, it's hard to venture far without hearing the high, reedy whistle of the Cedar Waxwings that nest throughout the park.

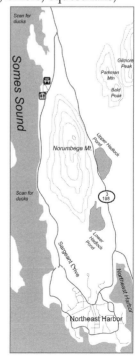

❼ Somes Sound is the only natural fjord bordering the Atlantic in the United States. Glaciers gouged a valley between two peaks and when the glaciers receded, the sea rushed in. Birding here is unremarkable in summer, spectacular in fall foliage, and interesting during the winter. All the usual Acadia sea ducks are seen here, and since Somes Sound is more sheltered from ocean breezes, the ducks are sometimes more readily observable. The ocean scenery on this road is lovely. In winter, cascading ice flows encrust the cliffs. In spring breeding season, where Sargeant Drive leaves the shoreline and enters a mature forest, Blackburnian and Pine Warblers inhabit the white pines and oaks. There is a small park in this area that is mostly used by weekend picnickers and volleyball enthusiasts. Look for Common Yellowthroats, American Redstarts, and Chestnut-sided Warblers in the shrubs surrounding the park. In the secondary growth behind, look for Black-throated Green Warblers and Northern Parula. These give way to canopy warblers in the mature trees behind. There is a portable toilet in summer. The park is unmarked but the open gates should be apparent.

Directions: on the approach to downtown Northeast Harbor, look for a sign that points to Sargeant Drive along Summit Road. Bear right again on Millbrook Road, leading to Sargeant Drive, which hugs Somes Sound until returning to Route 198.

8 Pretty Marsh is a tiny village that contains a park picnic area of cathedral-like quality. Tall cedar, spruce, and hemlock trees tower above it, making a pleasant home for nuthatches and woodpeckers. A short walk to the shoreline overlooks Pretty Marsh Harbor. Toilet facilities are available.

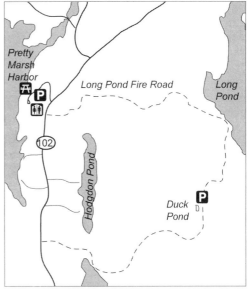

Just beyond the picnic area, look for the Long Pond Fire Road. Equally good for bicycles and slow vehicles, it winds its way through a mixed forest that should produce a great variety of woodland species. Since it is off the beaten track, drive slowly with windows down and listen for songs in early summer, and the chatter of foraging flocks in late summer. The road brushes Long Pond at a popular launch for fisherman. Long Pond Road is about 4.7 miles long and exits onto the

Hodgdon Road on its south end. Returning along the main road to the original entrance creates a loop of 5.7 miles.

Indian Point Blagden Preserve is nearby. This Nature Conservancy preserve is located on land that escaped the devastating fire of 1947. At the entrance, an aged oak stands where it was planted on the day of President Abraham Lincoln's assassination. Tall red spruce, white cedar, and balsam fir dominate and there is an 8-acre stand of tamarack on the wetter ground in the center. The variety and maturity of the foliage supports abundant wildlife, numbering at least 12 species of warbler and 6 species of woodpecker, and including rarely seen Black-Backed Woodpeckers. There is more than a thousand feet of shoreline, which can be good for shorebirds. Harbor seals frequent the ledges offshore.

Directions: after crossing the causeway onto MDI, take Route 102/198 toward Somesville. In 1.8 miles, turn right onto Indian Point Road, then bear right at the first fork in 1.7 miles. The entrance is about 200 yards farther ahead and is marked by a small sign. From Somesville, reach Indian Point Road via Oak Hill Road. Turn left at the intersection and go 200 yards to the entrance.

9 **Beech Mountain** is just a pleasant hiking area eleven months out of the year. In September, if the winds are from the northwest, it's a hot spot for hawk watching and a popular alternative to Cadillac Mountain. Cadillac is usually preferred for its accessibility by car and for the presence of expert hawk-watchers to assist, but Beech Mountain often presents a closer view of the birds. Raptors from far up the coast fly a straight line toward Cadillac, but often skirt the edges upon passing the peak. Beech Mountain is the next major crest on the route south and its smaller size often "focuses" the birds around its cliff face. Furthermore, the preferred ledge for hawk watching overlooks a valley between peaks so that hawks can be seen as they flash beneath or above. Other birds such as irruptive crossbills, Evening Grosbeaks, and finches sometimes traverse the valley. A morning fallout of autumn warblers is also more likely to concentrate over the smaller, wooded Beech Mountain than the larger, treeless Cadillac.

Directions: on Route 102 just south of Somesville, take the right turn toward Pretty Marsh at the Post Office, then turn left and proceed 4 miles to Beech Mountain. Park on the right upon entering the lot and take the trail at the right-hand (northeast) edge of the lot. Follow it uphill for about a mile over sometimes steep and challenging terrain. It's short enough that reasonably fit birders can carry a spotting scope, portable chair, and picnic, with frequent pauses to admire the view. There will be several small ledges, but stop at the major ledge about 200 feet below the summit.

⑩ The Lurvey Spring Road is another lightly used road that can be good for birding. It runs through mature woods from Route 102 (just north of Southwest Harbor) toward Seal Cove, transiting though hemlock, gray birch, and beech as it leads to Long

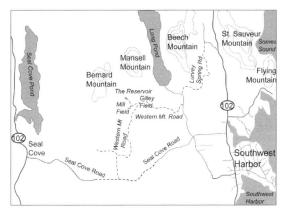

Pond Road and later Seal Cove Road. The Western Mountain Road branches off Seal Cove Road to the north and leads to several interesting areas hidden deep in Acadia. These roads also contain mature trees but the dampness of the woodland floor is signaled by the preponderance of fern, moss, and cedar. Follow the signs to a couple of interesting features: Mill Field and the reservoir. Both areas are adjacent to lesser-used trail entrances in this part of the park. The tiny reservoir is particularly interesting and the open space around the edge is attractive to a variety of warblers and passerines.

Directions: just over a mile south of Ikes Point on Route 102, turn west toward Echo Lake Beach, then left again onto Lurvey Spring Road toward Seal Cove.

⑪ Seawall in Manset is where some of the best birding on Mount Desert Island begins. South of Southwest Harbor, Route 102 makes a circuit loop, starting with a left onto Route 102A to Manset, later returning to Route 102 via Bass Harbor. Route 102A leads to a very rocky beach called Seawall. The ocean view is one of the best places for sea duck watching, especially in winter. Common Eiders, Buffleheads, Horned and Red-necked Grebes, Black Guillemots, all three scoters, both cormorants, Long-tailed Ducks, and Red-breasted Mergansers are present at various times. Look also for Bonaparte's Gulls, which sometimes flock in large numbers. This is a good place to use a spotting scope. In the immediate ledge area, stay alert for Purple Sandpipers in winter. Across the street, there are always ducks around whenever the pond is not frozen. Just beyond, a picnic area opposite the camp-

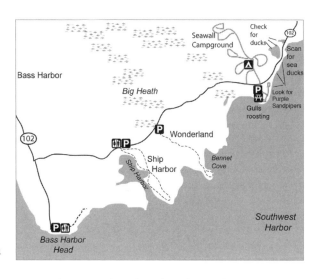

ground is plowed in winter and is populated with at least three species of gull. Farther along the road, be alert to the boggy area opposite the Wonderland trail. This is the Big Heath, and it offers the best opportunity for boreal birds that are not common on MDI. Palm warblers nest in early June. Yellow-bellied and Olive-sided Flycatchers are known to nest here, as do Lincoln's Sparrows.

Wonderland is the first of two trails that shelter nesting warblers. Given their proximity, Wonderland and Ship Harbor share much in common. Wonderland contains a higher ratio of conifers and open, dry ledges, so boreal species may be more likely here. Blackpoll Warblers can sometimes be found near the shoreline. From a dense, wet beginning, the trail transitions through white spruce and jack pine to an unusual concentration of blue-tinted white spruce and roses. Open areas are good for American Redstarts, Nashville Warblers, and Yellow-rumped Warblers. In a good cone year, look for both Red and White-winged Crossbills in the spruce trees. On offshore ledges, perched Bald Eagles are a common sight.

Ship Harbor is a longer trail that offers a bit more mature growth and habitat diversity than Wonderland, improving the opportunity for both coniferous- and deciduous-loving warblers. Be alert for crossbills. There is a summer composting toilet at the trailhead.

Bass Harbor Head Light is the grandest on the island. It is a popular tourist attraction, and the shrubs and secondary growth adjacent to the lighthouse and in the neighboring yards attract a fair share of common warblers. Toilet facilities are present at the far end of the parking lot.

Bass Harbor is the nearest thing to a quaint fishing village on Mount Desert Island. It is more sheltered, so Long-tailed Ducks, Buffleheads, Red-breasted Mergansers, Common Loons, Black Ducks, Mallards, and various gulls drift among the anchored boats in winter.

Swan's Island is reached by ferry from Bass Harbor. Though the island is not part of Acadia National Park, some vacationers go there to get away from it all. The year-round population of 350 doubles in the summer. The island's 7,000 acres contain 29 miles of paved road and many more private and woods roads. Coves are sheltered and deep and the hills are mostly spruce covered. Bicycles are often the best way to get around the island for birding and day-tripping. The ferry charges a fee for pedestrians and an additional fee for bikes.

⟢⟐⟐⟐⟣

41 Schoodic Point is a separate part of Acadia National Park. Although it shares some of the habitat characteristics of the larger park on Mount Desert Island, there are important differences. The Schoodic portion is more strongly boreal, with uncommon sightings of Spruce Grouse, Boreal Chickadee, and Black-backed Woodpeckers a possibility. The park loop road is closer to the water, with frequent pull-offs, making it easy to scan for waterfowl. Schoodic is one of the most exposed points of land anywhere on the coast and one of the best places to scope for distant sea birds.

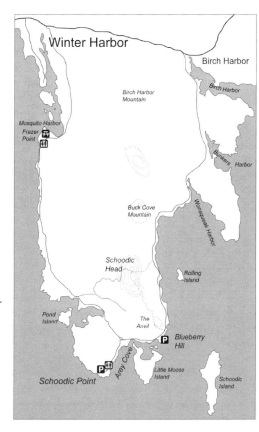

Directions: from Route 1, follow the signs to Winter Harbor along Route 186 to Schoodic Point.

Frazer Point: The first contact with salt water after entering the Park Loop Road is a causeway called Mosquito Harbor, worth a brief stop. In season, Belted Kingfishers forage over the wide tidal river. Immediately afterward, pull into Frazer Point. The open space and low shrubbery entice warblers, and the picnic area provides a wide-open look at the channel. Good binoculars or a spotting scope are required, because the sea ducks tend to stay rather distant here. There is a seasonal rest room.

Schoodic Head: For the next couple of miles, proceed through low coniferous forest with a smattering of birch trees. Through spring and summer breeding season, this is a warbler paradise. At about 2.3 miles beyond Frazer Point a gravel road appears on the left. The road climbs a mile up Schoodic Head, followed by a few hundred yards of footpath to the summit. The road is closed in winter, but even in summer birders often elect to park at the bottom and hike the length. The spruce-fir mix is adequate for boreal specialties. Spruce Grouse, Black-backed Woodpeckers, Yellow-bellied Flycatchers, and Boreal Chickadees occur here but none are common. Swainson's Thrushes are present. In irruptive seasons, it's a good area for White-winged and Red Crossbills. Barred Owls and Northern Goshawks patrol the woods around the summit. Beyond the Schoodic Head Road, there is a marshy pond attractive to Great Blue Herons. A half-mile later there is a salt marsh that should be checked for Nelson's Sharp-tailed Sparrows.

Schoodic Point: Continue along, lingering for a quick scan wherever there is water. Where the road forks right to Schoodic Point and becomes two-way traffic, take the time to check the birds of Arey Cove. At any time of year expect Common Eiders, Red-breasted Mergansers, and Black Guillemots. All three scoters are found here during the year. In winter, it's a good chance for Red-throated Loons. Schoodic Point extends into the Atlantic, and Northern Gannets may be passing in any season but mid-winter. It's a good spot for occasional Black-legged Kittiwakes in late summer and fall. Harlequin Ducks are becoming more common in winter. Expect the usual suspects: Common Eiders, Common Goldeneyes, Long-tailed Ducks, scoters, cormorants (Double-crested in summer; Great in winter), Horned and Red-necked Grebes, loons, Buffleheads, and Black Guillemots. There are plenty of gulls around, so don't overlook a chance Glaucous or Iceland in winter.

Continuing eastward there is another trail towards Schoodic Head opposite the parking lot for Blueberry Hill. Ruby-crowned Kinglets and many warblers lurk along the beginning of this trail in spring and summer. These include American Redstart, Nashville, Chestnut-sided, Black-throated Green, and Yellow-rumped. Spend ample time scanning the waters off Blueberry Hill. In winter, Great Cormorants are abundant and Thick-billed Murres have been sighted on multiple occasions.

To exit the park, follow the road to Birch Harbor, turning left to remain in the Acadia area or right to continue toward Washington County.

━━➤-◦-◄━━

Additional Sites:

a **The Little Deer Isle Causeway** was purchased in 2004 by the Island Heritage Trust, which has made parking and viewing more accessible. Route 15 to Deer Isle/Stonington crosses a suspension bridge over Eggemoggin Reach onto Little Deer Isle, and then turns sharply left to cross a causeway onto Deer Isle. Birding from the bridge is impossible and there is little room to park on the far side, so birders typically zoom by. However, the causeway can sometimes be interesting depending on season and tide. At low tide, the area is mostly unproductive mud flats. At high tide, eiders, loons, scoters, and grebes are all possible. Bonaparte's Gulls may be visible on the wing and such unusual species as Lesser Black-backed Gull have been found roosting on the rocks on the other side of the road. Surf and White-winged Scoters are often seen in the cove along the causeway and Bald Eagles have nested on the island.

Scott's Landing is a 22-acre parcel across the street from the causeway beach. It is a mix of abandoned blueberry fields, moraines, marsh, woody wetlands, mature and young woodlands—an above-average spot for open-area warblers like American Redstarts, and another good place to scan for sea ducks.

b **Barred Island Preserve** is a quiet sanctuary of The Nature Conservancy and the Island Heritage Trust that can be hard to find. The trail squeezes between two tracts of privately owned woods through a stand of spruce/fir that is interrupted by yellow birch, some white birch, and a little red and striped maple. The forest floor is carpeted in moss, and interpretive signs on the trail will explain the unusual lichens that grow here. This is the domain of Swainson's Thrushes, Golden-crowned Kinglets, Black-burnian Warblers, and Blue-headed Vireos. Boreal Chickadees have been noted here in the past, though their numbers appear to have dwindled. The last quarter of the mile-long trail emerges onto glaciated ledges punctuated by white spruce. The margin between cliff and forest is likely to contain Northern Parula and Black-throated Green Warblers, while the openly spaced spruces are known for Common Yellowthroats and Song Sparrows. Barred Island lies at the end of the trail. At low tide, hikers may clamber onto the island, returning before the tide begins rising again.

Directions: follow Route 15A south from Deer Isle through the village of Sunset. A half mile after passing the golf course, look for the sign to Goose Cove Road on the right and follow 1.2 miles to the preserve parking lot on the right. There are no signs for the preserve from the main road. The parking lot has room for only a few cars and a sign admonishes visitors to return later if they find the lot full. Do not park in the road. Avoid straying onto private property.

C **Crockett Cove Woods** is also a preserve of The Nature Conservancy and the Island Heritage Trust. Unlike the balsam and white spruce that cover Barred Island Preserve just a few miles away, white pine, oak, and red spruce cover many of its 98 acres. This diversity accommodates a greater variety of warbler species. Black-capped Chickadees are common and Boreal Chickadees are possible, though rare. There are 18 interpretive stops along the nature trail.

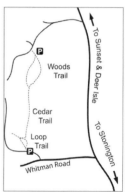

Directions: from Sunset, continue south about three miles beyond the Sunset Post Office. Turn right onto Whitman Road, and then another right onto Fire Lane 88. The preserve entrance is just ahead, marked by room for a couple of vehicles, a small sign, and a registration box. From Stonington, the preserve is two miles west along the Shore Road, then turn left onto Whitman Road.

d **Stonington** has exceptional sea kayaking, due to its sheltered location and many small islands. It provides a good chance to see many of Maine's common seabirds, and perhaps harbor porpoises and harbor seals as well. There are many lobster boats working these waters, so personal experience or outfitter assistance is recommended. Find more information through the Maine Island Trail Association at www.mita.org and the Maine Association of Sea Kayak Guides at www.maineseakayakguides.com.

For kayaking, boat trips, and even cruises to see Atlantic Puffins, Old Quarry Adventures is a fine local choice. Check www.oldquarry. com for schedules. Captain Bill Baker makes regular summer trips to Seal Island, an island 20 miles offshore that is part of the Maine Coastal Island National Wildlife Refuge. This puffin trip offers several advantages. The trip goes far enough out to sea that encounters with pelagic species are common. Besides the multitude of puffins and Razorbills, the island is a good place to look for Great Cormorants in summer at the southernmost tip of their summer breeding range. Like all puffin colonies, the island supports a healthy population of Common and Arctic Terns, too. Early season trips afford an additional bonus: a chance to see Purple Sandpipers before they leave for their northern breeding grounds in late May.

e **The Old Settlement Quarry** is managed by the Island Heritage Trust. Although small, it takes a while to explore it fully because of the views and the fascinating history of the site as explained by several interpretive signs. The trail to the quarry and many of the surrounding paths traverse mixed habitat with lots of spruce and fir. The sounds of Winter Wrens, Swainson's Thrushes, and drumming Ruffed Grouse accompany a good walk on this preserve. Weedy vegetation around the quarry attracts sparrows, especially during migration.

Directions: take Route 15 towards Stonington, turning left onto Oceanville Road. In just under a mile, past the sign for Webb Cove Road and Old Quarry Adventures, look for a granite sign on the right and the entrance to the preserve.

f **The Edgar M. Tennis Preserve** was once a coastal farm and some of the pathways and foundations still remain. A registration box at the entrance may contain brochures that explain the history of the farm, which is now state property managed by the Island Heritage Trust. The spruce/fir habitat is typical of coastal sites in the area and there are a fair number of common birds to enjoy while walking the trails. Look for Bald Eagles and Ospreys along the shore, and seals hauled out on the ledge.

Directions: go about 1.3 miles from where Greenlaw intersects Sunshine and take a right onto Tennis Road. Continue on until you find the preserve register box on the left followed by a small parking area.

g **Isle au Haut** lies 8 miles due south of the Deer Isle/Stonington peninsula. Acadia National Park manages about half of the island. The remainder is private and access is limited. Accommodations on the island are also very limited. There are five seasonal lean-tos operated by the park at Duck Harbor, and advance registration is necessary. For birders, Isle au Haut's big claim to fame is its large population of wintering Harlequin Ducks. About

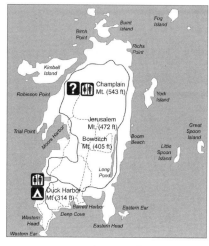

100–200 ducks make up the largest known concentration on the east coast. However, there are no public boat trips to witness this spectacle. Maine Audubon offers a trip in some years, but these have dwindled as Harlequins have become more regular in southern Maine.

There are no birds to be found on Isle au Haut that cannot be found on the mainland. Because of its proximity to other islands, it is not a big migrant trap like Monhegan and Matinicus farther south. Still, the park limits visitation to 50 people a day, and since there are limited accommodations and the mail boat from Stonington is a bit pricey, the one thing you can be sure of is that you won't see a crowd. For mail boat and lodging information, visit www.isleauhaut.com.

h **Stanwood Wildlife Sanctuary** in Ellsworth is also known as Birdsacre. The 130-acre wildlife reserve is full of nature trails, picnic areas, and more than 100 species of birds. More importantly, Birdsacre serves as a rehabilitation center for ducks, songbirds, hawks, and particularly, owls. Originally the home of Cordelia Stanwood, noted ornithologist, photographer, and writer, it was purchased in 1960 by Chandler Richmond upon her death. Richmond preserved and expanded the property until 1984 when stewardship was handed over to his son, Stanley Richmond, and his daughter, Diane Richmond Castle. Some of the nature trails are wheelchair-accessible and all are popular with hikers and birders. Be sure to visit the owl rehabilitation center.

Directions: the sanctuary is on the east side of Route 3 just beyond where it diverges from Route 1 in Ellsworth.

ℹ Prospect Harbor's sardine processing plant attracts hundreds of gulls. In winter, Iceland gulls are regularly found among them, probably sitting on the roof of the plant or roosting among the Herring and Great Black-backed Gulls. Check the gulls resting on ice flows or islands in the adjacent estuary. It is one of the more promising places in Maine for Glaucous Gulls. While their white wingtips may not be immediately evident, their size alone—nearly comparable to a Great Black-backed Gull—helps them stand out in the crowd. They tower over Herring Gulls. This is the last active sardine canning plant in the U.S. and its future is uncertain. Should the plant close, the number of gulls will diminish, though the harbor will remain attractive to sea ducks.

Directions: the harbor and cannery are on Route 186 east of Birch Harbor.

Down East: Washington County

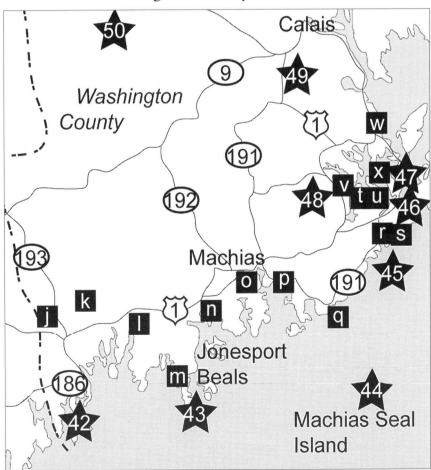

Official Maine Birding Trail Sites

⭐ 42 **Petit Manan:** A series of peninsulas extends up Maine's coast. Beyond Acadia National Park lies Petit Manan. Maine Coastal Islands National Wildlife Refuge encompasses five separate refuges along the Maine coast. Its 5,125 acres include 14 islands as far as 150 miles down the coast, where Pond Island rests next to Popham Beach State Park. However, the heart of the refuge is here on Petit Manan Point and the island of Petit Manan.

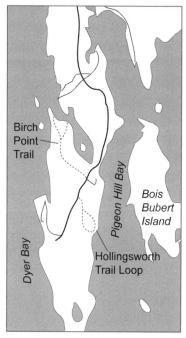

There are two trails on Petit Manan Point. The Birch Point Trail begins near the parking lot. A kiosk here is usually well provisioned with information, trail guides, and bird lists. The Birch Point Trail slopes gently over a variety of habitat during its 4-mile round trip. Blueberry barrens give way to boreal forest, which in turn yield to salt marsh. Boreal Chickadees are uncommon and Spruce Grouse are occasional in these woods. Canada, Nashville, Magnolia, Black-and-white, Black-throated Green, and Blackburnian Warblers are prominent. This is a favorite place for snowshoeing and cross-country skiing in winter.

The Hollingsworth Trail is a more rugged 1.5-mile round-trip that leads to the eastern shore of the point. Cobblestone beaches and very rugged shoreline extend southward for miles from here. The trail can be reached by driving or walking about a half mile from the parking lot at the Birch Point Trail. Another parking lot on the right and the trailhead on the left mark the spot. The road continues past the trail, serving a few private homes on the west side of the peninsula. The Hollingsworth Trail is more open, catering to Common Yellowthroats, American Redstarts, Chestnut-sided, and Yellow-rumped Warblers.

Petit Manan Island is the site of the second-tallest lighthouse in Maine, stretching 123 feet into the sky. The lighthouse is on the National Register of Historic Places. Petit Manan Island is one of the most important nesting islands on the entire coast of Maine. Its 10 acres provide nesting grounds for Atlantic Puffins, Common Eiders, Black Guillemots, Razorbills, Leach's Storm-petrels and all three of Maine's offshore breeding terns: Common, Arctic, and the endangered Roseate. It is also the largest known cold-water nesting site for Laughing Gulls. Naturally, like most other critical nesting habitats, it's off limits to the public. However, many of its resident species can be seen from shore.

Directions: Petit Manan Point lies at the end of Pigeon Hill Road. The turn onto Pigeon Hill Road from Route 1 is small and not well marked. It is 2.2 miles south of Milbridge or 2.9 miles north of Steuben on Route 1. Follow Pigeon Hill Road through a tiny village and fishing community to its termination at the refuge.

<hr />

43 Great Wass Island: The Nature Conservancy (TNC) has stewardship over one of Washington County's jewels. TNC snapped up much of this ecological treasure in 1978 for a number of reasons. Foremost, the peninsula stretches farther into the Atlantic than any other extension of the Down East mainland, at a point where Bay of Fundy and Gulf of Maine waters collide. Thus, it is virtually surrounded by the tempering effects of both, a mixture of moderate temperatures and constant humidity. Flora more common to Atlantic Canada reach the limit of their southern ranges here and some of Maine's rarest plants call the island home. The bogs (or heaths) on

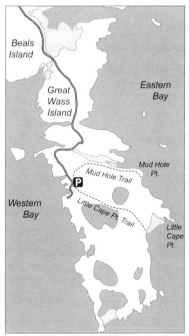

Great Wass are of a raised type that flourish in only the most extreme maritime environments. Depressions left behind by glaciers 10,000 to 12,000 years ago slowly filled with accumulating layers of sphagnum moss, creating an acidic bog habitat supportive of carnivorous plants and stunted shrubs.

The preserve is home to virtually all of the boreal species nesting

in Maine: Palm Warblers, Boreal Chickadees, Spruce Grouse, Yellow-bellied Flycatchers, Lincoln Sparrows, and Black-backed Woodpeckers. Most of Maine's other coniferous–loving woodland warblers are present, too: Blackburnian, Bay-breasted, and Blackpoll. In the deciduous woods along the road and in the parking lot, all of the hardwood-loving warblers may be found—especially Black-throated Green and Black-throated Blue, Northern Parula, and American Redstart. A Canada Warbler often turns up just a hundred yards along the trail, where boardwalks cross a boggy area. Common Loons, eiders and all three scoters cover the waters close to shore, and it can be one of the better places to chance upon an Atlantic Puffin in August. In winter, Common Murres, Thick-billed Murres, Razorbills, Harlequin Ducks, Black Guillemots, Red-necked and Horned Grebes are all possible. Bald Eagles, Ospreys, and Common Ravens nest on Great Wass and its neighboring islands. In any season, harbor seals haul out in great numbers off Cape Cove.

One trail exits the parking lot, diverging into two: the Mud Hole Trail and the Little Cape Point Trail 100 yards later. The left fork (Mud Hole) meanders through spruce and fir for 1.5 miles until it reaches a narrow cove. From here it winds east until reaching Mud Hole Point. The views of Eastern Bay and its islands are panoramic. The right fork (Little Cape Point) wanders 2 miles through a jack pine, spruce, and fir forest carpeted in thick moss. After about a mile, open ledges offer a glimpse of the preserve's best bog areas. Still farther, a bridge presents the opportunity to walk through the bog area and evaluate its unique vegetation more closely. Although either trail offers good birding, the Little Cape Point Trail is preferred for its length and a little more habitat variation. It is possible to combine both trails into a loop. A cairn and a red marker indicate the shoreline terminus for each trail. Simply walk the shoreline between them for a loop of about 5 miles. It is also possible to hike the shoreline the full 4.5 miles from Little Cape Cove south to Red Head, but you must return the way you came because from there the shoreline is private property.

Directions: from Jonesport, cross the bridge to Beals Island, then continue over the causeway onto Great Wass Island next to Alley Bay. Continue straight ahead, following the hardscrabble road as it turns to dirt and narrows. About three miles from Beals, look for The Nature Conservancy parking lot on the left.

⭐**44** **Machias Seal Island** provides the best offshore birding experience in Maine. Technically, it is disputed territory between the United States and Canada. Canada has maintained a lighthouse since 1832 and the island is staffed and supervised by the Canadian Wildlife Service. Their rangers enjoy the opportunity to share their 15-acre birding paradise. There are over 3,000 Atlantic Puffins nesting on the island, surrounded by even more Arctic and Common Tern nests. (Numbers may vary. The island experienced complete tern colony failures for several years during the writing of this guide.) Razorbills and Common Murres are also easy to see on the island. A series of blinds allow visitors to observe and photograph birds within arm's reach. The best time to visit is early June through mid-July, but there is good variety for as long as the tour boats go forth. Two commercial tours serve the island from the U.S., one from Jonesport, the other from Cutler. A Canadian tour boat also visits the island from Grand Manan.

The Norton family operates the granddaddy of them all: Puffin Tours out of Jonesport. The family moved to Down East Maine in 1760 and has operated the tour for decades. Captain Andy Patterson motors out of Cutler Harbor on the *Barbara Frost*, a custom forty-foot passenger vessel self-described as the fastest and best-equipped means to Machias Seal Island. His Bold Coast Charter Company also offers excursions to other sights Down East, including Cross Island, the northernmost island of the Maine Coastal Islands NWR.

Several conditions apply to Machias Seal Island boat tours. Departure times are tide and weather dependent. It is optimal to arrive at Machias Seal Island during high tide. All tours do their best to land guests on the island, but the landing is tricky. Guests are transferred to a small skiff and shuttled to shore. In high surf conditions, passengers will not be able to land at all. However, in this uncommon instance, the boats will moor in the lee of the island and good observations are still assured. In poor weather, the boats won't go out, which means that each operator requires a check-in with them the night before. For more information, contact Puffin Tours: 888-889-3222 or 207-497-5933, or www.machiassealisland.com. Bold Coast Tours at 207-259-4484, or www.boldcoast.com.

45 **The Bold Coast Trails** are terrific and seldom crowded. They would be worthy of hiking even if the birding weren't so good. The paths wind through some of the best boreal habitat in the state. This is a good place to find the warblers that prefer spruces, especially Bay-breasted, Canada, Blackpoll, and perhaps Cape May warblers. Spruce Grouse, Boreal Chickadees, Golden-crowned Kinglets, and

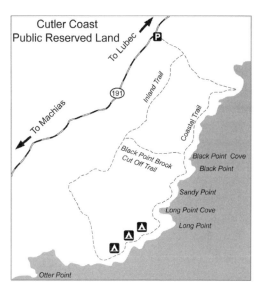

Brown Creepers are regularly encountered. Nearly 200 species have been recorded on or near this 2,190-acre area, including Merlin, Peregrine Falcon, and six owl species. Not only are Common Eiders and Black Guillemots easily observed from the coastal trail, but so are seals, porpoises, and sometimes whales. Black bear, moose, deer, bobcat, and coyote roam the preserve.

All of the trails pass through spruce-fir habitat, impenetrable to the sun. Several sections traverse cedar bog. The trails can be damp and slippery. There are narrow log boardwalks across the muddiest places, but the boardwalks themselves tend to be slick. The Coastal Trail requires up and down climbing over short sections. Therefore, good footwear and adequate hiking ability are required.

Directions: the Bold Coast trails are located along Route 191 between Cutler and Lubec. They are 17 miles southeast of Machias, three miles northeast of Cutler and about 10 miles southwest of Lubec.

---

46 **Quoddy Head State Park's** beauty and the birding in this area cannot be exaggerated. It is home to one of Maine's best-known lighthouses. First established in 1808, it was replaced by the current, candy-striped tower in 1858. Sail Rock, which sits offshore of the head, is technically the easternmost point in the United States. The birds that

roost on it vary by
the season: Double-
crested Cormorants
all summer, Black-
legged Kittiwakes
in late summer, and
Great Cormorants
throughout winter.
It requires good bin-
oculars or a spotting

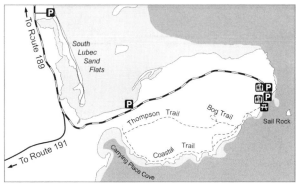

scope to find the Black-bellied Plovers, Ruddy Turnstones, and Purple
Sandpipers that often roost on this rock as well. This is one of the more
promising places in Maine to see Razorbills from land. Black Guillemots,
Red-breasted Mergansers, and Common Loons are normal; rarities such
as Pacific Loon are possible. Scoters linger offshore in all seasons except
mid-summer, joined by Long-tailed Ducks in winter. Boreal Chickadees
are sometimes encountered in the parking area near the pit toilet.

The picnic area is a good place to sit and wait for the birds to come
to the table. Warblers such as Magnolia, Yellow-rumped, Black-and-
white, Black-throated Green and American Redstarts work the fringes.
The park's 4.5 miles of trails traverse a variety of habitats. The Coastal
Trail pops in and out of the woods, providing great ocean views while
boreal species remain near enough to be heard. It passes Gulliver's Hole,
a unique narrow chasm formed by the erosion of a vertical fault in the
magma. The Thompson Trail is maritime boreal habitat. Black-capped
Chickadees are more common than Boreal Chickadees, but both are
possible. Golden-crowned Kinglets are abundant. The Bog Trail is
exceptional. Not only does it contain an interpretive boardwalk, but the
woodland border also normally produces Palm Warblers and Yellow-bellied Flycatchers. Olive-sided Flycatchers are possible. Lincoln's Sparrows
nest along the boardwalk and scold visitors in early summer.

In Washington County, Quoddy Head is the single best place to
bird in winter. Sea ducks and alcids are more common in winter. Bald
Eagles frequent the park and surrounding coves. There is an astonishing winter crop of berries on the road into the park, which makes
it possible in some years for American Robins to winter over by the
hundreds, perhaps thousands! Although snow may accumulate in the
picnic area and the trails may be too icy, the lighthouse area is often

windswept of snow so that good viewing is possible all year. Naturally, cold days with high winds are painful, but sunny, windless winter days are a coastal pleasure.

Directions: follow Route 189 toward Lubec 9.6 miles from the intersection with Route 1 in Whiting. Turn right on South Lubec Road and follow to the end. From Route 191 via the Boot Cove Road, bear right onto the South Lubec Road. The lighthouse area is straight ahead at the end. The picnic area and trails are in a separate parking area to the right. There are pit toilets in both locations. There is a small fee to visit Quoddy Head State Park, but none for visiting the lighthouse area alone.

⟶➤◦◄⟵

47 **The South Lubec Sand Bar** is one of Maine's best places to witness shorebird migration. Throughout August and early September, the mud flats fill with shorebirds. The best period is from the second week of August through Labor Day. Semipalmated Sandpipers and Plovers are the most numerous, but careful searching will turn up plenty of Least and White-rumped Sandpipers. Pectoral Sandpipers are few but noticeable as they tower above their cousins. Black-bellied Plovers are numerous and a few American Golden Plovers can often be found in their midst. Small flocks of Short-billed Dowitchers work both the mud flats and the pond margins. Hudsonian Godwits are occasional and Marbled Godwits are rare visitors. Buff-breasted Sandpipers pop in occasionally. Dunlin arrive later in the season. Horned Larks are likely along the spit and Lapland Longspurs are possible in autumn, often mixed in the same flock. The best time to visit is within 2–3 hours on either side of high tide, when birds are concentrated. Wherever shorebirds are present, Peregrine Falcons and Merlins are inevitable. Short-eared Owls sometimes roost in the grass. In winter, large concentrations of gulls also roost here and there is always the chance that Iceland and Glaucous Gulls will be among them. There is another overlook area on the South Lubec Road near Carrying Place Cove, which is always worth a stop. At the right tide, the birds may be closer to the outflow of the stream in that area.

Visiting the sand bar requires complete respect for private property. The state owns the farthest section of the bar, but the near sections, including the dirt access road, are clearly posted as no trespassing. It is permissible to park in the privately owned parking area, walk directly to the beach, and then down the beach to the state-owned part of the sand bar where large signs are obvious. If the lot is full, please bird elsewhere and return later. Never approach or disturb roosting shorebirds. There are no facilities.

Directions: the entrance is normally marked by a small sign that reads "Bar Road." It is a small, dirt road 1.9 miles from Route 189 along the South Lubec Road. Park only in the parking area. Go directly to the beach. Only the south end of the bar is owned by the state. From Route 191 via the Boot Cove Road, bear left onto the South Lubec Road and look for the right turn after Olson's Propane.

---

48 Moosehorn National Wildlife Refuge, Edmunds Division, is less than half the size of the Baring Unit, which is farther north, but its 8,781 acres include some of the most

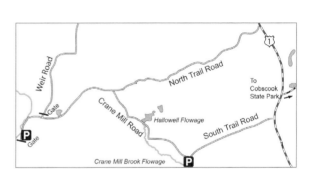

strongly tidal shoreland in America, with 24-foot fluctuations that alternately reveal and conceal mud flats for the shorebirds. Much of the shoreland section of this unit is managed by Cobscook Bay State Park. But what really makes the Edmunds Division attractive is a loop of dirt roads that plunge into exceptional mixed woodland and managed wetlands. Boreal Chickadees inhabit some of the thicker stands of spruce, and the refuge is particularly good for warblers, vireos, thrushes, flycatchers, and woodpeckers. Expect Black-and-white, Black-throated Green, Black-throated Blue, Nashville, and Magnolia Warblers. Try for Cape May, Canada, Blackburnian, and Bay-breasted Warblers. Northern Goshawks are regular nesters. Like the Baring Division of the refuge, The Edmunds Division is managed specifically for American Woodcock.

The South Trail Road turns west from Route 1 just south of the Cobscook Bay State Park entrance. The North Trail Road likewise turns west about a mile north of the park entrance. Both are marked with small kiosks. At the far end of South Trail Road, Crane Mill Road connects the two, creating a loop. The Crane Mill Brook Flowage is just a quick walk beyond the gate at the end of South Trail Road. It is worth a quick peek for waterfowl. The aspens behind the outflow are good for shrub-loving warblers and sparrows. Crane Mill Road passes another good flowage, Hallowell Flowage, in the middle of its mile-long stretch. Canada Geese, Ring-necked Ducks, and Hooded Mergansers are the most likely to be present.

Crane Mill Road intersects North Trail Road at the midpoint of its three-mile excursion into the woods. The first half of North Trail is especially good for warblers, vireos, and Swainson's Thrushes. The last half-mile follows a stream that flows through a burned area—a very good spot for Chestnut-sided Warblers and Swamp Sparrows. Along its length, the North Trail produces seven flycatchers: Alder, Least, Yellow-bellied, Olive-sided, Great-crested, Eastern Wood Pewee, and Eastern Phoebe. Just west of the North Trail intersection with the Crane Mill Road, Weir Road enters from the right. It is gated, but is a great walking trail past a series of small ponds. It is three miles along the Weir Road, one way, to Route 1. There are no facilities.

Directions: the South Trail Road is almost 4 miles north of the Route 1 intersection with Route 189. The North Trail Road is a mile farther north.

49 Moosehorn National Wildlife Refuge, Baring Division, is outstanding. In 1934, Congress passed The Federal Duck Stamp Act to raise money for the establishment of national wildlife refuges. Just three years later, Moosehorn NWR became one of the first refuges in the country. Recent acquisitions have expanded the total protection area of the refuge to 28,808 acres.

Moosehorn has many claims to fame. First among these are its American

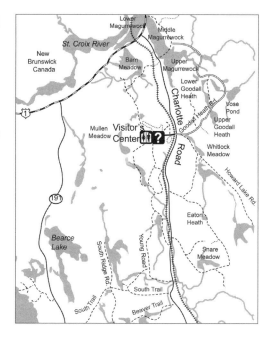

Woodcock study and restoration projects. Large tracts of the refuge are managed primarily for woodcock. Second in priority are the waterfowl, wading bird, and shorebird habitats. Four natural lakes are augmented by more than 50 manmade wetlands. It is an important breeding ground for many species and a stopover point for many more. Its third claim to fame is its forest management practices. The refuge is carefully managed through selective woodcutting and prescribed burning to yield a diverse woodland habitat. More than 220 species have been identified at Moosehorn, including over 20 warbler species. Approximately one-third of the refuge is part of the National Wilderness Preservation System.

The Baring Division is the larger of the two and provides most of the birding opportunities. On the northern edge, Route 1 runs through the refuge. Magurrewock Marsh, in its various upper and lower sections, teems with waterfowl in the spring. Many species linger to breed. Canada Goose, Wood Duck, Green-winged and Blue-winged Teal, American Black Duck, Mallard, Ring-necked Duck, Hooded and Common Mergansers, Common Loons, American Coot, and Pied-billed Grebes are all confirmed nesters. Snow Goose, Brant, Northern Pintail, Northern Shoveler, Gadwall, American Widgeon, and Lesser Scaup all pass through. Virginia Rail and Sora breed in Magurrewock Marsh. Marsh Wrens in late May can be heard buzzing all night long.

The most visible Bald Eagle's nest in Maine is right next to busy Route 1. Bald Eagles have shown sensitivity to human disturbance, but apparently that does not apply to the pair that has taken over a platform originally intended for Ospreys. An observation deck has been erected a discreet distance away, adjacent to the road, and offers excellent views from snowmelt through July when the birds disperse. At least three pairs of eagles nest within Moosehorn. Ospreys, undeterred, nest nearby on other platforms.

Expect some frustration in birding along Route 1. The road is heavily traveled at all times, with many large trucks, and the noise will challenge the best birding ear. It is possible to park near the railroad crossing on Route 1 just south of the Charlotte Road and walk the tracks into the center of the marsh. The tracks divide Lower Barn Meadow from Lower Magurrewock Marsh. Virginia Rails and Sora are present on either side. Marsh Wrens chatter incessantly. Kingbirds, Catbirds, and Yellow Warblers are prominent and Warbling Vireos have been found nesting at the end of this spur near the river. Do not go beyond this spur's junction with the main track along the river, because this track is still active and trains can appear with little warning.

The Charlotte Road divides the Baring Division from north to south. It also gets heavy traffic. Turning south off Route 1, the Charlotte Road passes by the largest portion of Magurrewock Marsh. Because the marsh is valuable nesting habitat, there are few opportunities for close observation. Resign yourself to good views from the roadside, even at the dam-controlled end of the marsh where Canada Geese abound. It takes no patience to see a Great Blue Heron and only a little patience to become aware of the many American Bitterns that are present. Their odd, thunder-pumping song can be heard for half a mile and they are frequently seen on the wing.

The Moosehorn offices and visitor center are located some three miles south of the Charlotte Road intersection with Route 1. It is often best to go there first, because the kiosk provides bird lists, trails maps, and detailed information about the refuge. Bathroom facilities are available. Also, there are two interpretive trails nearby. The Habitat Trail loops for 1.2 miles behind the center. It is good for common warblers such as Black-throated Green, Black-and-white, Magnolia, and American Redstart. The Woodcock Trail loops for 1/3 mile at the entrance of the access road. Since the primary management species of Moosehorn NWR is woodcock, this interpretive trail offers great insight. Woodcock are abundant throughout the season and vocal from late April through late May. Their lek displays are some of the most famous in the bird kingdom. This trail is handicapped-accessible.

There are 50 miles of dirt roads and trails in Moosehorn. All are good, but a few are best for birding. The Barn Meadow area encompasses an incredible diversity of habitat. At first, the trail leads through thin woods, good for American Redstarts, Magnolia and Black-throated Green Warblers, as well as Red-eyed and Blue-headed Vireos. Scarlet Tanagers are regularly heard but seldom seen. After a quarter mile, there is a substantial stand of large white pines on the right side of the trail where Pine Warblers sing as if on cue. Not long after crossing the railroad tracks, a service road circumnavigates a set of ponds regulated for water depth. Blue-winged Teal and American Black Ducks are the most likely nesters but be prepared for anything. Virginia Rail and Sora are often vocal. A dozen different warbler species are likely to be identified while circling the ponds. Stay alert for Wilson's Snipe, Eastern Bobolink,

Northern Harrier, and perhaps an uncommon Willow Flycatcher.

Directions: the trail entrance is obscure. Look for several boulders lined up next to the road just beyond the Magurrewock Impoundment on the Charlotte Road 3/4 mile from Route 1. The trailhead is on the far left side of the small field.

Just beyond the Magurrewock Impoundment, there is a parking lot and a paved path leading through a Bobolink-infested field to a small blind on the marsh. Canada Geese, Wood Ducks, and other dabblers may be present. Swamp Sparrows and Common Yellowthroats are easy to see here. Eastern Phoebes nest under the eaves of the blind and other flycatchers are nearby, including Alder and Yellow-bellied. Virginia Rails are secretive within the reeds. This trail is handicapped-accessible.

Directions: at 1.3 miles on the Charlotte Road, look for a small parking lot on the left.

At 3 miles along the Charlotte Road, a right turn leads to the Refuge headquarters. Opposite the entrance road to the headquarters, there is an entrance to two roads that can be birded on foot. The gate for the left fork is normally open for vehicle traffic, which allows cars a limited distance to some of the wetlands. Gated trails lead along the Goodall Heath Road to the Vose Pond Road for an excellent loop around several ponds and flowages, plus heath and mixed hardwood stands. Veery is the predominant thrush in this area. The road is good for many species of warblers, Blue-headed and Red-eyed Vireos, Wilson's Snipe, and a variety of waterfowl. Be on the lookout for moose.

The stretch of Charlotte Road south of Refuge headquarters is boreal forest. Saw-whet Owls are thick along this stretch of road and can be heard calling before dawn from late winter to June. They often seem to be in vocal competition with the Whip-poor-wills, which are also common along this road as well as along the refuge's many dirt roads.

At the southern end of the Baring Division, another nice walking loop takes birders through more good waterfowl flowages. This area is particularly good for moose. A loop using the South Trail, South Ridge Road, and Beaver Trail is just over three miles long. Parts of it pass through enough mixed forest and wetland habitat to provide an unusually high diversity of species.

Directions: look for South Trail on the west side of Charlotte Road approximately 6 miles from Route 1. Beaver Trail is only 0.3 mile beyond. South Ridge Road connects these two trails for an easy loop, but it's wise to bring a map, as all trails look alike.

50 **Downeast Lakes Land Trust** in interior Washington County is famous for the undeveloped lakes that make a visit so worthwhile. The tiny village of Grand Lake Stream sits at the outflow of West Grand Lake, the center of a robust hunting and fishing tradition since the 19th century. The traditional sporting camps and lodges here are marvelous places to stay while exploring the area. Beginning with an initial conservation purchase of 27,000 acres, the Downeast Lakes Land Trust has been working to protect the natural beauty of the Farm Cove Community Forest since 2001, while continuing to improve its water access and hiking trail systems.

The Little Mayberry Cove Trail begins at the outlet dam and follows the shoreline for 2-1/2 miles through mature hemlock forest. Black-throated Blue Warblers, Scarlet Tanagers, and Eastern Wood-Pewees are common among the many songbirds found along the trail.

The Pocumcus Lake Trail provides two loops: one loop is 1.3 miles long, the other 3.6 miles. This trail begins in secondary growth forest and proceeds through thick vegetation into a mature canopy forest. Northern Parula, Black-throated Blue and Blackburnian Warblers are plentiful. Near the lake, the white pines harbor Pine Warblers and any damp tangle within the forest is likely to shelter a Canada Warbler. It's a good trail for Ruffed Grouse and, judging by the abundance of moose droppings along the trail, it's also a pretty good corridor for wildlife in the thick woods. The trailhead is located 7.5 miles from Grand Lake Stream on the Fourth Lake Road.

Wabassus Landing at Mile 6 deserves a visit. Check the flowage on both sides of the road for waterfowl. Then walk the short road to the landing. The warblers, thrushes, kinglets, and nuthatches are particularly numerous along the road, with an abrupt change in species among the bushes at the landing.

For a chance to see Boreal Chickadees and other boreal forest birds, walk the ITS 84 snowmobile trail to the west from the Third Lake Road about 0.75 mile south of the Fourth Lake Road. The trail passes through spruce wetlands and crosses Hayes Brook, a small tributary to the Machias River.

On the way to and from Grand Lake Stream, stop at Big Musquash Stream about five miles east of town. This large, grassy wetland often yields a view of an American Bittern as it flies around the marsh. Bobolinks, Swamp Sparrows, swallows, and raptors are regular treats, and on rare occasions Short-eared Owls have been noted here.

Directions: from Route 1 in Indian Township, 2 miles north of Princeton, turn west onto Grand Lake Stream Road and follow to the village. The land trust office is in the center of the village, opposite the convenience store. Additional maps and information are available during business hours, and at www.downeastlakes.org.

Additional Sites:

j **The Narraguagus River** flows briskly through downtown Cherryfield. Although the fastest route along the coast on Route 1A bypasses the town, it can be worth a brief stop for a chance to see Bald Eagles over the river, or the swallow show that takes place in the summer. Several buildings adjacent to the bridge at the intersection of Routes 1 and 193 have historically sheltered Cliff Swallow nests. Barn Swallows nest under the bridge and Tree Swallows nest in the adjacent yards. This confluence of swallows is enjoyable.

k **Blueberry barrens** are extensive in Washington County, but the barrens along Route 193 are some of the most visible. To find Upland Sandpipers and Vesper Sparrows, it is not necessary to trespass into the fields, where chemical spraying and bee hives make that inadvisable. The birds can usually be spotted from the road. Although blueberry bushes can conceal Upland Sandpipers, they prefer thinner or bare ground cover and are more likely to be observed in the open. Vesper Sparrows are most easily seen while they are singing or flitting about the blueberries.

Directions: Route 193 runs between Route 1 and Route 9, the two main arteries through Washington County.

l **Addison Marsh** is an uncommonly large salt marsh for this part of the coast, so there is a better opportunity for finding large wading birds here. Canada Geese, American Black Ducks, and Mallards are usually present, while other waterfowl are more sporadic. This is a good place to look for Nelson's Sharp-tailed Sparrows. Savannah Sparrows are also present, so look carefully. Check for shorebirds in the mud flats under the bridge and by the public boat landing west of the marsh. Black-bellied Plovers are likely anywhere along the mud flats of Pleasant River during the summer and autumn, joined by Semipalmated Plovers and Sandpipers in August.

Directions: from Columbia Falls on Route 1, take Addison Road south to the village. Once through the village, stop at the bridge that spans Pleasant River and the salt marsh. Park and scout very carefully. There is little room on the bridge itself. Upon crossing the bridge, note the left turn onto Wescogus Road that leads toward Jonesport.

m **Jonesport:** This is the quintessential "Maine fishing village." One of the tour boats to Machias Seal Island leaves from here. (See 44.) In town, upon entering from Route 187, most of the shorefront consists of homes, shops, and working docks. Enjoy the ambience, and then cross the bridge over Moosabec Reach to Beals Island. Continue straight ahead along Beals Island, keeping Alley Bay on the left. The causeway to Great Wass Island is just over a mile ahead. Scan for shorebirds at mid-tide. At high tide, some shorebirds may be roosting on the ledges near the far end of the causeway. In May and June, a handful of non-breeders often turn up in this location, including Red Knots and Ruddy Turnstones. Take pains to scope out the small rocky promontories extending into the flats.

n **Tide Mill Creek Conservation Area** is a relative newcomer to conservation. The roads and trails are narrow and rough—precisely why it is a good place to look for boreal species, especially Spruce Grouse. The entrance road is worth exploring for warblers. There is a small parking area at the end of road. From the lot, there are three apparent trails. Each is similar, winding through thick spruce vegetation until reaching Tide Mill Creek and Tenney Cove. Both are part of Chandler River's flow to the sea at Roque Bluffs. There are no facilities.

Directions: from Route 1, east of Jonesboro, take Roque Bluffs Road toward Roque Bluffs. Follow 1.4 miles and look for a small dirt road entrance and an equally small sign. There is a gate that is closed to traffic in the off-season, and the area is closed to all-terrain vehicles in all seasons.

o **Machias:** At the confluence of the Machias and East Machias Rivers, fresh water meets tidal water. In the downtown area, Route 1 crosses a small causeway. Park on the near end at Helen's Restaurant.

Check the river behind the Machias Motor Inn for ducks and check the trees on the far side for Bald Eagles. They nest in the taller trees and are usually observable. Also check the river at high tide below where the East Machias River cascades into the tidal zone. (This is where Route 191 splits off eastward over a bridge in East Machias.) It is a lively place for cormorants, mergansers, and gulls any time of year, but especially when fish are moving upstream to spawn.

p **Route 191** has some small and easily overlooked hot spots that make this road interesting. Five miles from Route 1, watch for Looks Canning Company on the right. If the tide is high, shorebirds and gulls will be pushed ashore for easier viewing. The road continues away from the shoreline for a few miles, regaining the ocean at Little Machias Bay. From late summer through autumn, take the turn toward the obvious antenna fields. This is the site of the world's largest Very Low Frequency radio transmitter—once used to communicate with U.S. Navy vessels around the world. The base is off limits, but the access road leading up to the gate has been a favorite place for Whimbrels in late summer and early fall. Flocks of thirty or more are commonly found in the blueberry fields on either side of the road or roosting on the mud flats in the bay below.

In November and December, sea ducks return to Little Machias Bay in good numbers. Scan for scoters, grebes, mergansers, eiders, cormorants, and Long-Tailed Ducks. Continue along Route 191 through Cutler. The harbor can be counted on for Black Guillemots and Common Eiders year round.

q **Western Head** is just south of Cutler Harbor, located on Destiny Bay Road. It is one of the many gems conserved by the Maine Coast Heritage Trust. The 3-mile loop winds through spruce-fir forest typical of harsh maritime climates. Bald Eagles invariably nest here and Merlins often do. Spruce Grouse, Boreal Chickadee, and Black-backed Woodpecker should be looked for, as well as a great variety of warblers, including Blackpoll and Bay-breasted. Swainson's Thrush and Winter Wren are very common. Look for crossbills feeding on spruce cones on the exposed cliff. The coastal views of Cutler Harbor should turn up Common Eider and Black Guillemot. As Razorbills disperse from nearby Machias Seal Island, they may occasionally be seen from the head or even in the mouth of the harbor. The trail is wet and rough in places. It also crosses private property at the preserve entrance, so be sure to remain on the trail. There are no facilities.

Directions: just south of Cutler Harbor, turn onto Destiny Bay Road. (The road sign is not visible from the north.) The road is just north of Head of the River Baptist Church on Route 191. A small parking lot is located one mile from the turn.

r **Boot Head Preserve,** protected by the Maine Coast Heritage Trust, is a 690-acre site encompassing spruce/fir forest, peat bog, rocky coast, and a pebble beach. The round-trip hike is less than 3 miles, but it packs a wallop over its short distance. It is a good spot for Spruce Grouse, especially in

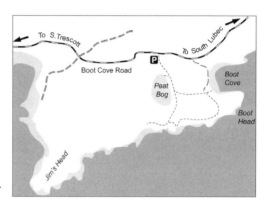

the first quarter mile to the peat bog overlook. Yellow-bellied Flycatchers, Lincoln's Sparrows, and Palm Warblers nest in the bog. It's usually pretty easy to find Northern Parula, American Redstart, and Yellow-rumped, Black-throated Green, and Nashville Warblers here. Ruby-crowned Kinglets are vocal in early summer and Golden-crowned Kinglets anytime. Boreal Chickadees forage sporadically through the area. The beaches and the overlook from Boot Head are scenic. There are no facilities.

Directions: the preserve is reached via the Boot Cove Road, also known as the South Trescott Road. The turn is 11.2 miles northeast of Cutler, and provides a 6-mile shortcut between Route 191 and Quoddy Head State Park. At the Route 191 intersection, there is an old general store with the name Fitzhenry's Store still visible. Proceed 2 miles and look for a small parking area. The trailhead is not visible from the road but there is a small sign in the woods just beyond the lot.

s **Hamilton Cove Preserve** lies just a mile and a half north of Boot Head. Trails through its 376 acres stretch for 3 miles, encircling a major portion of the cove. Unlike Boot Head, this trail winds through early succession habitat consisting mostly of alders and small stands of spruce. It's good for open area warblers such as Chestnut-sided, Wilson's, and Common Yellowthroat. A small stream runs through this property, creating more marsh and fen, so there are better chances for American Bittern, American Black Ducks, American Woodcocks, and assorted flycatchers. Catbirds work the shrub margins and Hermit Thrushes work the woodland margins. All three accipiter hawks have turned up on this small preserve and both Merlin and Northern Harrier breed here. Common Eiders and Red-breasted Mergansers are normally found in the cove. There are no facilities.

Directions: on Boot Cove Road, the parking lot is 3.5 miles from the Route 191 intersection, and 1.5 miles from Boot Head Preserve. It is 2 miles from South Lubec Road near Quoddy Head.

t **Commissary Point** is a 433-acre Maine Wildlife Management Area frequented by deer, moose, hare, bobcat, and occasional bear. There is a hiking trail leaving from the parking lot that loops around Rocky Point. Blackburnian Warblers are likely in the parking lot and Golden-crowned Kinglets prevail in the woods. The abandoned mud road that extends beyond the gate runs through 3/4 of a mile of dense secondary growth that is good for Blue-headed and Red-eyed vireos, American Redstarts, and warblers such as Magnolia, Black-throated Green, Black-throated Blue, Black-and-white, and Ovenbird. The road ends in an area of regenerating grassland. Bay-breasted and Blackburnian warblers are uncommon; American Redstarts, Common Yellowthroats and Chestnut-sided Warblers are typical. There are no facilities.

Directions: along Route 189, Commissary Point Road is 1.8 miles east of the intersection with Route 1. Follow it 0.4 mile to the parking lot at the gate.

u **Morong Point** is another 350-acre Maine Wildlife Management Area. There are no developed trails, but an easy 2.2-mile round trip follows obvious paths through a mixture of wooded stands and grassy fields. Nature has nearly reclaimed this former farm, but apple trees and flowering bushes suggest its former status. The area is now managed largely for American Woodcock but there is a large intertidal zone with a salt marsh at the point. Canada Geese, American Black Ducks, Buffleheads, Common Goldeneyes, mergansers and teal sometimes find shelter in this marsh area. The birding is similar to Commissary Point. There are no facilities.

Directions: follow Route 189 eastward 5.6 miles east from the intersection with Route 1. Turn onto Crow's Neck Road and turn right onto a dirt road at 1.8 miles. Follow for 0.6 mile, over a wooden bridge, and park in the small parking lot at the gate.

V **Cobscook Bay State Park** is notable for its boat ramp and its camping area, both of which are seldom crowded. Campsites are loosely spaced in both forested and shrub habitat, making it possible to find a variety of warblers without leaving the picnic table: American Redstart, Magnolia, Black-throated Green, Chestnut-sided, Black-and-white. Bald Eagles and Merlins nest in the park. There are two short trails. The Nature Trail is a two-mile round trip following a blazed loop through alternating stands of hard- and softwood. Much of the trail parallels Burnt Cove and sections of boardwalk provide water views. The Shore Trail is only a 3/4 mile round trip that winds through the woods and campsites to the boat ramp. The park is mostly sheltered from the open bay, so ducks and herons seek the relative calm of the cove.

Directions: follow Route 1 north to Edmunds. Signs for the park are clearly posted. The park entrance is a short distance down the South Edmunds Road.

W **Gleason Point Park** is worth a quick visit. In addition to being a pleasant picnic area, it offers a good view of the boundary waters of the Western Passage between the United States and Canada's Deer Island. Double-crested Cormorants predominate, but the tidal mud flats of Little River and Gleason Cove are good for shorebirds in season. The channel waters are strongly tidal, producing a lot of aquatic life. Scoters, mergansers, Black Guillemots, Buffleheads and Long-tailed Ducks dive for food, while Bonaparte's Gulls, Black-legged Kittiwakes, and Common Terns forage from the sky.

Directions: the park is reached from Shore Road just north of its intersection with Route 1.

X **Eastport** is America's easternmost city. There are three prime reasons to bird Eastport. The first is the several mud flats that are good for shorebirds in season. The best mudflat is at Carrying Place Cove, where there is a convenient parking area and interpretive signs.

On the way there you'll pass several other mud flats, though each requires care and discretion in parking and walking.

The second reason is the *Sylvina W. Beal*, a 50-passenger schooner that cruises good birding waters. Its principal purpose is sight-seeing and whale-watching, but this 80-year-old sailing vessel ventures into waters where Bonaparte's Gulls and Black-legged Kittiwakes are abundant in late summer. Call 207-853-2500 for information and bookings on the *Sylvina W. Beal*.

The third reason is **Shackford Head State Park**. This area is historically famous because five vessels that served in the Civil War were burned for salvage in its coves. Many tons of metal were removed from the smoldering ash. The site was selected because of the extraordinary tides. It was possible to beach the deep draft ships at high tide, torch them at low tide, and then recover the brass and iron on subsequent low tides. The park also shelters some of the oldest marine fossils, perhaps over 400 million years old.

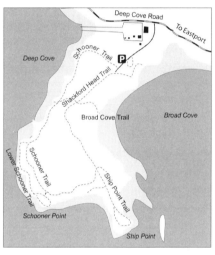

Shackford Head is 173 feet above sea level, with dramatic views and difficult footing on some trails. Shackford Head Trail is level and comparatively easy. Boreal Chickadees are present but uncommon. Shorefront trails such as Schooner and Ship Point Trail can be wet, slippery, jagged, loose, winding, and vertically challenging. They require agility and good footwear. Blackburnian, Bay-breasted, and Blackpoll warblers appear along these trails, as well as more common species such as Magnolia, Black-and-white, and Black-throated Green warblers. Hermit Thrushes thrive on the head and are encountered often. Sea ducks and Common Terns are abundant along the shoreline. Spotted Sandpipers and all the common peeps are available in season at low tide.

Directions: from Route 1 in Perry, take Route 190 to Eastport. Where 190 makes a sharp left turn at an Irving station, make a sharp right turn onto Deep Cove Road. Follow the signs to Shackford Head or the Marine Technology Center.

MAINE LAKES AND MOUNTAINS

From civilized Sebago Lake in the south to wild Richardson Lake in the north, the cry of the loon is taken for granted. Between these two lakes lie several mountain ranges, exceptional state parks, and 47,000 acres of the White Mountain National Forest. The Androscoggin and Saco Rivers drain the heavy snows of the White Mountains through this region, gathering the flow of their tributaries along the way.

In Androscoggin County, the twin cities of Lewiston and Auburn make up Maine's second largest urban area. Lewiston is home to Thorncrag Nature Preserve, which overlooks the city. Sites along the Androscoggin River, which separates Lewiston and Auburn, attract a fine assortment of birds.

Oxford County is simple and uncrowded. Resorts are small, lakes are peaceful, and hiking on trails is a solitary ex-

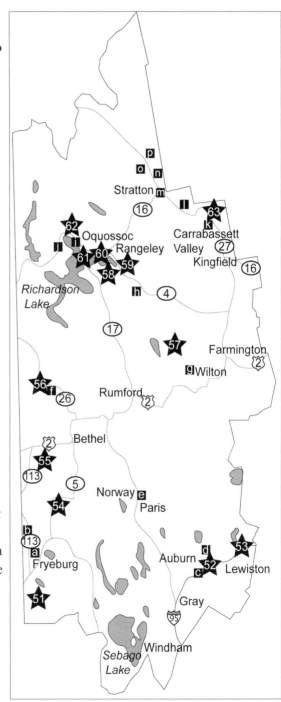

perience. As with everywhere in Maine, development pressure is growing, but local residents are sensitive to it and supporting of land trusts that uphold the tradition of public access to Maine's nature and wildlife.

The White Mountain National Forest is not confined wholly to New Hampshire. Maine's share, including Evans Notch, is harmoniously quiet compared to the rest of the national forest in crowded New Hampshire. The clear mountain waters of Wild River tumble through the region and many of the flat pools are popular for their substantial trout populations. Moose are also common. Farther north, Grafton Notch State Park provides another good escape from crowds and offers some of the best mountain climbing in New England. Within this Maine Lakes and Mountains Region, birds of southern New England may be found on the lower end, while species of the boreal forest are found just 90 minutes away on the upper end.

Norway is a lovely lakeside community near Paris. Fryeburg is a quiet town most of the year, but activity picks up whenever there is good paddling on the Saco River or during the hugely popular Fryeburg Fair in October. Conversely, Bethel is bustling primarily in the winter due to its proximity to Sunday River, a major ski resort. Summers are quieter and the hospitality industry caters to golfers, mountain bikers, hikers, and birders.

The Carrabassett Valley's biggest claim to fame is Sugarloaf, a world-class ski mountain. American Olympians train on its slopes. Though winter is the busy season, mountain hiking and bicycling in the area are first class. The Appalachian Trail winds over the Bigelow Range. The communities of Kingfield, Stratton, and Eustis are geared toward active people. Thus, the area retains an impressive sense of vitality throughout the year, but loses the crowds in spring and summer. For birders, that means the best of both worlds.

The Carrabassett Valley winds between Sugarloaf and the Bigelow Range along Route 27 and the Carrabassett River. (A second valley on the back side of Bigelow is also described in the Kennebec River Valley section.) This road from Kingfield all the way to the Canadian border is one of the most scenic routes in the state. It gets pretty wild and remote from Eustis through Chain of Ponds to Coburn Gore and there are few opportunities to get off the highway and bird, but a drive to the border can be a pleasant way to spend that part of the day when the songbirds are at their quietest.

Trip planning: www.WesternMaine.org or 888-688-0099.

Official Maine Birding Trail Sites

⭐ **5** **Brownfield Bog** is valued by Maine birders because it contains species more common to southern New England. It is the most reliable location in Maine to find Yellow-throated Vireos. From the parking lot it is occasionally possible to simultaneously hear the songs of Red-eyed, Blue-headed, Warbling, and Yellow-throated Vireos. Baltimore Orioles are common along the woodland edges. Blue-gray Gnatcatchers are more common here than anywhere else in the state,

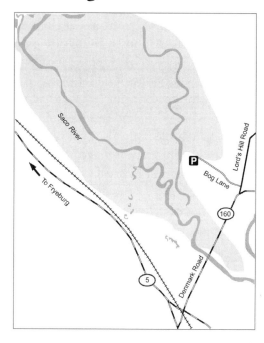

and there are also better odds of finding either of the Yellow-billed or Black-billed Cuckoos or the Willow Flycatcher.

The bog is part of the Saco River complex. It has probably been a good spot for waterfowl since the last ice age. But a little dynamite was used to improve it, blasting new potholes for ducks decades ago. (The dynamite shack is still on the edge of the parking area.) Any of the ducks may be present in migration season. Mallards, American Black Ducks, Wood Ducks, Ring-necked Ducks and Pied-billed Grebes are particularly prevalent in breeding season, though Blue-winged and Green-winged Teal also nest here. Hooded Mergansers and Common Goldeneyes compete with Wood Ducks for the nesting boxes posted around the wetland. Least Bitterns, Wilson's Snipe, and Virginia Rails are hidden among the reeds. The access road is narrow and muddy. Trails can be damp and buggy. Be prepared.

Directions: from Route 5/113 in Brownfield, turn east on Route 160 (Denmark Road). This intersection of several roads is signaled by a series of blinking lights. Proceed 1.4 miles and turn onto Lord's Hill Road, then take an immediate left onto Bog Lane. (There is currently no other sign to indicate the property.)

52 **Thorncrag Nature Preserve** overlooks Lewiston from the highest point in the city. The Stanton Bird Club has managed this 310-acre preserve for over 80 years and maintains three miles of easy trail. The sanctuary consists mostly of mature pines and hardwoods. Cellar holes, stone walls, and orchard remnants adjacent to the trails give evidence of its agricultural history. Fields atop the hill are typically good places to watch for hawks, both resident and migrating. Wood and Hermit Thrushes are woodland residents. Ovenbirds, Black-throated Green, and Pine Warblers are also typical of the woods, while American Redstarts and Chestnut-sided Warblers work the field edges. Common Yellowthroats nest in brushy thickets and Yellow Warblers are regularly sighted around the open fields. Eastern Wood-Pewees are heard throughout early summer. Scarlet Tanagers prefer the mature deciduous stands, while Baltimore Orioles are often conspicuous in the open areas near orchards. There are no facilities.

Directions: the sanctuary is reached from Sabattus Street (Route 126) in Lewiston. Look for the Hannaford Supermarket and turn onto adjacent Highland Spring Road. One trail entrance is at the end of Highland Spring Road. To get to the other, turn left onto Montello Street, then right onto East Avenue, and park at the end of the road near the Montello Heights Reservoir.

———◆◦◆———

53 **Sabattus Pond** is remarkable in autumn, as the water level is drawn down to rid the lake of potential algae blooms from phosphorus. This exposes extensive mud flats, creating ideal feeding habitat for migrating sandpipers. Surprising numbers of Semipalmated, Least, and White-rumped Sandpipers are joined by Pectoral Sandpipers, Black-bellied Plovers, Greater Yellowlegs, Short-billed Dowitchers, Killdeer, and later-arriving Dunlin. Stay alert for American Golden Plovers and Sanderlings, too. Merlins and Peregrine Falcons are regularly attracted to this smorgasbord.

As the shorebirds depart, waterfowl move in. From October until the pond freezes over, anything can happen. Regulars include Mallards, American Black Ducks, Ruddy Ducks, Hooded Mergansers, Common Goldeneyes, Green-winged Teal, American Widgeons, Northern Pintails, Ring-necked Ducks, both species of scaup, and American Coots. Even saltwater migrants such as scoters, grebes, Buffleheads,

Long-tailed Ducks, and Red-breasted Mergansers are possible to see. Bald Eagles find this abundance appetizing. Late in the season, flocks of Common Mergansers gather and the mud flats again become populated with small numbers of American Pipits, Snow Buntings, Horned Larks, and Lapland Longspurs. Most of the available birding is from a small park and boat launch called Martin Point on the southwestern corner of the pond. Ample parking and a pit toilet are available.

Directions: a new Maine Turnpike exit to Sabattus may not show on older maps. Take Exit 86 from the Maine Turnpike and head west on Route 9. In 1.3 miles, Route 9 will turn left. Instead, proceed straight through the light for another 0.3 mile to Sabattus, and then turn right onto Elm Street and right again on Lake Street to the park at Martin Point.

---

54 **The Greater Lovell Land Trust** has built an impressive inventory of birding opportunities in western Maine. Formed in 1985, the trust continues to grow. These are some of its productive properties:

• **Sucker Brook Preserve** is a 32-acre nature trail in Lovell. It begins and ends on Horseshoe Pond Road. The trail is best known for its profusion of increasingly rare Cardinal Flowers in August. Birders will find it more productive from April through July. Many common warblers, woodpeckers, and flycatchers nest within the preserve and they are likely to reveal themselves to anyone spending quiet time on top of the viewing platform located at the trail's halfway point. This platform overlooks a bog that may contain waterfowl when flooded.

Directions: from Route 5, take the West Lovell Road over the Narrows, past the Kezar Lake Marina. Bear

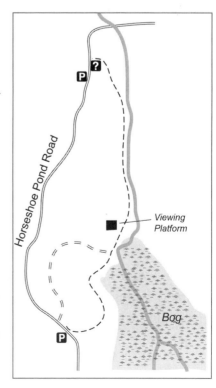

left onto Foxboro Road, then right at New Road. Turn right at Horseshoe Pond Road.

• **The Bradley & Heald Pond Preserve** is reached via Slab City Road. The Heald Pond Preserve trail is reached first. It follows a jeep path, skirting the west side of Heald Pond. The forest is mature and highly diverse, featuring birch, beech, oak, ash, and aspen. Pockets of hemlock and balsam fir contribute to the woodland mix. Watch for birds rising from beneath your feet. Ovenbirds and Hermit Thrushes have both been observed nesting in the middle

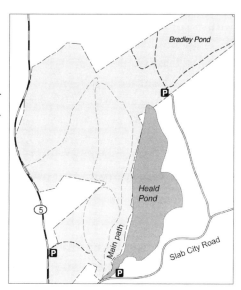

of this lightly used path. Black-throated Green Warblers and Northern Parulas are likely as well. Toward the end of the trail, the habitat becomes a little damper and more stunted. Be watchful for moose.

• **The Bradley Pond Preserve** is part of the same parcel as Heald Pond but the access trail begins from a different parking lot. It loops through hardwood forest to a woodland bog. Though the habitat on these trail systems is not overly coniferous, Yellow-bellied Flycatchers have been heard singing in both.

Directions: from Route 5, turn east onto Slab City Road. The 2.4 mile Heald Loop Trail begins on Slab City Road 500 feet west of the Fairburn parking area at the south end of Heald Pond. The Bradley Pond Trail is reached via Heald Pond Road just a little farther down Slab City Road.

55 A lightly used portion of the **White Mountain National Forest** extends into Maine just below Bethel and even many Mainers are unfamiliar with its attractions. Route 113 skirts the west side, passing through Evans Notch, with access to scenic overlooks, trailheads, and campgrounds. Most of this route is mixed hardwood with some hemlock and balsam fir. Veery, Swainson's Thrush, and Hermit Thrush are everywhere. Warblers are likely to be Black-throated Green, Black-throated Blue, Blackburnian, Black-and-White, Northern Parula, American Redstart, Yellow-rumped, and Magnolia. Three miles south of Gilead on Route 113, the turnoff toward Wild River passes a pond that often contains Hooded Mergansers and may hold other waterfowl. Belted Kingfishers and Great Blue Herons readily use this pond. The road continues into New Hampshire where Wild River Campground is located. Mountain trails at the southern

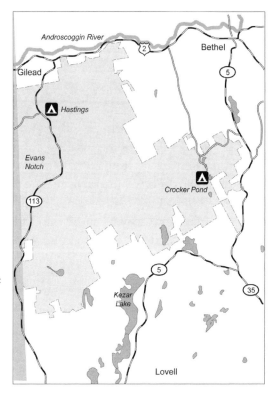

end of Route 113 in the White Mountain National Forest rise into the high elevation spruce zone, where Bicknell's Thrushes, Boreal Chickadees, Gray Jays, and Blackpoll Warblers may be present, but trails at the north end near Hastings Campground do not reach sufficient elevation to find these boreal specialties.

Crocker Pond is a small campground (7 sites) on the east side of the forest. The access road and many of the wetlands in this area are extraordinarily rich, both in birds and moose.

• An auto tour begins at Patte Brook, where tour maps are normally stocked. An early stop along the road leads to an opening in the woods. This path is alive with warblers and thrushes, though the area is also prone to ticks in the first half of summer. Take precautions. Expect Black-throated Green, Black-and-White, Magnolia, Yellow-rumped, and Nashville Warblers. Watch for Ovenbirds, Northern Parula, Common Yellowthroats, and American Redstarts. Veeries, Swainson's, and Hermit Thrushes are all possible, as well. Winter Wrens are common.

• Albany Mountain is a relatively easy hike. The view from the summit is partially obscured. The forest passes through habitat for many woodpeckers, thrushes, and Scarlet Tanagers.

• Patte Marsh is a 45-acre wetland improved when the U.S. Forest Service and Ducks Unlimited cooperated to repair an outlet dam in 2002. The shallow pond is ideal for moose and they are often present. Waterfowl can be abundant in spring and fall.

• Broken Bridge Pond is another good stop for ducks and moose. Common Mergansers frequent this particular flowage. Hooded Mergansers can be expected in any of the local ponds. Beyond this stop there is another gated road that opens the forest canopy enough to enable good views of warblers along the edge.

• The road ends at Crocker Pond. Park in the parking area and walk back along the access road for the many warblers, vireos, woodpeckers, thrushes, wrens, kinglets, chickadees, nuthatches, and creepers that inhabit this forest. Expect Eastern Phoebes around the campground and the pond, and Least and Great-crested Flycatchers along the road. Accipiters use the road as a hunting corridor, with Sharp-shinned, Cooper's, and Northern Goshawks all possible. Barred Owls take over at dusk. There is a hiking trail on the far side of the parking lot that leads to Round Pond. The mile-long walk is relatively flat and easy, though damp. Bird activity is frequently close to the trail.

Directions: Crocker Pond may be reached from Route 2 via Flat Road in West Bethel or from Route 5 in Albany just south of Songo Pond. Follow the signs. Crocker Pond Campground has pit toilets and there is a freshwater hand pump at the parking lot's entrance.

⟫•0•⟪

56 **Grafton Notch State Park** is extraordinarily popular with hikers. The Appalachian Trail twists over some of the prettiest summits in Maine, including Old Speck and Baldpate Mountains. Between the peaks, Bear River plummets alongside Route 26 through scenic drops with names like Screw Auger Falls, Mother Walker Falls Gorge, and Moose Cave Gorge.

There is no easier place in Maine to find Philadelphia Vireos than at the Appalachian Trail parking lot. These vireos dominate the dawn chorus, along with Hermit Thrushes, Winter Wrens, and Least Flycatchers. While enjoying this treat, stay alert for Peregrine Falcons that nest on the cliffs above. Red-eyed and Blue-headed Vireos are also common throughout the park. Most of Maine's warblers enjoy the mixed forest that abuts Route 26, including Black-throated Green, Black-throated Blue, Northern Parula, Blackburnian, Nashville, Magnolia, Black-and-white, American Redstart, and Yellow-rumped.

Spruce Meadow Picnic Area marks the transition to boreal habitat in the northern end of the park. Boreal Chickadees can be found here. This boreal zone extends for another three miles beyond the park boundary. Check for Black-backed Woodpeckers in the wet spruce areas alongside the road but be wary of the heavy logging trucks that hurtle along this highway. This is also a likely spot for moose.

Boreal habitat is common at the higher elevations of the park. A day of hiking can mean an encounter with any of these: Gray Jay, Spruce Grouse, Black-backed Woodpecker, Boreal Chickadee, Yellow-bellied Flycatcher, Bay-breasted Warbler, and Blackpoll. Bicknell's Thrushes are present throughout the stunted spruce of the Mahoosuc Range above 3,000 feet. A substantial number have been documented on Baldpate Mountain.

———◆———

57 Mt. Blue State Park is second only to Baxter State Park as the largest state park in Maine. It contains several hiking peaks and a lakefront camping area. Center Hill is reached shortly after driving into the park. A short, interpretive trail brings visitors quite close to breeding Hermit Thrushes and Winter Wrens, which are apparently accustomed to visitors and less shy than usual. American Redstarts are plentiful in the overlooks, and many of the most common warblers are present. Scarlet Tanagers are often audible from the parking lot.

Mt. Blue (3,167 feet) is a popular hike, though the pace is relentlessly uphill, the footing uneven, and the views limited. This mountain offers the potential for all six of Maine's breeding thrushes. Wood Thrushes and Veeries are sometimes heard around the deciduous base of the mountain. Hermit Thrushes are typically audible for the first 15 minutes of the climb, replaced by Swainson's Thrushes for the remainder of the trek to the summit. In the thick spruce zone on top, a Bicknell's Thrush may be heard, though it is rare. (Nearby Tumbledown Mountain is a better bet.) Scarlet Tanagers like the mature hardwoods around the parking lot. Black-throated Blue and Blackburnian Warblers dominate most of the trail, with Winter Wrens, Brown Creepers, and Red-eyed Vireos for company. American Redstarts, Nashville and Magnolia Warblers appear in the transition zone from birch to spruce. Blackpolls, Bay-breasted Warblers, Yellow-bellied Flycatchers, and Boreal Chickadees may be found around the summit.

The campground on Webb Lake in Weld offers campsites in a mature forest featuring beech, birch, white pine, and hemlock. There is a foot trail around the perimeter, but because there is little change in elevation or forested habitat, the species diversity is below average. Expect Hermit Thrushes and Red-eyed Vireos.

Directions: from Route 2 in Wilton, turn onto Route 156 and follow the signs to the park in Weld.

---

58 Rangeley Lake State Park is popular primarily for camping and swimming, but a trail winds along the edge that yields many of Maine's common songbirds. Mixed forest habitat shelters many species of warblers: Black-throated Green, Black-throated Blue, Chestnut-sided, Blackburnian, Pine, Magnolia, Nashville, Black-and-White, Northern Parula, American Redstart, and Common Yellowthroat. Blue-headed and Red-eyed Vireos are widespread. Woodpeckers include

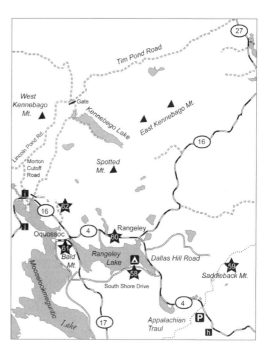

Downy, Hairy, Yellow-bellied Sapsucker, Northern Flicker, and Pileated. The understory is home to Hermit Thrushes, Veeries, and Winter Wrens. Campsite reservations may be made by calling 207-287-3824.

Directions: from Route 4, turn onto South Shore Drive. The park is approximately 5 miles ahead on the right. From Route 17, turn onto South Shore Drive. The park is approximately 3 miles ahead on the left.

59 **Saddleback Mountain** is a large ski area on the outskirts of the town of Rangeley. It is a reliable place to find Bicknell's Thrush, though the climb is strenuous and unsuitable for many people. Saddleback Mountain management is accustomed to hikers accessing the summit via their ski trails and has marked the proper routes. Stay on trails, because alpine vegetation is fragile and off-course wanderers are hard to find in an emergency. Check for a hiking trail map at the base lodge. There is little relief during the vertical, hour-long ascent. Mud, soft sand, and loose pebbles are common hazards on these trails. Once above 3,000 feet, birders are free to enjoy Blackpolls, Bay-breasted Warblers, Boreal Chickadees, Gray Jays, and Spruce Grouse. The Bicknell's Thrush is notorious for singing only at dawn and dusk, but its call notes may occur at any time.

Directions: from Route 4 just south of Rangeley, turn onto Dallas Hill Road and follow the signs. Watch for moose.

60 **Hunter Cove** is a property of the Rangeley Lakes Heritage Trust. Several trails wander through mixed habitat to a cove on Rangeley Lake. A thick stand of young spruce near the parking lot sometimes harbors Boreal Chickadees and Gray Jays. Blackburnian Warblers are common over the first few hundred yards of the trail, along with Red-eyed Vireos, American Redstarts, Northern Parula, and Magnolia, Nashville, and Black-throated Green Warblers. Cape May Warblers have appeared annually. The trails are often damp and tangled, requiring waterproof footwear, but it is these conditions that encourage Canada Warblers to nest here.

Directions: the entrance is on the west side of Route 4 between Rangeley and Oquossoc, at the foot of Dodge Pond Hill opposite Dodge Pond.

61 **Bald Mountain** is a 2,443-foot knob that separates Rangeley and Mooselookmeguntic Lakes. There is an observation tower on top that provides a superb 360-degree view. The bottom two-thirds of the ascent pass through mature hardwood forest, with plenty of Black-throated Blue and Black-throated Green Warblers, interspersed with Blackburnian Warblers, Brown Creepers, Least Flycatchers, many Winter Wrens, Hairy, Downy, and Pileated Woodpeckers, and Yellow-bellied Sapsuckers. After 45 minutes of upward hiking, the forest begins its transition to balsam and spruce. This also marks the transition from

Hermit to Swainson's Thrushes. As tree growth becomes stunted, Magnolia and Nashville Warblers and American Redstarts forage readily. Blackpolls, Dark-eyed Juncos, and Yellow-bellied Flycatchers are likely. The summit is thickly covered in spruce. Watch for Boreal Chickadees and Gray Jays. White-winged and Red Crossbills are possible.

Directions: the trailhead is on Bald Hill Road less than a mile from the end of Route 4 in Oquossoc.

62 **The Boy Scout Road** is designated by that name on newer editions of the DeLorme Maine Atlas. Older maps provide no name at all. A small sign identifies the area as a project of the Rangeley Lakes Heritage Trust. This dirt road provides excellent birding through a mix of habitats. Most of its three-mile length shadows an alder stream that is thick with Swamp Sparrows, Northern Waterthrushes, Veeries, American Catbirds, Common Yellowthroats, and Belted Kingfishers. The road begins in deciduous forest but changes to mixed habitat and then thick spruce in a relatively short distance. This accounts for the good variety of birds to be found here, including Canada Warblers, Golden and Ruby-crowned Kinglets, Yellow-bellied and Olive-sided Flycatchers, and both Blue-headed and Red-eyed Vireos. Canada Jays are occasionally encountered in the spruce stands and may share these woods with Swainson's Thrushes, Boreal Chickadees, Spruce Grouse, and Bay-breasted Warblers. This road is lightly traveled by a few private landowners and a handful of fishermen.

Directions: the Boy Scout Road is on the east side of Route 16 just 1.3 miles after its split with Route 4 in Oquossoc.

63 **Bigelow Preserve** is remarkable. The Appalachian Trail ascends the highest peaks, while other spurs scale the remaining ridgeline. All are well tended by the Appalachian Mountain Club. Trailheads begin in a hardwood zone dominated by Hermit Thrushes, Least Flycatchers, Scarlet Tanagers, and Yellow-bellied Sapsuckers. Warblers are primarily Blackburnian, Northern Parula, Black-throated Green, Black-throated Blue, and Ovenbirds. The Black-throated Blue Warblers persist as the trail winds upward into a mixed zone with more balsam and yellow birch. Beyond here, Swainson's Thrushes begin to replace

Hermits. One or two hours into the climb, the spruce zone begins, often abruptly. Black-poll Warblers and Yellow-bellied Fly-catchers become audible. Where stunted birches fight the spruces

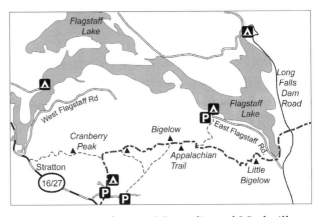

for control of the slope, American Redstarts, Magnolia and Nashville Warblers find the sparse, sunny exposure they enjoy. Dark-eyed Juncos join the chorus and the chance to hear Bay-breasted Warblers increases. After the birches give up the fight, the remainder of the mountain-top is boreal. Blackpolls and White-throated Sparrows are abundant, Boreal Chickadees and Yellow-bellied Flycatchers are common, Gray Jays are present, and Spruce Grouse are possible. There is no logging at these heights, so dead trees remain standing and attractive to Black-backed Woodpeckers. At an elevation of 3,000 feet, most mountains are in the krummholz zone–an impenetrable zone of short, stunted spruce. In a band that roughly follows the Appalachian Trail from the White Mountains to Katahdin, this is the zone for Bicknell's Thrush.

Bigelow Mountain is a strenuous hike that will take most of a day to complete. Bicknell's Thrush habitat at the top of the mountain is extensive, but by the time most hikers have reached it, the quarry is silent save for occasional call notes. Patience scanning from a ledge above the krummholz may be rewarded by the view of a foraging thrush among the spruces. Cranberry Peak offers another possibility. This peak barely surpasses 3,000 feet and the zone for Bicknell's Thrush is small, but the summit may be reached in as little as two hours.

Directions: a major trailhead is located prominently on Route 27 that accesses all trails on both sides of the road. An alternative set of trailheads is located within the Bigelow Preserve on Stratton Pond Brook Road. This entrance is easily overlooked. It passes a few private cottages before entering the preserve. At 0.8 mile the Cranberry Peak trailhead is located just 100 yards down Public Lands Road. The Appalachian Trail is at 1.0 mile, with a larger parking area for the Stratton Pond trails at 1.5 miles. There are no facilities.

Additional Sites:

a The Saco River dominates southern Oxford County. Extraordinary efforts are made to keep this river clean because it provides irrigation and drinking water to communities along its course. Its cool, clear waters have made it a favorite recreational river and many outfitters and campgrounds have sprung up. For adventurers who are adept at paddling with binoculars, an early summer paddle can provide glimpses of warblers foraging in the overhanging tree branches. The river is lined with secluded sandy beaches that invite swimming on warm days. It is best to avoid weekends, which are just a little too popular. While all of the area outfitters can supply rental canoes, they will also ferry your own boat for a fee. The float from Fryeburg to Brownfield is the most popular.

b Fryeburg Harbor refers to a large floodplain of the Saco River located just above Fryeburg. A sod farm and other flat fields are notorious for attracting shorebirds from August through October, usually after a soaking rain. Look for Killdeer and American Golden Plover. Sandpipers in-

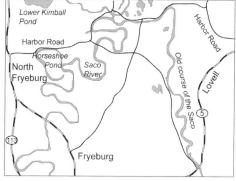

clude Solitary, Pectoral, Semipalmated, and Least. Greater and Lesser Yellowlegs are often present, and Short-billed Dowitchers are occasional. The farmland draws Northern Harriers year-round, and American Pipits, Snow Buntings, and Rough-legged Hawks late in the year. This is also a good time to be alert for American Tree Sparrows. Both the Saco River and lingering wetlands isolated by its meandering course are places to see Hooded Mergansers, and nearby Lower Kimball Pond gets its share of Snow Geese and Canada Geese in November.

Directions: from Fryeburg, take Route 113 north to North Fryeburg and turn east onto Harbor Road. Or from Route 5 in Lovell, turn west onto Harbor Road just north of the Fryeburg town line.

c Riverside Cemetery is located very close to the center of Lewiston, on the bank of the Androscoggin River. This is where local birders greet returning songbirds in the spring. Migrants using the river for navigation often fall out in the mature trees surrounding the cemetery and especially in the foliage along the river itself. Many common warblers remain to nest, typically including Common Yellowthroat, Black-throated Green, Northern Parula, American Redstart, Chestnut-sided, Yellow, and Pine Warblers. Scarlet Tanagers that inhabit the mature woodland next to the cemetery regularly forage along the river's edge. Warbling Vireos and Baltimore Orioles are likely along the water's edge. There are no facilities. As in all cemeteries, please be quiet and respectful of plots.

Directions: the entrance is at the end of Riverside Street, which turns off Route 202 in Lewiston just a half-mile north of Central Maine Medical Center, or a quarter mile south of Veterans Memorial Bridge.

d **Gulf Island Dam** provides an ice-free section of the Androscoggin River below its outflow in any winter. Common Mergansers are certain in colder months, often accompanied by Common Goldeneyes, and sometimes by Hooded Mergansers. Gull flocks may contain an Iceland or Glaucous Gull in winter. Check the power poles on the opposite bank for nesting Bald Eagles, which typically set up housekeeping before the end of April. Canada Geese and an assortment of migrating waterfowl may be found in the open water of early spring. Ospreys arrive in mid-spring. The road hugs the riverbank for 1.5 miles before ending at the security gate.

Directions: from Route 202 in Lewiston, turn left onto Switzerland Road 1.3 miles north of the Veterans Memorial Bridge.

e **Cornwall Nature Preserve** in Paris is 147 acres of mixed hardwood and white pine. The trail system also winds through field edges and by a few wetlands, assuring species diversity.

Directions: from Route 26 just 0.3 mile from the center of Paris, turn east onto Paris Hill Road and follow 1.8 miles to the parking lot on right.

f **Step Falls Preserve** is private land supervised for public use by The Nature Conservancy. This half-mile trail meanders alongside Wight Brook as it tumbles from an improbable height in the woods. On hot days, this is a popular place for locals to bask on rocks and splash in the pools. Amid the red maples near the parking lot, Red-eyed Vireos are likely. Upon entering the hemlocks, expect a scolding from one of the many Blue-headed Vireos that nest here. Blackburnian and

Black-throated Green Warblers are present in good numbers, but the main attraction is the scenic beauty of the falls itself.

Directions: from Route 2 in Newry, turn onto Route 26 and proceed north approximately 7.5 miles. The trailhead is on the east side of the bridge over Wight Brook. This area is just south of Grafton Notch State Park. Please respect neighbors' property and stay within the bounds of the preserve. The preserve is open during daytime hours and dogs are not allowed.

g **The Foothills Land Conservancy** is a unique stop on the way to Mt. Blue State Park. Just north of Wilton, these grasslands are located only 0.2 mile off Route 156. The fields are maintained for grassland birds and butterflies. Mowed paths guide visitors around the edges, where American Catbirds and Yellow Warblers are numerous. The paths lead to a wetland area where ducks are likely to be present, especially in spring and fall.

Directions: from Route 156, turn west onto Pond Road. A parking area with an information kiosk is just ahead on the right.

Just beyond the Foothills Land Conservancy are the mountains of Tumbledown (3,038 feet), Little Jackson (3,434 feet), and Big Jackson (3,535 feet). Located within Maine Public Reserve Land a short distance west of Mt. Blue State Park, they offer birding similar to Mt. Blue, and better views. Because they are a little off the beaten track, expect to encounter fewer people. There is also a better chance for Bicknell's Thrush. All are strenuous climbs.

Directions: from Route 142 in Weld, take the Byron Road (which becomes the No. 6 Road shown on the DeLorme Maine Atlas). The preferred trailhead is 2 miles from the beginning of the Byron Road and 0.8 mile in on the Morgan Road. The Loop trail begins 5.5 miles from the beginning of the Byron Road.

h **Smalls Falls** is a popular stop along Route 4 on the way to the Rangeley Lakes area. On warm summer days, families picnic and swim beneath the cascade. The rushing water makes it difficult to hear the Black-throated Green and Blackburnian Warblers that nest among the mature pines. Red-eyed Vireos and Ovenbirds are present. Picnic tables and pit toilets are available. For the next mile along Route 4, moose are particularly common. The Appalachian Trail crosses the road three miles ahead, and this portion of the trail can be used to reach the summit of Saddleback Mountain for a try at Bicknell's Thrush.

Directions: the rest area is well marked on Route 4 in Madrid just be-fore Township E. The Appalachian Trail is also well marked, with an ample parking lot.

i **Cupsuptic** is about five miles north of Oquossoc on Route 16. The habitat becomes highly boreal, and Boreal Chickadees are a common occurrence among the roadside spruces. Gray Jays are regular camp robbers at the Cupsuptic Campground. Black-backed Woodpeckers have been noted in the beaver flowage up the road.

j **The Forest Legacy Trail** is another property of the Rangeley Lakes Heritage Trust. This trail leads downward toward Cupsuptic Lake along a jeep path. It passes through mostly open hardwood and woodcut edges, so even though the variety of songbirds is not as pro-lific as other properties, the birds are often easier to see. Black-throated Blue Warblers are especially common. Other warblers include Com-mon Yellowthroat, American Redstart, Magnolia, Nashville, Chestnut-sided, Black-throated Green, Black-and-white, and Ovenbird. In a couple of places, Canada Warblers can be heard from damp tangles only a few yards into the woods. Hermit Thrushes are most com-mon but Swainson's Thrushes can also be heard from damper conifer stands down the hill. The mixed habitat is particularly good for Ruffed Grouse, and all of the common woodpeckers are present.

Directions: follow Route 16 from Oquossoc through Cupsuptic. The trail is on the east side of Route 16, 10.1 miles from the intersection of Routes 4 and 16 in Oquossoc.

k **The Sugarloaf Outdoor Area/Carrabassett Ski Touring Center** is a boon for cross-country skiers in the winter. In summer, it is practi-cally deserted. Maintenance crews and mountain bikers keep the trails free of fallen limbs and overgrowth. In its mixed forest habitat, most of the more common warblers are present: Black-throated Green, Black-throated Blue, Northern Parula, American Redstart, Nashville, Magno-lia, Black-and-white, Common Yellow-throat, Chestnut-sided, Oven-bird, Canada, and Yellow-rumped. Hermit Thrushes, Veeries, Winter Wrens, Brown Creepers, Ruby and Golden-crowned Kinglets and Red-eyed and Blue-headed Vireos are usually vocal. Chipping Sparrows surround the parking lot. Trails may be buggy and damp in spring.

l **Caribou Pond Road** is just a couple miles beyond the entrance to Sugarloaf . It is a privately owned logging road that is best avoided when wood harvesting operations are underway. However, it is a generally reliable site for Philadelphia Vireos in the vicinity of Mile 2. Red-eyed Vireos elsewhere along the road encourage study and comparison. Many warblers, thrushes, woodpeckers, and Least Flycatchers are also obvious. The road condition deteriorates beyond four miles from Route 27.

m **Stratton** is a village with inexpensive lodging, dining, and outfitting. Just west of the village on Route 27, the North and South Branches of the Dead River flow into the shallow backwater of Flagstaff Lake. Diving ducks appear regularly. Expect Common Loons and Mergansers. In some periods, the water level is drawn down and substantial mud flats are revealed. Shorebirds are likely in migration. Dabbling ducks, particularly Mallards and American Black Ducks, are usually in view along the water's edge and in lingering puddles. Wilson's Snipe populate the grassy borders of the lake.

n **Maine Public Reserve Land** on the west side of Flagstaff Lake can be reached from Route 27 in Eustis. The access is via Flagstaff Road. Immediately upon turning off Route 27, the road crosses a causeway that yields terrific views of waterfowl habitat. The site is normally good for swallows and flycatchers. Continuing forward, and bearing right at an intersection, the road passes through a stand of red pines that

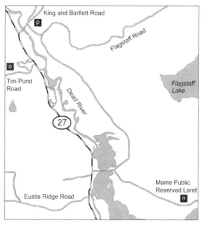

has been regularly thinned. Beyond this stand, mixed habitat prevails the rest of the way to the primitive campsites on the lake. These woods are particularly active with Blackburnian, Black-and-white, and Black-throated Green Warblers. Despite the lack of mature white pines, there are also a surprising number of Pine Warblers, Blue-headed Vireos, and Golden-crowned Kinglets. Brown Creepers are plentiful and even Boreal Chickadees are encountered occasionally.

o **Tim Pond Road** enters from the west just over two miles farther on Route 27. This is a major logging road that serves the working forest north of Rangeley. As such, it can be muddy, dusty, rough, and clogged with 100,000 pound logging trucks. But it can also be an adventurous way to reach the Rangeley area while investigating the many spruce stands along the 25 miles of dirt road. The thickest stands are around Miles 2, 8, and 13. Chances are good for Boreal Chickadees, Gray Jays, and Bay-breasted Warblers. The road follows a ridgeline, so raptors are a good bet, particularly Merlins, American Kestrels, Northern Harriers, and Sharp-shinned Hawks. Because the road rides the ridge, there are few damp, boggy places until the road dips at Mile 17 to intersect with the Kennebago Road. It is also possible to find Spruce Grouse in this area.

After the intersection, the route becomes the Lincoln Pond Road. About three miles ahead, a well-marked trail ascends West Kennebago Mountain. All of the boreal specialties are known to be in the spruce zone atop the mountain and Bicknell's Thrush are possibile. Bay-breasted Warblers, Blackpolls, Dark-eyed Juncos, Yellow-bellied Flycatchers and Swainson's Thrushes dominate the chorus at elevation. Return to pavement via the Morton Cutoff Road. Or take a little more time and follow the Old Lincoln Pond Road to civilization. At its mid-point, there is a memorial that marks the site of a B-17 crash that occurred on July 11, 1944.

p **The King and Bartlett Road** intersects Route 27 from the east, a mile west of Tim Pond Road. The route ahead is gated at three miles, but there is a nice spruce stand before the gate that is good for Boreal Chickadees. Instead, most adventurers turn right after crossing the bridge and follow the road to the back side of Flagstaff Lake. Most of the habitat is mixed, making it particularly favorable for Ruffed Grouse. There are also several good spruce stands up to Mile 8 that encourage Gray Jays, Boreal Chickadees, and Bay-breasted Warblers. Although the road winds completely around the back side of the lake, the birding is only average and road conditions can be rough. Enterprising explorers with high road clearance might be tempted to find Grand Falls, a spectacular waterfall on the Dead River. There are no signs, but the left turn is after Mile 9, just over a small bridge. It is three miles to a right fork, another four miles to a gate, and one last mile on foot to the falls.

THE KENNEBEC VALLEY

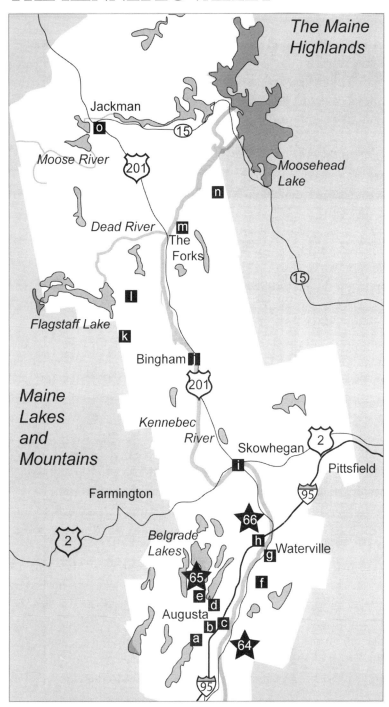

The Kennebec River defines a significant part of Maine, both in its geography and in its history. From its headwaters at Moosehead Lake, the river flows 150 miles to the sea. The river provided a major transportation route, first for Indians, later for colonists. During the Revolutionary War, Benedict Arnold led American troops up the Kennebec in large open canoes (called bateaux) for an ill-fated assault on Quebec City. Later, the river carried logs downstream to mills in Madison and Waterville as recently as the 1970s. Shadowing the river, Route 201 became an overland route to Quebec, conveying commerce and immigration in both directions. A scenic byway has been established along this route called the Kennebec Chaudiere. Rest stops and way stations are embellished with informational kiosks and historic markers.

Augusta is the state capital. It rests so close to the Kennebec River that Water Street in the downtown section lives up to its name when the river floods. Visitors who have dealings with state government are delighted to find that there are quality places to pursue birds nearby.

Waterville sits on the Kennebec River less than 30 minutes north of Augusta. Waterville is the service center for a group of lakes and ponds just west of the city that is collectively known as the Belgrade Lakes. The Kennebec Highlands, located next to the lakes, is a major land conservancy area that provides superb birding.

Bingham to Jackman is a corridor that seems specifically designed for people who love the outdoors. Each town provides outfitting and guiding services for sporting enthusiasts. An entire community of white-water rafting companies sprang up in the 1970s at The Forks, the confluence of the Kennebec and Dead Rivers. The tourism amenities offered here add a touch of modern polish to the traditionally rustic nature of the area. Moose are common along Route 201, presenting a daytime distraction and a nighttime traffic danger .

Trip planning: www.KennebecValley.org or 800-393-8629.

Official Maine Birding Trail Sites

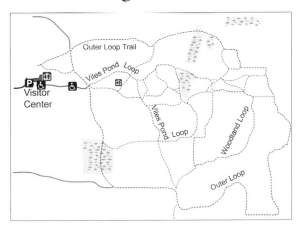

⭐**64** **Pine Tree State Arboretum** contains fields, marshes, ponds, gardens, copses of maples, and stands of pines, making it one of the favorite destinations for local birders. Walking trails meander through the preserve. This green space near the Kennebec River must be very attractive to migrants, because returning songbirds often arrive here first. Two dozen warbler species pass through, and some stay to breed, including Yellow, Black-and-white, Black-throated Green, Chestnut-sided, Pine, and Magnolia Warblers, as well as American Redstarts and Common Yellowthroats. Bobolinks and Savannah Sparrows nest in the grasslands. Eastern Bluebirds and Tree Swallows occupy the birdhouses. On a fine spring evening, look for Wilson's Snipe circling above the wetlands in its mating flight display. The same wetlands conceal Sora that are heard more often then seen. Great-crested, Least, Alder and Willow Flycatchers occur in the arboretum. The Viles Visitor Center is open Mon–Fri, 8am–4:30pm. Dogs are allowed on leash.

Directions: in Augusta, on the east side of the Kennebec River, follow Hospital Street (Route 9) one mile to the visitor center on the left. The visitor center is not easily seen from the road, but it is just past the entrance to athletic fields on the same side of the road.

⭐**65** **The Kennebec Highlands** took an already terrific lakes region of the state and made it even better. In 1998, the Belgrade Regional Conservation Alliance began a project to preserve 6,000 acres of prime undeveloped habitat, including the highest peaks in Kennebec County, several streams, many wetlands, and five ponds. The area is interwoven with old logging roads, hiking paths, and multi-use trails. The bulk of the Kennebec Highlands is west of Belgrade Lakes Village on the far side of Long Lake. Two mountain trails are located on the near side, just north of town.

The prevailing habitat throughout the Kennebec Highlands is northern hardwood forest. It is relatively dry and mature. As Maine becomes more boreal farther north, Wood Thrushes disappear. But here, they are found in equal numbers with

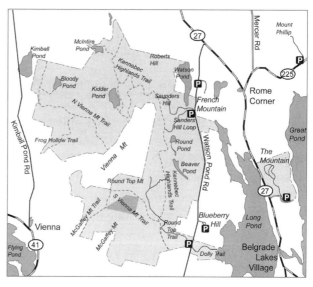

Hermit Thrushes and Veeries. Common warblers include Blackthroated Green, Black-throated Blue, Blackburnian, Northern Parula, Yellow-rumped, and Ovenbird. Common Yellowthroat, American Redstart, Chestnut-sided, Nashville, and Yellow Warblers are found around open areas. Canada Warblers nest in damp, forested areas, while Pine Warblers inhabit large stands of white pines. Typical flycatchers include Eastern Wood-Pewee, Great-crested, and Least. Red-eyed Vireos are abundant, Blue-headed are common, and Warbling are occasional near water's edge. Ruffed Grouse are plentiful, as are Pileated, Downy, and Hairy Woodpeckers, Yellow-bellied Sapsuckers, and Northern Flickers. Also expect Scarlet Tanagers and Rose-breasted Grosbeaks. Most of the forested habitat is similar, but each trail has its own characteristics. The Official Trail Map and Guide is inexpensive and is available at local markets. Visit the Web site at www.belgradelakes.org. Below is an abbreviated synopsis of the best birding trails.

• **The Kennebec Highlands Trail** serves as the backbone of the main preserve. It runs along the ridge in front of the higher peaks and connects the access paths to the larger trail network. It is predominantly hardwood, hemlock, and white pine, and the species listed above are typical. Vienna Mountain is the tallest peak and its exposed summit can offer fair hawk-watching in September.

The following trails are all reached via the Watson Pond Road, which runs the length of Long Pond on its western side. The road intersects Route 27 about 5 miles north of Belgrade Lakes Village.

• **French Mountain Trail** is the first trail encountered on Watson Pond Road, less than a mile south of Route 27. The trail provides a big payoff for little effort. The short, 0.4 mile climb to the summit justifies its popularity with a splendid vista of Whittier Pond in the foreground and Long Pond beyond. The view looks over the tops of some pines that might bring you to eye level with a Pine Warbler. Nashville Warblers also nest near the top. Broad-winged, Red-shouldered, and Red-tailed Hawks are all possible in the valley below.

Directions: the parking area is indistinct. There is room for two to four cars on the expanded shoulder where the trail begins, on the left side of Watson Pond Road. The pull-off is opposite two houses, less than a mile south of the junction with Route 27. There are no facilities.

• **The Sanders Hill Loop** is one of the best of these trails because it crosses several habitats. The trail starts at the trailhead parking lot and proceeds up an old logging road. Before long, a spur exits to the left in a boggy area that often produces Northern Waterthrush and might yield a Yellow-bellied Flycatcher. Listen for Canada Warbler, too. The trail continues southwest until intersecting the Kennebec Highlands Trail. Turn right and follow 0.7 mile, looking for the return trail on the right. The return crosses the summit of Sanders Hill, drops through a boulder field, and eventually traverses the inflow of Watson Pond for another opportunity to encounter forested wetland species.

Directions: the trailhead parking lot is on Watson Pond Road 1.3 miles south of the Route 27 intersection.

• **Blueberry Hill** is a pleasant picnic spot requiring only a few minutes to appreciate. A scenic overlook of Long Pond is the main attraction, but the trees surrounding the parking lot are likely to contain American Redstarts. The shrubbery at the field edges is home to Song Sparrows, Common Yellowthroats, and Eastern Towhees. Dark-eyed Juncos and White-throated Sparrows like these shrubs too. This can be a good vantage point for hawks in the valley.

Directions: the entrance is on the left of Watson Pond Road 3.6 miles south of its intersection with Route 27. There are no facilities.

• **Round Top Trail** begins at the southern end of the preserve. The trail itself is a 3.9-mile round trip, though the hike can be extended along the Kennebec Highlands Trail. The trail is moderate, sometimes traversing granite ledges. The species variety is typical, with enough wet spots to provide a chance for Canada Warbler, and enough deciduous trees to guarantee White-breasted Nuthatch. The South Vienna Mountain Trail to the summit of Kennebec County's highest hill, Vienna Mountain, is reached about halfway up the path.

Directions: the trailhead is located on Watson Pond Road, four miles south of its junction with Route 27. The ample parking lot is next to the entrance to Wildflower Estates. There are no facilities.

• **The Mountain Trail** is the first trail encountered north of Belgrade Lakes Village on Route 27. It was the initial parcel to be acquired by Belgrade Regional Conservation Alliance in 1998. The main artery of the preserve is an old logging road, which makes for easy walking and a wide view of the surrounding woods. It is short but heavily populated with birds. All of the region's warblers may be present, with a better than average chance of Scarlet Tanagers and Rose-breasted Grosbeaks. Ruffed Grouse and Wood Thrush particularly favor this trail. There are two scenic loops at the top, one that overlooks Long Pond to the west, and one that overlooks Great Pond to the east. The entire round trip is less than two miles.

Directions: one mile north of the village on Route 27, turn east onto Mountain View Drive. The parking area is 0.3 mile ahead on the left.

• **Mount Phillip Trail** is another short trail that ends with a pleasant view. The 0.6-mile footpath proceeds almost straight up to the summit, over a moderate grade. This trail is dominated by mature oaks and pines, with one impressive stand of mature hemlocks. Blackburnian Warblers dominate the treetops. Black-throated Green and Black-throated Blue Warblers are almost as common. The partial clearing at the peak offers views of Great Pond to the south and the Kennebec Highlands to the west.

Directions: the trailhead is inconspicuous. From Route 27, turn onto Route 225 and proceed 1.5 miles. Park in the wide, unpaved pullout on the left, opposite Starbird Lane. The trail begins at the far end of the pullout, about 50 yards ahead. There are no facilities.

★ **66** **The Good Will-Hinckley School** was established in the 19th century as a home and school for troubled youth. Its founder, George Hinckley, believed that the area's rural nature would help to build character and motivate young people to improve their lives. He was correct. The campus was built with walking trails and arboretums that continue to feed the soul today. The backbone is a loop of trails that starts behind the L.C. Bates Museum. The Dartmouth Trail is nearly a mile long, and returns via the Bowdoin Trail. There are several side trails, cut-offs, and extensions that provide alternative paths. Black-throated Green and Blackburnian Warblers, Northern Parulas, Winter Wrens, Hermit Thrushes, and Eastern Wood-Pewees are normally easy to find in the woods. Wood Thrushes and Brown Creepers are present in smaller numbers. Side trails that lead to the adjacent fields provide an opportunity to find Bobolinks, Indigo Buntings, Northern Harriers, and Wild Turkeys. Check the farm pond for Warbling Vireo, Sora, American Bittern, and Wilson's Snipe.

The L.C. Bates Museum is worth a stop on its own merits. The natural history exhibits feature a mounted display of Maine birds and 19 dioramas of native species in their habitats by Impressionist artist Charles D. Hubbard. The museum organizes programs, tours, and bird walks on the property, and is open Wednesday through Sunday (closed Sunday in winter).

Directions: from I-95, take Exit 133 and turn north toward Skowhegan. The campus is about 5.5 miles ahead on the left.

—➤•◆•◄—

Additional Sites:

a **Jamies Pond** is a Maine Wildlife Management Area in Hallowell. Mature hardwoods prevail, providing a home to Ovenbirds, Winter Wrens, Red-eyed Vireos, Scarlet Tanagers, Rose-breasted Grosbeaks, Eastern Wood-Pewees, and Black-throated Blue Warblers. Thrushes include equal

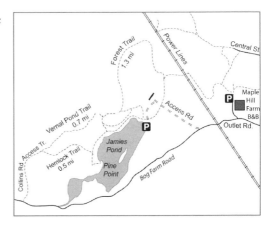

numbers of Hermit, Wood, and Veery. Other breeding warblers likely to be encountered include Black-throated Green, Black-and-white, and Blackburnian. Canada Warblers lurk in dense, tangled underbrush. On forest edges, expect American Redstarts, and Magnolia, Nashville and Chestnut-sided Warblers, and Least Flycatchers. Several other foot trails surround the pond and adjacent hills. The pond offers the additional opportunity to scan for Bald Eagles, waterfowl, and flycatchers.

Maple Hill Farm is located near Jamies Pond and borders the trail system. Besides being a fine B&B and small convention center, it provides excellent habitat on its own property. The extensive fields are mowed later in summer, ensuring a thriving population of Bobolinks and Savannah Sparrows. Wild Turkeys work the field edges under the trees, while Indigo Buntings, Baltimore Orioles, and Scarlet Tanagers sometimes forage in the branches above. The farm buildings attract swallows and the birdfeeders lure sparrows, cardinals, titmice, and finches. The power lines on the hill behind the fields should be checked for Prairie Warblers, which reach the northern edge of their range here. Access to the snowmobile trail system is available at the rear of the parking lot and at the top of the field. Birders are encouraged to park and enjoy the entire area, but please check in at the front desk to let the owners know you are there. (They can provide a free trail map.) The woodland species are the same as those for Jamies Pond.

Directions: from Water Street in Hallowell, turn up Central Street, proceed 1.5 miles. Turn left onto Shady Lane for 0.4 mile, then right onto Outlet Road. Follow Outlet Road past Maple Hill Farm Inn, then turn right onto the small road that leads to Jamies Pond. Though there are no directional signs to Jamies Pond, the route to Maple Hill Farm Inn is well marked.

b **Vaughan Woods** is located minutes away from the capitol. It is hard to overstate the historic significance of Vaughan Woods, or the generosity of the Gibson family in conserving it for future generations. Its location was a site of substantial trading between the earliest Europeans and Native Americans. In the late 1620s

it was part of a patent granted to the Plimouth Colony. In 1791, the grandson of Benjamin Hallowell (for whom the town is named) settled here. Charles Vaughan built a flour mill, a wharf, and extensive farms. In 1797 his oldest brother, Benjamin, arrived and transformed the property into an agricultural masterpiece. In the 1930s, great grandson William Warren Vaughan removed several dams and buildings, and constructed a series of paths and stone bridges that remain today as Vaughan Woods. In 1988, George and Diana Gibson began arrangements with the Kennebec Land Trust to forever protect these woods. Diana is a 7th generation descendent of Benjamin Hallowell and a 5th generation descendent of Benjamin Vaughan. Birders will find old-growth stands of pine and hemlock, as well as oak and beech. Warblers, vireos, and flycatchers move about the canopy while thrushes and Ovenbirds rule the under story. Vaughan Brook tumbles through the heart of the woodland, which has attracted nesting Louisiana Waterthrushes in recent years on the northernmost edge of its range. A field hidden in the woods contains Bobolinks, Savannah Sparrows, and sometimes Eastern Meadowlarks.

Directions: from Water Street in Hallowell, turn up Central Street, drive three blocks, turn left onto Middle Street, and follow to the end. A small parking lot marks the trail entrance. There are no facilities.

c **The Kennebec River Rail Trail** is a paved path that runs along the Kennebec River from downtown Augusta to downtown Hallowell. It is popular for walkers in all seasons, but species of interest to summer birders are limited primarily to common warblers, Double-crested Cormorants, and occasional Bald Eagles. In winter, however, Common Mergansers, Common Goldeneyes, and even Barrow's Goldeneyes are often found where flowing water keeps the river ice-free. In migration, eiders and scoters use the river as a flyway to their northern breeding grounds and are sometimes seen passing in large numbers. In winter, check the ornamental trees around the State House for Bohemian and Cedar Waxwings feeding on lingering fruit.

Directions: there are multiple access points from the main road along the river.

d **Augusta Airport** has featured nesting Prairie Warblers for many years, joined by Brown Thrashers and Eastern Towhees in the surrounding brush. Field and Grasshopper Sparrows and Willow Flycatchers are also possible, especially in the gravel pit area north of the runways that is reached by the small dirt road extending west of the parking area behind the cemetery.

Directions: from Western Avenue at the National Guard Armory in Augusta, drive up to and past the airport. Turn left into the cemetery just past the airport and look for a dirt parking area in the far right corner.

e **The Messalonskee Lake** boat ramp is often an easy place to see the Black Terns that arrive in mid- to late May. The boat channel runs through excellent marsh habitat before entering the lake. Dabbling ducks and Pied-billed Grebes are likely. Virginia Rails may call at any time of day. Warbling Vireos and Baltimore Orioles are common among the trees along the shoreline. Northern Harriers are regularly seen above the marsh.

This is a good place for an adventure by canoe, but make sure to clean all plant matter off the hull before launch and upon takeout. The lake has been plagued with invasive species in recent years and there is a intensive effort underway to avoid spreading the problem. Also, be very careful not to paddle close to the Black Tern nesting areas. Rather than hiding in place, chicks tend to scatter, making them easy prey for Snapping turtles, pickerel, bitterns, and other predators. Stay alert for the Sandhill Cranes in the area. They are rare breeders in Maine, but pairs have been nesting in this area for many years.

Directions: the boat launch is obvious on Route 27, 3.5 miles north of the split with Route 23.

f **Natanis Golf Course** is one of Maine's finest courses. It's also where Purple Martins nest. Martins are uncommon in Maine, but one colony is well established in the martin houses behind the clubhouse in Vassalboro. While there, look for Rough-winged Swallows over the water hazards. Baltimore Orioles are also a common sight. It is not necessary to venture onto the course or into the path of golfers. These target species are readily observable from the parking lot and from the immediate rear of the clubhouse.

Directions: follow Route 201 north of Augusta for approximately 6 miles to Webber Pond Road. Turn right onto Webber Pond Road and the course is about 2 miles ahead.

g **Fort Halifax** in Winslow is where the Sebasticook River flows into the Kennebec River. The current keeps the water ice-free, creating one of the more likely places to find Barrow's Goldeneye in winter. Common Goldeneyes and Mergansers are regular here, as well as Mallards and American Black Ducks. Fort Halifax is the recreation of a historic blockhouse that served to protect colonial interests at this important river junction, and the park that surrounds the fort provides several good vantage points of the Kennebec. There are sidewalks on both sides of the bridge, providing a safe, upstream view of the Sebasticook River.

Directions: from Waterville, cross the bridge into Winslow, turn right onto Route 201/137, and follow for half a mile to Fort Halifax on the right, just before the bridge.

h **Perkins Arboretum** is part of the Colby College campus. The campus commands the high ground of Mayflower Hill, overlooking the city of Waterville. Just downhill from the campus buildings, a large woodland separates the college from the residential neighborhoods of town. This is Perkins Arboretum. Enormous hemlocks at the heart of the arboretum indicate that these trees have not felt a saw

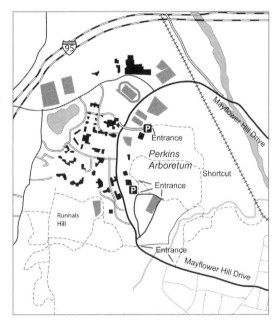

blade in many decades. This is the realm of Ruffed Grouse, Ovenbird, Veery, Eastern Wood-Pewee, Red-eyed Vireo, and typical canopy warblers such as Blackburnian, Black-throated Green, and Northern Parula. Toward the outer edges of the forest, Black-throated Blue and Nashville Warblers gain ascendancy. Canada Warblers call from damp tangles. Black-and-white Warblers are found throughout the arboretum. Cooper's Hawks and Barred Owls have nested regularly here for many years. Broad-winged Hawks are often present.

There are two distinct sections. A wide dry path dips into the woods in a horseshoe shape that has its entry points next to Hill House, behind the tennis courts, and behind the parking lots opposite the dormitories on the south end of campus. This runs through a birdy section of shrubs, secondary growth, and pines. Expect American Redstart, Chestnut-sided Warbler, Common Yellowthroat, and American Catbird. Besides the ubiquitous Red-eyed Vireo, Warbling Vireo has been found here. Veeries often pop out from the deeper woods. These deeper woods are reached from several points on the southeast side of the arboretum. Two entrances on Mayflower Hill Drive are unmarked. The best entrances are from the parking lots. Follow the signs (or follow the edge of the woods down the hill alongside the old playing fields). Yellow Warblers, Tufted Titmice, Baltimore Orioles, and flycatchers are common along the field edge. The trail enters the deeper woods below the fields. There are four color-coded trails. The blue and yellow trails terminate on Mayflower Hill Drive. The white and red trails run on opposite banks of a stream in the heart of the preserve. Both terminate on the railroad track on the far edge of the preserve. The red trail can be muddy on the far end. Footing throughout the arboretum is occasionally challenging and damp.

Trails continue up Runnals Hill on the opposite side of Mayflower Hill Drive, behind the president's house. House Wrens are common and Field Sparrows have been found in some years. Rose-breasted Grosbeaks and Eastern Bluebirds appear regularly.

Directions: From Waterville, proceed up Mayflower Hill Drive to the campus. From the Waterville-Oakland exit of I-95, turn onto Kennedy Memorial Drive, then onto Second Rangeway. Follow around the campus to Mayflower Hill Drive.

i Several major routes converge with the Kennebec River in **Skowhegan**. The river is dammed at the center of town and there may be no place in Maine where it is easier to see Rough-winged Swallows. These frequently mix with Cedar Waxwings in the summer, hawking insects over the outflow of the dam. Downstream at the edge of town, the river widens. Mallards, American Black Ducks, and other dabblers are frequently present, often joined by Common Mergansers, especially in winter. Though still fast flowing, the river deepens along a roadside rest area east of town. Common Loons and a variety of swallows are often seen in this section.

j **Bingham** is a good place for gas and food, since towns are few and far between along Route 201. In Bingham, a major hydropower dam impounds the Kennebec River, creating Wyman Lake. If time permits, sneak over to the western side of the lake for a visit to Houston Brook Falls. An easy trail extends several hundred yards through a mixed hardwood and hemlock forest to a surprise waterfall in the woods. Expect encounters with Black-throated Green and Blackburnian Warblers, Blue-headed Vireos, Winter Wrens, and Hermit Thrushes.

Directions: on the southern edge of town, Route 16 turns west toward Kingfield. Immediately after crossing the bridge, turn right and follow the road 3-1/2 miles to the Pleasant Ridge Plantation Transfer Station on the right. The trailhead is at the far edge of the ample parking area. There are no facilities here. A boat launch and picnic area 2.4 miles from the Route 16 intersection provide facilities, a pleasant view of the lake, and an opportunity for Common Loons.

k **Long Falls Dam Road** leads to the back side of Bigelow Preserve (detailed in the Maine Lakes and Mountains Region) and Flagstaff Lake. Over the first dozen miles it passes through several small communities. Beyond these, birders will share the road only with a few campers, fishermen, an occasional logging truck...and many large tankers. This is where Poland Spring taps Maine's cool, clear, mountain water and carries it off to be bottled. Just over halfway to Long Falls Dam, the forest makes a transition from hardwood to boreal habitat rich in moose. Boreal Chickadees and Gray Jays arc present year-round. In irruption years, crossbills have been abundant along this road.

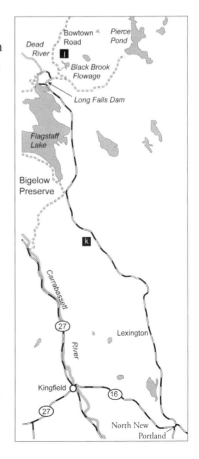

One resource to tap in this area is Claybrook Mountain Lodge. Maine Audubon has staged many of its warbler and boreal species trips from this traditional sporting camp. Greg and Pat Drummond willingly point birders in the right direction and share the unusual species to be found on their own property. Philadelphia Vireos are sometimes seen from the porch. A pair of Louisiana Waterthrushes pushed the limits of their northern range to nest here in 2002. Visit www.claybrookmountainlodge.com.

Bigelow Preserve is reached via Big Brook Road. (The Carriage Road from Carrabassett Valley enters near its beginning.) The five-mile road is smooth, lightly traveled, and conducive to good birding. There are many hardwood warblers in breeding season, usually very visible. Ovenbirds, Hermit Thrushes, Winter Wrens, and Least Flycatchers are equally noisy but more difficult to see. As the road continues through more mixed habitat, both Hermit and Swainson's Thrushes sometimes come out of the woods to land on the road, foraging in plain view. There is a pleasant camping area and the Safford Brook Trail at the end of this road. The trail presents a panoramic ascent of Bigelow Mountain that includes a wide boreal zone, topped by a substantial high-elevation spruce belt inhabited by Bicknell's Thrush.

l **Black Brook Flowage** is well hidden and rarely visited. Before reaching Long Falls Dam, look for a right turn toward Cobb's Camps on Pierce Pond. This road passes through a good boreal section and a clear-cut area where Lincoln's Sparrows can be heard singing. At about three miles, there is a T intersection. The right turn leads to Pierce Pond. Instead, turn left and proceed half a mile along the Bowtown Road, looking for a jeep path into the woods. The road widens to allow parking next to some boulders along the right-of-way. The jeep path is a short, level walk to Black Brook flowage. Cape May Warblers nest along this path. It ends at an excellent wetland where moose and Gray Jays compete for attention. Waterfowl are likely, particularly Hooded Mergansers. Stay alert for Wilson's Snipe. Sections may be wet, so waterproof footwear is suggested. This section of the Bowtown Road is also particularly good for Boreal Chickadees, Spruce Grouse, and Gray Jays.

m **The Forks** sits at the confluence of the Kennebec and Dead Rivers. There are many places to stay, eat, and adventure. Rafters enjoy both rivers, so outfitters proliferate. There is a picnic area where Moxie Lake Road turns east from Route 201. Warbling Vireos are commonly heard along the river's edge. A trailhead located 1.9 miles up this road leads to Moxie Falls, a family friendly hike to one of the most scenic waterfalls in Maine. The trail is 0.6 mile one-way, sloping gently downhill toward the river, and descending stairs on the final approach. The woods are predominantly hardwood with some balsam fir. Featured warblers are Black-throated Blue, Black-throated Green, Northern Parula, Blackburnian, Black-and-white, and Yellow-rumped. Red-eyed and Blue-headed Vireos are present. Hermit Thrush, Brown Creeper, Golden-crowned Kinglet, and Winter Wren round out the chorus.

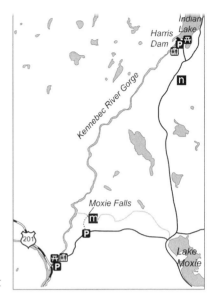

n **Harris Dam** impounds Indian Pond on the Kennebec River. The fabled Kennebec Gorge begins at the outflow, and this is where rafting companies launch their adventures. Many of the rapids are notorious, especially Magic Falls—so named because of its ability to make whole rafts disappear. Before noon, the area is uncomfortably hectic and best avoided. But after lunch, the commercial rafters have cleared out and it can be an interesting area to explore. Best of all, the eight-mile access road from Lake Moxie to Indian Pond runs through a strongly boreal habitat where any of the four specialties–Gray Jay, Boreal Chickadee, Spruce Grouse, and Black-backed Woodpecker–may turn up. The adjacent power lines make a good corridor for almost all of Maine's hawks, including the uncommon Red-shouldered Hawk.

Directions: from The Forks, follow Lake Moxie Road to the lake, stopping at Moxie Falls if desired, then turn left toward Indian Pond. Access to the Harris Dam recreation area is free but it requires a gate check-in.

o **Jackman** is the last established community in Maine before reaching Canada on Route 201. From Lake Parlin to the border, spruce begins to dominate the forest and the chance of a moose encounter increases. Route 201 is too busy to stop easily for birding, despite the appealingly boreal habitat. Logging roads intersect the main highway but the truck traffic is often heavy and discouraging. Jackman is an important hub for snowmobile and all-terrain vehicle trails. It is also a major stop on the Northern Forest Canoe Trail, which links waterways from New York to Maine. Several canoe trails, especially the Moose River Bow Trip, are among the most popular in Maine. Jackman does not have as many walking trails as other places in the Maine woods, so birding here requires a sense of adventure. Establishing headquarters at one of the area's traditional sporting camps is a fine option. Most have their own local trails; for example, try the Last Resort on Long Lake. Not only is its trail system fun to bird but this section of the lake is also great for waterfowl, snipe, rails, and eagles. See: www.lastresortmaine. com. Several of the major logging thoroughfares are wide enough to avoid problems with trucks and these can be used as boreal routes to other valleys on the birding trail, with stops as desired at spruce stands and beaver flowages.

THE MAINE HIGHLANDS

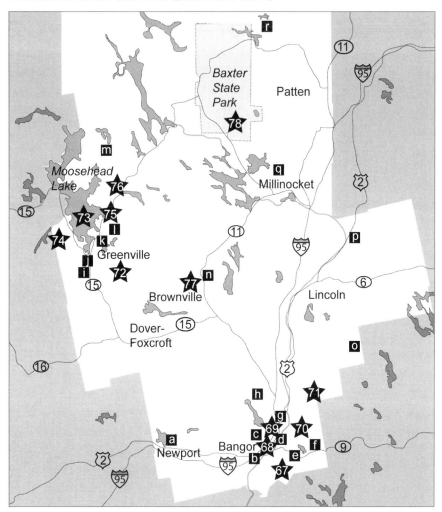

Bangor is the gateway to northern and interior Maine, and is also just an hour's drive from Acadia National Park. The Bangor vicinity has a little bit of everything. The Penobscot River is tidal through the downtown area, rising and falling as much as 16 feet. Above the tide line, the river is a migration route for sea ducks and a gathering point for freshwater ducks. The Caribou Bog complex extends rare raised bog habitat right to the doorstep of the Bangor Mall. The City of Bangor and the University of Maine in Orono maintain large forested recreational corridors and trails. Gardens and orchards are among the first places in Maine where irruptive Pine Grosbeaks and Bohemian

Waxwings show up in winter. Significant spruce-fir boreal tracts occur nearby at Sunkhaze Meadows National Wildlife Refuge.

Greenville to the west lies at the southern tip of Moosehead Lake. Moosehead is Maine's largest lake—in fact, it is the largest lake within a single state east of the Mississippi. In spite of its size and cool, clear water, much of the lake shore is undeveloped. Many of the nearby lakes and ponds are remote and protected by conservation. The area is famous for its large moose population, and Greenville is home to the Moosemania Festival every spring. The region boasts scenic mountains and rushing rivers. There is a diversity of wildlife habitats over a relatively small area. Beech and birch predominate through most of the forest, but spruce, balsam fir, cedar, and tamarack take over in the cooler, damper areas. This creates an important transition zone between the southern hardwood forest and the boreal spruce-fir forest of Canada. These zones are home to Maine's boreal bird specialties: Spruce Grouse, Black-backed Woodpecker, Canada Jay, and Boreal Chickadee. White-winged and Red Crossbills can often be found, sometimes year-round. At least twenty species of warbler breed here. Bicknell's Thrush can be found on area peaks above 3,000 feet.

Millinocket to the north lies at the southern entrance to Baxter State Park. The park stands as a monument to the love of Governor Percival P. Baxter for his native state of Maine. Even before Baxter served as governor from 1921 to 1925, he launched an effort to set aside more than 200,000 acres of forest to be preserved forever as wilderness for the people of Maine. It took him 32 years to assemble 28 parcels of land, along with a legal trust to protect the park in perpetuity. The influence of mountains and latitude produces an ideal breeding ground for Maine's coveted boreal species. Spruce and Ruffed Grouse are regularly seen picking gravel from the Park Tote Road. Boreal Chickadees are commonplace. Black-backed Woodpeckers, and the even rarer Northern Three-toed Woodpeckers, are known nesters. Gray Jays are notorious camp robbers, especially at Chimney Pond Campground. Philadelphia Vireos are reliable in several spots. Yellow-bellied Flycatchers and Lincoln Sparrows may be found in boggy areas. Though Fox Sparrows are at the southern edge of their breeding range, they are sometimes heard singing along the trails and in boreal areas. Blackpoll and Bay-breasted Warblers are present in many areas. Moose find the mud ponds irresistible, and moose photo tours are now available. Black bear, white-tailed deer, eastern coyote, bobcat, and varying or snowshoe hare are just some of the mammals that thrive in the park.

Trip planning: www.TheMaineHighlands.com or 800-91-MOOSE.

➡➤◦⬅⬅

Official Maine Birding Trail Sites

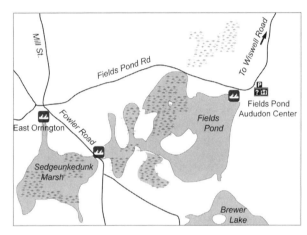

67 Fields Pond Audubon Center is on Fields Pond Road at the Holden-Orrington town line east of Brewer. The sanctuary encompasses 190 acres of fields, wetlands, forest, lakeshore frontage, plus a 22-acre island. The fields are ringed by bluebird boxes and the grasslands support Bobolinks and Savannah Sparrows. The forest contains a variety of warblers, thrushes, and woodpeckers. The nearby Sedgeunkedunk Stream Marsh is one of the best places in the area for early spring waterfowl, many of which remain to nest. Continue driving south along Fields Pond Road to reach the marsh. It is also possible to paddle to the marsh from the center itself. Canoes and snowshoes are available seasonally for rent. The center also contains a small birding store with books, optics, and supplies. The center is open Wednesday through Sunday (and other times when staffed). The property is open to visitors dawn to dusk, seven days a week.

Directions: from I-95, take Exit 182 to I-395 in the direction of Brewer. Proceed over the Penobscot River, and then take the Parkway South exit from I-395. Turn left from the exit, continue on Parkway South to a four-way junction. Turn left on Elm Street, which becomes Wiswell Road in about a mile. Continue on Wiswell Road to Fields Pond Road, turn left, and follow to the center on the left.

68 Bangor City Forest and the **Orono Bog Walk** are included in a 680-acre forest tract owned by the City of Bangor. The property features about nine miles of hiking and biking trails and four miles of access roads. It offers a close-in tract of mature woods with a variety of warblers, thrushes, and other woodland birds, all of which are easy to see because of the width of the trails. The Orono Bog Boardwalk was constructed in 2003. This spectacular 4,200-foot-long boardwalk loops through peat and bog habitats, providing views of specialty breeders such as Lincoln's Sparrow and Palm

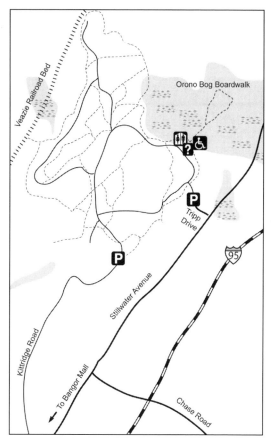

Warbler. A host of other common warblers is readily observable, particularly Black-throated Green, Yellow-rumped, Black-and-white, and Nashville Warblers. Interpretive signs along the boardwalk accurately depict where certain species are likely to be found, including the Canada Warbler that is regularly heard singing near its sign. The open horizon of the bog makes it easier to see raptors at a distance, including uncommonly seen species such as Red-shouldered Hawk and Northern Goshawk. The boardwalk is wheelchair-accessible, and is open from May through November.

Directions: from the end of Hogan Road north of the Bangor Mall, turn right onto Stillwater Avenue, then travel about 1.3 miles to Tripp Drive. (Look for small signs to the Bangor City Forest and the Bog Boardwalk.) Drive into the Bangor City Forest parking lot at the end of the road, park, and follow the East Trail about 0.25 mile to the boardwalk.

69 **Newman Hill Preserve** is also
known locally as the Taylor Bait Farm,
although it is no longer commercially
active. Its shallow ponds have a local
reputation for attracting waterfowl in
the spring and shorebirds in the fall.
While part of the preserve is protected with easements by the Orono
Land Trust, much of the site is private
property and must be respected. Stay
on roads.

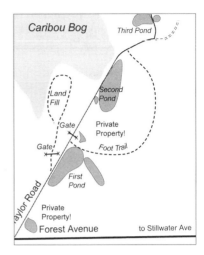

The first pond is less than a mile
along Taylor Road. It is best for
Hooded Mergansers, Pied-billed Grebes, and American Bitterns. The
marsh on the opposite side of Taylor Road contains Virginia Rails. A
second pond is reached by walking past the gate that marks the end of
legal parking and past the private house on the right. American Black
Ducks, occasional Common Mergansers, and teal sometimes congregate in this pond. Stay alert for otters. There is a third pond a short
hike beyond this point that is smaller and less likely to contain interesting species. There is also a foot trail that winds over Newman Hill.
The trailhead is well marked just beyond the first pond, and it reenters
the roadbed after the second pond.

*Directions: from the Bangor Mall, go north on Stillwater Avenue to
Forest Avenue. Turn left, proceed 1.4 miles, and turn right onto the Taylor
Road. Park only where designated along the first pond and stay on marked
trails and roads. The best birding is from the road itself so there is no need to
trespass on private property.*

70 **Leonard's Mills** is a restored logging mill and pioneer settlement.
The mile-long access road provides a predictable warbler environment
in May and June, with a variety of habitats over a conveniently short
trek. The road begins with secondary growth on the right, good for
Chestnut-sided Warblers and American Redstarts. Just ahead, beyond
the forestry offices, the secondary growth supports several warbler
species, including Blackburnian and Black-throated Green Warblers,
and plenty of Ovenbirds. Upon reaching the open power lines, note
any active Osprey nests on the towers. Check the tall trees where Great

Blue Herons have been colonial nesters in recent years. Wet areas contain Swamp Sparrows and American Bitterns. Just beyond the power lines, as the road makes a transition to more mature forest, Nashville

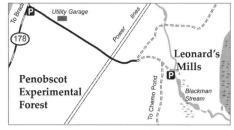

Warblers and Veeries have been prevalent. The mature pines support a good number of Black-throated Blue, Blackburnian, and Pine Warblers, as well as Northern Parula and Eastern Wood-Pewee. The museum complex is interesting, and there is a nature trail on the far side of the grounds. There is a gated road beyond the parking lot that leads toward Chemo Pond. Local traffic is restricted and sparse, allowing for more opportunities to search for thrushes and wood warblers, as time permits.

Directions: located on Route 178 in Bradley, halfway between Brewer and Milford. Watch for the sign. Park at either end of the access road. There is room for several vehicles at the beginning of the road, and a large parking area at the end.

⭐ **Sunkhaze Meadows National Wildlife Refuge** is 20 minutes from downtown Bangor. Getting there is half the fun. It's a vast expanse of peat land, marsh, and wetland forest, though the interior is accessible only by canoe and then only by dragging the boat over occasional beaver dams. The obstacles and the slow flow mean a long paddle, requiring plenty of time. This is a breed-

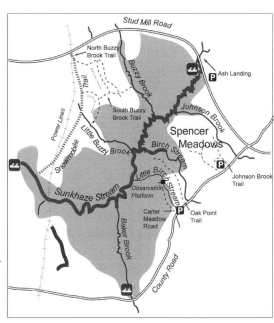

ing habitat for American Black Ducks, Hooded Mergansers, Ring-necked Ducks, and both species of teal. Marsh Wrens are common and noisy. Nelson's Sharp-tailed Sparrows breed here. American Bitterns and Great Blue Herons are abundant. Yellow Rail and Sedge Wren have been found within the marsh, but both are very rare.

Several clusters of foot trails are available along the edges of the refuge. The Carter Meadow Road offers an excellent 2-mile round trip to an observation platform. This is the best view of the entire Sunkhaze Meadow from land. It's also one of the better places near Bangor to chance upon moose. Least Flycatchers are abundant over the first section and Boreal Chickadees have been noted along the trail. A parking area and interpretive sign are just north of the trail entrance. The Oak Point Trail is about 1.5 miles long. It is wet in the spring, though boardwalks help in the most challenging places. This trail traverses mostly upland forest but it does approach the peat bog. The Johnson Brook Trail loops for about three miles through upland forest. A section through a cedar swamp also relies on boardwalks in the wettest areas. A parking lot and map kiosk serve this trailhead. All three trails begin on the County Road. The Buzzy Brook Trail System is accessed from the Stud Mill Road close to where the power lines cross. The trail begins within the gated McLaughlin Road.

There are three waterway entrances by canoe. The shortest are from Baker Brook on the County Road, and at the Ash Landing Trailhead of Sunkhaze Stream on the Stud Mill Road. They are often obstructed and might be impassible in low water. The longest but easiest way is at the western end where the Sunkhaze Stream crosses under Route 2 on its way into the Penobscot River. Expect an upstream paddle against current in the spring and a low-water paddle in a dry season. Nonetheless, this route usually encounters the fewest obstacles. Overall, it's best to contact the NWR office at 207-236-6970 for current information.

The County Road skirts the border of the refuge and provides a shortcut to the Stud Mill Road. From Milford, northbound on Route 2, turn right onto the County Road soon after the intersection with Route 178. The next eight miles traverse multiple woodland and marsh habitats. Barred and Saw-whet Owls can be heard at night on the stretch beyond the Milford Transfer Station. In the winter, finches and crossbills are possible, and crossbills will stay all summer in irruptive years.

The Stud Mill Road marks the northern boundary of the refuge. It is one of the roads that makes Maine "Maine." This gravel superhighway runs from Route 2 in Milford to Route 1 in Princeton, crossing the Union, Narraguagus, and Machias Rivers en route. About five miles east of its intersection with the County Road, boreal habitat becomes entrenched along the roadway. Gray Jays, Boreal Chickadees, and Yellow-bellied Flycatchers occupy this zone. Whip-poor-wills nest in scrubby areas. They are deafening in the spring, particularly beyond the Maine Conservation Youth Camp on Pickerel Pond. All stream crossings are worth an extra peek for warblers and thrushes. Much of the vegetation alongside the road has been cleared for power transmission lines and a natural gas pipeline. These provide good habitat for American Kestrels, and the occasional Merlin and Sharp-shinned Hawk. In winter, it has become a hunting corridor for owls and it can be possible to see numerous Barred Owls in the sunlight of late afternoon.

The total distance from the Stud Mill/County Road intersection back to Route 2 is about three miles. Returning south on Route 2 will complete a 12-mile loop. Visit Ash Landing, a mile south of the County Road intersection. The view from the edge of this wetland often produces an unusual raptor or flycatcher. Hooded Mergansers and Wood Ducks are regular occurrences. Check the bridge that crosses the Sunkhaze Stream about 2.3 miles south of the intersection. Cape May Warblers have nested here over multiple years.

———— ❖ ————

72 **Borestone Mountain** is a Maine Audubon sanctuary that is a local favorite for family hikers. Two-thirds of the hike follows an easy dirt road, and a new hiking trail alternative was added in 2003. American Redstarts are often apparent right in the parking area along the low trees and shrubs by the road. Because Borestone has been protected for over 100 years, the mature hardwoods enveloping the first third of the trail are particularly good for canopy birds such as Red-eyed Vireos, Scarlet Tanagers, Blackburnian Warblers, and Northern Parula. The vegetation changes gradually during the ascent, leaving behind the maples and embracing birches and beeches. Here, Blue-headed Vireos, Magnolia, Black-throated Blue, and Black-throated Green Warblers quickly become commonplace, with a good chance for Ruby-crowned

Kinglets. Then, as the hardwoods
mix with stands of evergreens
(mostly red spruce), more Hermit Thrushes, Golden-crowned
Kinglets, and Winter Wrens
become noticeable. The usual
chickadees, nuthatches and woodpeckers are always present.

The trail plateaus upon approach to the visitor center. The
thicker evergreen forest is home
to Canada Warblers, and Northern Goshawks are seen regularly.
In winter, during irruptive years,
an astounding number of crossbills can be heard chattering
throughout this section.

Audubon's visitor center
is two-thirds of the way up
the mountain, adjacent to one
of the three mountain ponds.
The three ponds are pleas-
ingly known as Sunrise Pond
on the near right, Sunset Pond
out of sight on the distant left,
and, of course, Midday Pond in
the middle. The water in these
ponds is so clear it is possible
to see 50 feet below the surface.
There are occasional Common
Mergansers in the ponds but the

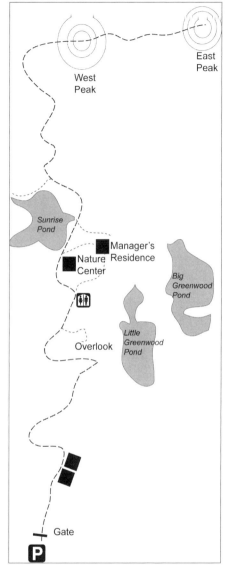

harsh alpine climate supports little aquatic life, so ducks are uncommon. At the visitor's center, feel free to make an extra donation. It is
a challenge for Audubon to maintain this incredible facility. Through
the early nineties, the nearby cliffs were a hack site for the reintro-
duction of Peregrine Falcons. Many of the falcons that fledged here
went off to urban skyscrapers and bridges from Portland, Maine, to
Baltimore, Maryland.

To ascend the rest of Borestone Mountain, follow the trail around the visitor center. The ascent is strenuous and will require some clambering over boulders, but the view is spectacular, especially in foliage season. Aside from more Winter Wrens, Hermit Thrushes, and White-throated Sparrows, the birding is ordinary to the summit, but the 360-degree views from the top make the hike worthwhile.

The road on the way to Borestone Mountain is pleasantly birdy. Stop at the Wilson Stream bridge and enjoy the Barn Swallows that nest under it. A mile later, stop and spend a few minutes at the railroad tracks. The trees are full of Red-eyed Vireos and with a little more patience Scarlet Tanagers may reveal themselves. It's not unusual for Sharp-shinned Hawks to cruise the rail line. This is an active track of the Canadian Pacific Railway, so beware of trains.

Directions: just after passing north through Monson, bear right onto the Elliotsville Road. Follow 7.5 miles to Big Wilson Stream Bridge. Turn left at the intersection and follow signs another mile to Borestone parking lot. Parking is at the base of the mountain. The lot fills early on nice days so you may have to join the others parked along the roadside. A privy is available near the visitor center.

⟢—⬩⊙⬩—⟣

⭐ **73** **Moosehead Lake** is Maine's largest lake. It drives this area's rural economy. Most of the surrounding forest is managed for timber harvesting, and there are many remote logging roads open to public access for traditional sporting activities. The combination of remoteness and access has made the region famous. Several float plane companies offer tours of the area by air, and there is even a Fly-In festival for float planes in the fall. A converted steamship, the *Katahdin*, operates as a museum and provides boat tours in summer. Visitors can expect fine dining and excellent accommodations unassociated with any chain restaurant or brand-name hotel. Birders should consider the Moosehead area as a destination that rivals the Maine coast. Its remote rivers, streams, and ponds are unparalleled.

The Moosehead Lake region is famous for its large moose population and Greenville is home to the Moosemania Festival every spring. These animals are a thrill to see, but remember that they can also be a real traffic hazard. In the spring, they seek highway shoulders for winter road salt and relief from woodland insects. Moose show little sense about traffic, often wandering onto the road. Furthermore, their eyes are less apt to reflect light than those of deer and their dark coloration can make them nearly invisible at night. Though moose can be encountered at any time of day, they are most often seen near dawn and dusk.

Maine also has the largest population of black bears east of the Mississippi and encounters with eastern coyotes are a regular occurrence. Beavers can be seen in every small and slow-moving body of water and they generally

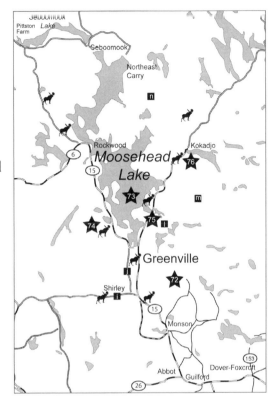

become active and visible in the late afternoon. Otters are common in shallow, slow moving waters.

On the west side of Moosehead Lake, two outflows of the Kennebec River cross under Route 15. The East Outlet is about 10 miles north of Greenville Junction. There is a small parking lot and a dirt road just north of the bridge. This is an excellent road for a warbler walk, since there is little traffic. The first section of this road is the best, traversing a mix of mature hardwoods and conifer species. Canopy warblers such as Blackburnian, Pine, Northern Parula, Bay-breasted, Black-throated Green, and Black-throated Blue are relatively easy to view. At 1.5 miles, just past a gate, there is a regenerating clear-cut where sparrows and flycatchers can be added to the day's list. At all times be alert for Boreal Chickadees. The road continues 5.5 miles to a dead end at the Kennebec River in Somerset Junction. It is usually drivable and there are a couple of stream flowages that offer chances for Common Yellowthroat and Wilson's Warblers but the remainder of the road is not as productive as the first 1.5 miles.

The West Outlet is about 16 miles north of Greenville Junction. North of the bridge, look for a dirt road leading west called Somerset Road. This road also traverses mature hardwood growth and offers many of the same birding opportunities as the East Outlet. However, this road continues for 26 miles to Route 201, and there are homes on the outlet ponds, so it tends to be more heavily traveled. On the other hand, the road brushes past several good views of river, ponds, and productive wetland areas, so a walk or slow drive can be equally pleasurable.

Rockwood is the last sure chance for gas and supplies. It is here that Route 15 turns west along the Moose River, heading for Jackman. However, by turning right and crossing the bridge in Rockwood, the Moosehead adventure continues. The Birches Resort lies just a few miles ahead. Beyond The Birches, a well-traveled dirt road extends far into the North Maine Woods. (There is an access fee at 17 miles.) The historic Pittston Farm sits 20 miles north of Rockwood on Seboomook Lake. Just beyond it, the Golden Road is an unpaved artery that runs east/west from Millinocket to Quebec. Its primary purpose is to serve Maine's working forest, but it also serves as the main access to many remote areas, including the Allagash Wilderness Waterway farther north.

In Rockwood, turn right and cross the bridge over the Moose River. From here, it is 17 miles to the Maine North Woods Association Checkpoint and 20 miles to historic Pittston Farm. (Hence the name of this road is the 20 Mile Road.) The first few miles cross through the Moosehead Wildlands, 11,000 acres of multiple use forest area. Nearby, The Birches is an associated complex of lodge and cottages that offers excellent accommodations and dining year round. It also maintains a system of cross-country ski trails that can double as birding trails in the spring. There are additional side roads all along the access to the West Branch area. Some are little used and can be walked without concern for traffic. Others lead to private property and signs that request privacy should be heeded. One road leads to Tomhegan Wilderness Resort, another excellent four-season sporting camp.

The 20-Mile Road leads through experimental plantings of red pine and white spruce where regenerating clearcuts are home to breeding Lincoln's Sparrows and Mourning Warblers. Just before the checkpoint there is a large beaver flowage that is good for flycatchers and blackbirds. For birding above the checkpoint, see the next chapter on the North Maine Woods.

74 **The Little Moose Unit** of Maine Public Reserved Land contains several hiking trails, campsites, and the trailhead for Big Moose Mountain. This peak rises 3,200 feet into the Bicknells' Thrush zone, and a few have traditionally nested near the summit. The most reliable spot is reported to be just before the first tower. Remember that Bicknell's Thrush is vocal primarily at dawn and dusk. It is handy to be familiar with its call notes, sounding like WEER. Due to its preference for alpine habitat, Bicknell's Thrush is a late migrant, usually arriving after Memorial Day weekend. The mountain ascent is relatively short and steep through excellent birding habitat, transitioning from the Scarlet Tanagers of the lower elevation hardwoods, through zones of balsam fir and spruce over the 90-minute climb. Blackpolls, Bay-breasted Warblers, Yellow-bellied Flycatchers, Boreal Chickadees, and Spruce Grouse are found near the summit. The road through the Little Moose Unit is good for Ruffed Grouse, and Philadelphia Vireos have been noted near the Big Moose Mountain trailhead.

Directions: on Route 15, the North Road turns west 3.5 miles north of Greenville Junction. The trailhead for Big Moose is 1.3 miles from the intersection.

---

75 **Lily Bay State Park** is on the east side of Moosehead Lake, 8.7 miles north of Greenville. This is a popular park for camping, with semi-secluded sites, a boat launch, and a beach. Tall white pines near the shoreline are lively with Pine Warblers, and there is a fine assortment of other common warblers, vireos, and thrushes throughout the park. Canada Warblers and Winter Wrens are more often seen than heard during a morning walk along the access road.

---

76 **Kokadjo** is a tiny community 18.5 miles north of Greenville on the Lily Bay Road. During spring and summer, Barn, Tree, and Cliff Swallows fill the sky here. Cliff Swallows nest under the eaves of the buildings, Barn Swallows nest in the barn behind the store, and Tree Swallows take advantage of birdhouses and woodpecker cavities in the area. Birdfeeders outside the restaurant attract Purple Finches, Rose-breasted Grosbeaks, American Goldfinches, and Chipping Sparrows, often in large numbers. Common Loons, Canada Geese, and Mallards in First Roach Pond take little heed of people and are always quite close. For the next several miles north of Kokadjo, including side roads and the road east to Second Roach Pond, there are extensive spruce-fir forests that are very good for the boreal specialties. Listen for Cape May and Bay-breasted Warblers, Lincoln's Sparrows, and Gray Jays. Spruce Grouse are sighted regularly in the area. Harvested woodlots that are regenerating with maple and brambles are good places to look for a Mourning Warbler. The Appalachian Mountain Club's Medawisla sporting camps are on Second Roach Pond. This road also leads to the Nahmakanta Public Reserved Lands farther east.

Lazy Tom Stream is 1.5 miles north of Kokadjo, bearing left at the first fork, then left again toward Spencer Pond Camps. Just a few hundred yards from the turn, terrifically scenic Lazy Tom Stream crosses under the road. There is always something unusual here. Common Mergansers are often present and the wetland is full of Wilson's Snipe. Northern Harriers are a common sight over the bog. American Redstarts and Cedar Waxwings are usually obvious. Crossbills, particularly White-winged, may be around at any time of year.

———◦———

⭐ **The Piscataquis County Soil & Water Conservation District Demonstration Forest** is well-hidden and lightly used in the woods of Williamsburg west of Brownville Junction. The 180-acre tract is managed to demonstrate varying forestry practices, which also account for the bird diversity. In breeding season, it is loud with Eastern Wood-Pewees, Least and Yellow-bellied Flycatchers, and an abundance of Blackburnian and Black-throated Blue Warblers. Hermit Thrushes and Veeries are to be expected in the northern forest, but Wood Thrushes

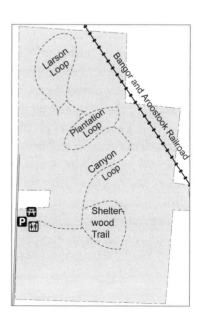

have been noted near the parking area. Several loop trails run through different habitats, the first of which is the Shelter Wood Trail. Initially, it traverses sparse pinewoods, but there is a dense coniferous stand on the back side that regularly produces a Ruffed Grouse.

The Canyon Trail (and the Plantation Loop and Larson Loops beyond) run through elevation changes that sometimes put hikers at eye level with canopy birds. Scarlet Tanagers and Red-eyed Vireos prefer the tops of these mature deciduous stands, while Ovenbirds may be found around the forest floor.

Directions: from I-95, take Exit 199 in Alton and follow Route 16 to Milo. Turn right onto Route 11 and follow to Brownville. Turn left onto High Street and continue north past the Moses Greenleaf monument along the Williamsburg Road. After the road turns to dirt and passes several mobile homes, the forest is 0.6 mile ahead across Penobscot Indian land, marked by a large sign. From the north in Brownville Junction, turn west onto Van Horne Road, then right onto Williamsburg Road. A privy is available at the entrance.

➠◦⋘

78 **Baxter State Park** is in the shadow of Mount Katahdin, Maine's highest peak at 5,271 feet. The mountain was both feared and revered by native tribes. A mighty spirit, variously named Pamola or Katahdin, was believed to live within or upon the twin peaks. Henry David Thoreau ascended the mountain in 1846 and wrote: "What a place to live, die, and be buried in! There, certainly men would live forever, and laugh at death and the grave."

Today, the Baxter State Park Authority takes seriously the mandate of keeping the park forever wild. Entrance gates regulate the number of people entering, and on busy days and weekends visitors may find themselves turned away from certain parking lots, particularly Katahdin trailhead parking lots, when full. In this case, motorists will be asked to choose another destination in the Park, where there is plenty of good birding. Camps and campsites at prime spots are highly coveted and reserved as much as four months in advance, using a rolling reservation system. Spontaneous campers can snap up any remaining available sites within two weeks of their planned arrival by calling Park Headquarters and making a phone-in reservation request, paying by credit card. Only one road runs through the park, with a few smaller roads that connect to camps and campgrounds. Old logging roads have been allowed to revert to forest or have been converted to footpaths. There are approximately 205 miles of hiking trails within the park, traversing a variety of habitats and ascending most of its peaks.

There are two entrances to Baxter State Park. The southern entrance is closer to population centers and receives heavier use because of its proximity to Mt. Katahdin, popular campgrounds, and historic sporting camps. This entrance is reached through Millinocket.

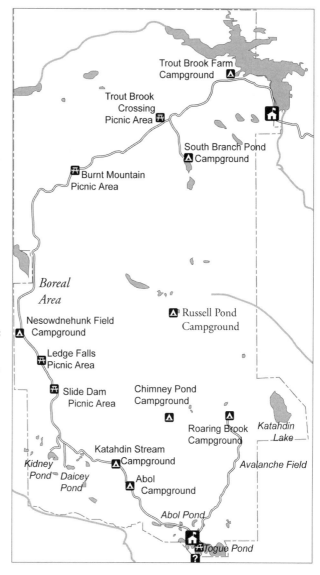

The quieter northern entrance is reached via Patten and Shin Pond. Though the road running through the park between these two checkpoints is just over 40 miles long, it takes half a day to drive it. Roads are narrow, the speed limit is only 20 mph, and the sightseeing is too dazzling to ignore. Park rules prohibit vehicles longer than 22 feet, higher than 9 feet, or wider than 7 feet. Motorcycles and ATVs are not allowed. Neither are dogs or other domestic animals. Camping is permitted only in authorized areas. For information, call 207-723-5140, write to Park Headquarters, 64 Balsam Drive, Millinocket, ME 04462, or visit www.baxterstateparkauthority.com.

Togue Pond Gate is at the southern entrance. There is a Visitor Information Center and a day use swimming area just south of the gate, located on Upper Togue Pond. Pine Warblers and Red-eyed Vireos dominate the tall pines in this vicinity, and it is also one of the more reliable places for Eastern Wood-Pewees. Common Loons are often visible on the pond from ice-out to freeze-over.

Immediately north of the entrance gate, the Park Tote Road forks left while the road to Roaring Brook splits right. Roaring Brook is immensely popular, both as a campground and as the trailhead for ascending Mt. Katahdin from the east. It often reaches its day use capacity early, and additional visitors are directed elsewhere. Local birders make this route their first priority in the morning, before traffic gets heavy. The first stop is at Helon Taylor Pond, on the left just after the split. This marsh can be good for dabbling ducks, American Bitterns, Swamp Sparrows, Alder Flycatchers, and such warblers as Wilson's, Palm, and Yellow. From here to Avalanche Field, the forest is mostly dry deciduous. Hermit Thrushes, Ovenbirds, Red-eyed Vireos, Black-throated Blue Warblers, and Least Flycatchers are audible everywhere from mid-May through mid-July. Beyond Avalanche Field, the forest type becomes more mixed, with an increase in spruce and fir. Swainson's Thrush takes over and there is an increase in Blue-headed Vireos and Black-throated Green Warblers.

On the final approach to Roaring Brook, tall deciduous trees return. This is one of Maine's hot spots for Philadelphia Vireo. The parking lot is long-famous for this species, but they compete with Red-eyed Vireos and the latter may be winning. Be careful to sort out individuals for an accurate identification. Least Flycatchers are numerous in the campground area. Woodpeckers include Downy, Hairy, and Yellow-bellied Sapsucker. While most of the trails leaving from the campground are intended to scale Mt. Katahdin and nearby peaks, birders make a beeline for Sandy Stream Pond. This short hike is relatively easy and level. The first quarter mile is full of Winter Wrens, Magnolia Warblers, American Redstarts, and occasional Blackpolls. On the approach to the pond (and most of the way around it) small boardwalks elevate hikers over the muddiest spots. Yellow-rumped Warblers,

Golden-crowned Kinglets, and four species of vireo are likely, though the Warbling Vireos prefer the open edges of the pond. Moose favor this pond and their tracks are everywhere. They are accustomed to people and take little notice of them. Common Mergansers, Ring-necked Ducks, and Common Goldeneyes are seen regularly in the pond. Swamp Sparrows and Common Yellowthroats are typical breeders around it.

On the back side of the Sandy Stream Pond, the trail leaves the wetland and proceeds either right (up South Turner Mountain), or left (up Russell Pond Trail). The latter can be used to make a loop back to the campground. The first few hundred yards of Russell Pond Trail are muddy with difficult footing, but it is also very boreal. Canada

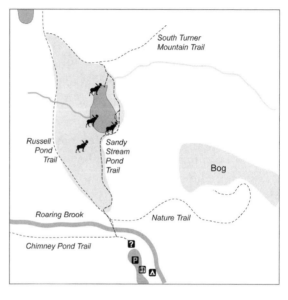

Warblers, Yellow-bellied Flycatchers, and Boreal Chickadees are encountered regularly. As the trail returns to a more mixed hardwood habitat, the chance for Philadelphia Vireo returns. Be sure to pay attention for a trail intersection 0.7 mile after the junction of the South Turner/Russell Pond trails; a left at this junction will lead you over 1.1 miles of forested, sometimes wet trail back to Roaring Brook campground. Visitors who go right at this junction, as some mistaken day hikers have, eventually find themselves at the backcountry campground of Russell Pond some six miles later, minus the food and equipment necessary for an overnight stay!

After returning to Togue Pond Gate and taking a right turn onto the Park Tote Road, the first section of the next few miles consists of mature deciduous habitat dominated by Hermit Thrushes, Ovenbirds, Least Flycatchers, and a medley of hardwood-loving warblers, particularly Black-throated Blue. After two miles, the woods begin a transition to mixed forest at Abol Pond. Check the pond for waterfowl. Possible dabblers include Wood Ducks, Blue and Green winged Teal, American Black Ducks, and Mallards. Potential divers include Hooded Mergansers and Ring-necked Ducks. A variety of warblers and flycatchers are typical of the wooded edges, and Lincoln's Sparrow is present near the culvert that connects the two water bodies.

After Abol Pond, the road's elevation rises steadily and the hardwood forest becomes intermixed with spruce, fir, and cedar. Swainson's replaces Hermit as the more common thrush. Stump Pond is a likely place to find moose, as well as the photographers who pursue them. The pond is surrounded by Swamp Sparrows and Common Yellowthroats. Snags are frequented by Nashville Warblers, Alder Flycatchers, and Cedar Waxwings. Ring-necked Ducks are common nesters in the pond. Common Goldeneyes are frequently present, and both Common and Hooded Mergansers can be seen regularly.

Abol Campground lies just beyond Stump Pond. From here to Nesowadnehunk Fields Campground, pockets of thick spruce increase the likelihood of Bay-breasted Warblers, Blackpolls, Boreal Chickadees, and both species of grouse. Ruffed and Spruce Grouse are drawn to the road for gravel, which they swallow to aid digestion. Northern Goshawks prey on grouse and are regularly encountered along the road, though brushes with Broad-winged Hawks are more common. The boreal forest pockets become more common at Katahdin Stream Campground, where campers have enjoyed the sporadic visits of White-winged Crossbills and Gray Jays. For the next few miles north, Bay-breasted Warblers and Blackpolls become more likely, though still unpredictable. The Grassy Pond trails offer moderate terrain through mixed forest while brushing several ponds that are often visited by moose. The last of these, Tracy Pond, is adjacent to the road and this pond is a good place to look for moose. Ring-necked Ducks and Common Goldeneyes are often sighted, and an Olive-sided Flycatcher on the back side of the pond has been a reliable treat for many years.

The access roads to the cabins of Daicey Pond and Kidney Pond offer enjoyable birding, especially because they are lightly traveled. The open parking area of Daicey Pond is populated with Chipping Sparrows, while Blackburnian and Pine Warblers are typical in the tallest pines. On the access road to Kidney Pond, a Bay-breasted Warbler is possible near both ends of the mile-long road, while Black-throated

Blue Warblers are known nesters throughout the middle portion. Eastern Wood-Pewees can be found in the trees that brush the stream. Barn Swallows and Eastern Phoebes nest under the eaves of the camps, and Hairy and Downy Woodpeckers join Yellow-bellied Sapsuckers in sharing the trees around the camp area. There is also a short nature trail that leads to potential moose sightings at the pond inlet beyond the cabins at Kidney Pond.

At Slide Dam Picnic Area, the road grazes Nesowadnehunk Stream in a particularly scenic spot beneath Doubletop Mountain. American Redstarts, Common Yellowthroats, and Chestnut-sided and Nashville Warblers are seen regularly foraging among the alders on the stream edge, while Veeries are in the woods just off the roadway. This scene repeats itself wherever the stream brushes the road, while Canada Warblers may be expected in the damper thickets.

Nesowadnehunk Field Campground is one of the largest open expanses in the park, making it attractive to sparrows and goldfinches, and a pair of nesting Merlins that feed on them. Trees on the edge of the fields are often noisy with Golden-crowned Kinglets. Boreal Chickadees in the spruce thickets near the campground are sporadic but never surprising. Just beyond the campground, the Park Tote Road becomes choked with bogs and spruce. This four-mile stretch is the most thickly boreal tract along any section of roadway in the park. Likely warblers include Bay-breasted, Blackpoll, Magnolia, Canada, Nashville, and Palm, along with many of the more common species. Boreal Chickadees and Yellow-bellied Flycatchers are frequently seen. Spruce Grouse, Gray Jays, and Black-backed Woodpeckers are possible, and a Northern Three-toed Woodpecker has been a recurrent rarity.

Beyond the Nesowadnehunk boreal stretch, which diminishes after the access road to Camp Phoenix, mixed forest habitat prevails all the way to Trout Brook Farm Campground. Maple, birch, and fir are characteristic. There are enough boreal patches to encourage the presence of Spruce Grouse, but it's even better habitat for Ruffed Grouse. Red-eyed Vireos and Least Flycatchers are abundant. Around the campground, Merlins, Evening Grosbeaks, and Spruce Grouse are possible.

The road to the South Branch Ponds traverses hardwood forest filled with Hermit Thrushes, Ovenbirds, and Black-throated Blue Warblers. Merlins often nest in the campground area and they are noisy neighbors once the young have begun demanding food. The Pogy Notch Trail skirts the east side of the ponds. It is relatively flat and fairly easy going, though damp in spots. Red-eyed Vireos are common, Philadelphia Vireos are present, and American Redstarts are remarkably abundant.

Mt. Katahdin dominates the park, but there are many other peaks that reward moderate to strenuous hiking with spectacular views. Most ascents in the park pass through several habitat zones. Mature trees at the bottom are habitat for warblers such as Blackburnian, Black-throated Green and Northern Parula. At higher elevations, a boreal zone of thick spruce provides Blackpolls, Bay-breasted Warblers, and Swainson's Thrushes, which can be heard through mid-July. This zone is good for Black-backed Woodpeckers, Boreal Chickadees, and Spruce Grouse. In the krummholz, a dense zone of stunted spruce and aspen normally above 3,000 feet, Bicknell's Thrush makes its home. Locating this species requires a familiarity with both its song and call notes. The song resembles the downward spiral of a Veery but with a hiccup in the middle. The penetratingly loud call notes can be characterized as "WEER!" The calls are usually heard more often than the song. Bicknell's Thrush tends to be vocal only at dawn and dusk, necessitating an ascent or descent in darkness. It can sometimes be heard from Chimney Pond Campground, located halfway up the east side of Katahdin. Due to its alpine habitat preference, this bird typically arrives late and should be looked for in June. Gray Jays are also visitors to Chimney Pond, and they think nothing of stealing food from the picnic tables of unwary campers. Expect Dark-eyed Juncoes, Yellow-rumped Warblers, White-throated Sparrows, and oodles of Winter Wrens at these elevations. Another alpine denizen is often found on the tablelands of Mt. Katahdin: American Pipits nest around Thoreau Spring at the conjunction of the Abol and Hunt Trails just above 4,600 feet. (Stay on trails: the sedge grass is fragile and the birds are ground nesters.) Common Ravens enjoy the thermals the mountain provides and even Northern Goshawks sometimes leave the woods to ride these air currents. Migrating hawks regularly pass the summit from mid-August through September.

Directions: south entrance—From I-95, take Exit 244, turn west on Route 11/157, and follow through Medway, East Millinocket, Dolby, and Millinocket. From downtown Millinocket, follow signs along Route 157 to the park. North entrance—From I-95, take Exit 264, turn west toward Sherman. Continue to Route 11 north through Patten, then turn left on Route 159 toward Shin Pond. Follow to the park.

Additional Sites:

a **Sebasticook Lake** in Newport is an unusual lake. It attracts an impressive number and variety of waterfowl, principally in late autumn. Many of the dabbling ducks show up along the margins. Diving ducks, including Greater and Lesser Scaup, visit the open waters in the middle of the lake. It can be impressive for Ruddy Ducks from mid-October to freeze-up. The lake is intentionally drawn down in the fall to prevent the buildup of phosphorous. This exposes mudflats that attract shorebirds in autumn. Greater and Lesser Yellowlegs are seen regularly around this time. Pectoral Sandpipers are noteworthy. Black-bellied Plovers are occasionally numerous. Dunlin may persist late into the shorebird season. Snow Buntings, Horned Larks, American Pipits, and Lapland Longspurs occur along these flats late in October and November.

In downtown Newport, a boat launch ramp within a small park provides a good vantage point for seeing diving ducks in mid-lake. A good place to scan for dabblers is from the Durham Bridge Road on the eastern side of the lake.

Directions: Newport is located at Exit 161 on I-95. Exit toward Newport, proceed past the fast-food restaurants, and bear right at the traffic lights. Turn left onto North Street and follow around to the park at the end. From downtown Newport, the park is at the end of Elm Street. For Durham Bridge Road, continue through downtown Newport approximately 3 miles along Route 2. Turn north onto Stetson Road, follow for two miles, then turn left again onto Durham Bridge Road. It is 1.3 miles to the causeway bridge.

b **Essex Woods** is a Bangor city property that surrounds a productive wetland. It is surprisingly birdy despite being located next to an Interstate highway. Warbling Vireos, Yellow Warblers, and American Redstarts are abundant. Baltimore Orioles, Scarlet Tanagers, and Chestnut-sided Warblers are common. Blue-winged Teal, Pied-billed Grebes, American Bitterns, and Green Herons are likely breeders, and it should be easy to find Mallards and American Black Ducks. The trail begins atop Essex Street Hill and follows a paved path 0.25 mile downhill to where it splits in a T intersection. Choose the right trail to circle the wetlands, enjoying waterfowl and open-area birds. Take the left trail for Scarlet Tanagers, Baltimore Orioles, and other forest canopy birds.

Directions: from I-95, turn off onto Broadway in Bangor, go right off the ramp, and turn right immediately onto Alden Street. A quick series of turns will follow from Alden to North French to East Broadway to Lancaster Avenue, which will end on Essex Street nearly opposite Watchmaker Street. Essex Woods is at the end of Watchmaker.

c **The West Penjajawoc Grasslands** are maintained as bird habitat by the Bangor Land Trust. This 13-acre parcel is overrun with ground-nesting Bobolinks and Savannah Sparrows, so it is important to stay on the mowed path. Tree and Barn Swallows are common. Because of the expansive field of view, Common Ravens and raptors are often seen along the tree line—primarily Broad-winged Hawks and Northern Harriers, but occasionally Sharp-shinned and Cooper's Hawks.

Directions: from the Stillwater end of Essex Street, drive approximately three miles, passing Chestnut Trail, and turning right onto Fox Hollow Lane. Stay on Fox Hollow Lane until the cul-de-sac parking area at the end. A kiosk contains maps and information.

d The entire length of the **Penobscot River** can hold many surprises. During the warmer months, Double-crested Cormorants are everywhere. In winter months, gulls congregating on the ice flows sometimes include an Iceland or Glaucous Gull. The best place to search for unusual winter gulls is from the parking lots adjacent to the Sea Dog Restaurant on the riverfront in downtown Bangor. The Brewer side of the river offers good vantage points from the Muddy Rudder Restaurant as well as from sites near the Veterans Remembrance Bridge on South Main Street. Common Mergansers and Common Goldeneyes are found wherever the river is free of ice from Bangor to Old Town. Barrow's Goldeneyes move into the river in the cold months too, particularly just upstream of Eastern Maine Medical Center. Bald Eagle populations have rebounded and they can now be expected along the entire river any time of year.

On the Brewer side, Route 9 follows the river much of the way to Eddington Bend. At this point on the Penobscot, Route 9 turns abruptly east on its way to Canada, while Route 178 continues upriver to Milford and Old Town. Pull into the parking lot at the Eddington Salmon Club and scope the rapids. This stretch remains open even in the coldest of winters. Common Goldeneyes, Common Mergansers, and even occasional Horned Grebes and Buffleheads are apt to be here. American Black Ducks and Mallards winter along all of the ice-free sections of the river from Eddington Bend to Milford and can be seen readily from shore especially near the dams in Old Town. This is also a good place to see Bald Eagles in winter.

In summer the dam in Old Town is entertaining because of the abundant swallows that cavort over the whitewater. Tree, Barn, Cliff, and Rough-winged Swallows can all be present.

e **Floods Pond Road** on the Eddington/Clifton line on Route 9 is ideal for birding while biking, rollerblading, walking the dog, or even pushing a baby stroller. It's the access road to Bangor's water supply. As such, it is paved and plowed year-round. Furthermore, it is gated and only a few pond residents are allowed vehicle entry. The woods contain an assortment of vireos, woodpeckers, thrushes, kinglets, occasional Indigo Buntings, and many common warblers, including Canada Warblers. There is enough spruce and fir stands that the road offers one of the better chances for crossbills in the winter and occasionally even in summer. A small marsh located a mile from the parking lot often contains ducks, and sometimes Northern Waterthrush. A mile farther down the road, there is a larger pond on the right that frequently has a few ducks. Three miles from the parking area there is another gate marking the beginning of the waterworks area; public access is not allowed beyond this gate.

Don't be surprised to see moose and deer on this road at dusk.

Directions: Floods Pond Road is on Route 9 in Eddington, just a few hundred yards east of the intersection with Route 46. Look for the gated access road.

f **Chick Hill** rises above Route 9 in Clifton. It is shown on some maps as Peaked Mountain. The summit has always been a popular hike, especially in fall foliage season. It can now be reached by car along the rough road that services the cell phone tower. Decades ago a fire tower graced this same spot. The peak provides spectacular 360-degree views from its bald top, and it's a good place for hawk-watching in autumn.

Directions: follow Route 9 east past Parks Pond in Clifton. Shortly after the pond, there are two left turns that both lead to Chick Hill. Take the second, Chick Hill Road, and follow to the end. Park near (but not in) the school bus turnaround and walk to the summit.

g **The University of Maine** campus is dotted with special and unusual plantings, from ornamental gardens to ivy-covered walls. In winter, it is one of the most likely spots in the entire state to find Bohemian Waxwings. In irruptive years, Pine Grosbeaks flock to the Littlefield Ornamental Garden and its crab-apple grove. During the summer, Cliff Swallows have traditionally built their mud nests on the Collins Center for the Arts and the nearby Donald Corbett Center building. House Finches are regular at campus feeders. Common Nighthawks are often present at dusk and probably nest on campus.

University (Demerritt) Forest is similar to the Bangor City Forest. It is a summer residence for many breeding warblers, and at least four thrushes and five woodpeckers. It is mixed deciduous and conifer with large stands of mature woods. It is an experimental forest with large monocultural tracts of thinned trees that offer uniquely clear birding views. The trails are frequently used by bikers, hikers, dog-walkers, and cross-country skiers, but the shared use seldom detracts from the birding. In the winter, it can be a good place for crossbills.

Directions: take Exit 193 off I-95 and proceed one mile north along Stillwater Avenue toward Old Town. At the McDonald's Restaurant, a right turn leads to the campus. A left onto College Avenue Extension leads to the University Forest, 1.1 miles ahead. Look for the gated gravel road on the right, with a parking lot opposite the gate on the left.

h **Hirundo** is located nearly 30 miles north of downtown Bangor. It is a private wildlife refuge on Route 43 between Old Town and Hudson, owned by the University of Maine and managed by a trust. There are over 2,500 acres that contain mixed stands of hardwoods and conifers. Deciduous-loving warblers

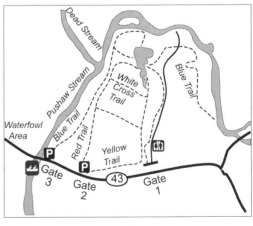

are common here, as are Eastern Wood-Pewees and Least Flycatchers. Two streams and a pond attract waterfowl, American Bitterns, Great Blue Herons and Swamp Sparrows. Gated roads provide access to the refuge. Visitors should register at Gate 3, where maps and directions are available at the house. Trails are open daily 9-4, in summer 9-5.

Pushaw Stream and Dead Stream meet in Hirundo and provide one of the area's best river paddles. Both flow slowly through river bottom-land accented with nest boxes for Wood Ducks and Hooded Mergansers. American Bitterns are common in the rushes. Warbling Vireos, Northern Waterthrushes, and a host of warblers sing through much of May and June.

Directions: from I-95 north of Old Town, take Exit 197 onto Route 43 toward Hudson. Follow five miles northwest to Hirundo.

ℹ Shirley is 4.5 miles north of Monson on Route 15. Coming from the south, make a quick check of Spectacle Pond while passing by. Enjoy the Common Loons that are usually visible from the bridge, but look for moose in the back of the pond. Then continue another two miles looking for a left onto the Lower Shirley Corner Road. Follow this road three miles to a pond directly on the edge of Shirley Mills. Pull over at the picnic table, and scout the pond. Common Loons are certain. Various ducks are possible. At this intersection, there are three directions from which to choose. Ignore the dirt road to the south. The road to the left leads to West Shirley Bog. (The dirt road skirting the right side of the pond is the B&A Railroad Bed North Road to Greenville.)

The first mile of the road to West Shirley Bog is paved. The remaining dirt road is often rough. Ignore any side roads, slow for all moose-watching opportunities, and continue to the outflow under the bridge. Settle on the bank and observe. Wilson's Snipe are often active. American Bitterns are near, but secretive. In migration, look for Greater Yellowlegs and Solitary Sandpiper. Spotted Sandpipers frequently flutter from rock to rock. Watch over the far side of the marsh for a Northern Harrier. Look far down the marsh for Canada Geese,

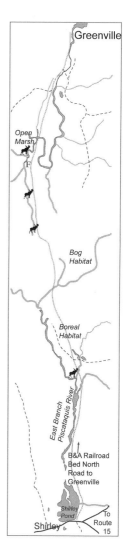

Greenville

Open Marsh

Bog Habitat

Boreal Habitat

East Branch Piscataquis River

B&A Railroad Bed North Road to Greenville

Shirley Pond

Shirley

To Route 15

Common Mergansers, American Black Ducks and Blue-winged Teal. Tune in to the variety of warblers around. The streamside aspens contain Magnolia Warblers and sometimes a Wilson's. American Redstarts are in the low branches of the woods; Black-throated Green Warblers are in the higher branches. Common Yellowthroats and Yellow-rumped Warblers are likely. A Canada Warbler might be across the road near the stream, sometimes calling from the wet thickets. At all times be on the lookout for Gray Jays. They occasionally visit the spot looking for a handout from campers and fishermen. In all water conditions except frozen, this is a lovely paddle. Besides waterfowl and moose, it is a haven for beaver and otters.

J **B&A Railroad Bed North Road** is also known as the Shirley Bog Road and, at one time, it was a railroad bed. Today, it is part of ITS 85, a snowmobile trail that is a component of Maine's Interconnected Trail System (ITS). The road is maintained for spring and summer vehicle traffic, though it can be a little rough. This road has some of the best bog and boreal habitat in the region. Boreal Chickadees, Gray Jays, and Spruce Grouse are in the spruces. Palm Warblers, Lincoln's Sparrows, and Olive-sided Flycatchers are in the bogs.

At the intersection in Shirley, take a look in the wet area on the right side of the road, opposite the pond. Red-winged Blackbirds and Common Grackles are all about. Wood and American Black Ducks occasionally hide in the back. In May, it's a good place to find migrating Solitary Sandpipers. Common Yellowthroats and Swamp Sparrows are abundant. American Bitterns are present and often seen.

The road passes in and out of wooded habitat, stream edges, and bogs for several miles. An open area at the end of five miles signals a subtle switch to spruce trees. For the next 0.3 miles this is the spot to scout for Boreal Chickadees, Yellow-bellied Flycatchers, Gray Jays, and Spruce Grouse. Ruby and Golden-crowned Kinglets are commonplace in summer. Cape May and Bay-breasted Warblers have been noted here.

For the next mile, the road resumes its streamside passage. When the road returns to the woods, it obscures a large bog on the right side and wetlands on the left. Alder and Olive-sided Flycatchers are frequently heard calling from the bog, and a search of the tallest dead trees often yields a sighting. Northern Waterthrushes and Canada Warblers are regular denizens of the wetlands.

Northward from the bog, the concentration of warblers is impressive. Expect Ovenbird, Northern Parula, American Redstart, Black-throated Green, Black-throated Blue, Nashville, Black-and-white, Pine, and Blackburnian Warblers. Gray Jays in the bog sometimes investigate activities on the road in this area.

After seven miles, the leading edge of the main flowage appears on the left. On this end of the flowage, dabbling ducks, Hooded Mergansers, and Pied-billed Grebes are more common. On the northern end toward Greenville, about a mile beyond, diving ducks such as Common Goldeneyes and nesting Ring-necked Ducks are more likely. American Bitterns are frequently seen. Scan the tall trees on the far bank for an Osprey or Bald Eagle. On a clear day, Common Ravens are usually seen soaring around the mountains beyond the bog.

Directions: from Shirley, as described above. From Greenville: proceed through town on Route 15 to Greenville Junction, near the waterfront park and boat launch area. Turn left onto Depot Road and follow straight ahead until it becomes B&A Railroad Bed North Road.

k **Scammon Ridge**, on the east side of Moosehead Lake just above Greenville, is one of the better mature forests in the area. Tall balsam fir, thick yellow birches, and elderly beeches predominate. Expect many canopy warblers such as Blackburnian, Northern Parula, Black-throated Green, and Black-throated Blue. Ovenbirds and Winter Wrens are common at ground level. The suggested birding route winds 8.1 miles behind the ridge and traverses several excellent beaver flowages before exiting along Mountain View Lane.

Directions: from Route 15 in downtown Greenville, take the Lily Bay Road north one mile and turn right onto Scammon Road.

l **Elephant Mountain**, like much of the woods east of Moosehead Lake, has been heavily logged. There are now vast stretches of secondary regrowth, experimental plantings of spruce and pine, and mixed hardwoods. American Redstarts, Magnolia, Chestnut-sided, and Nashville Warblers are found in abundance in these areas. Tennessee Warblers are present in small numbers. This is also an area of small ponds and beaver flowages. As a result, the back country contains a warren of identical dirt roads that crisscross the area, making it easy for birders to lose their way. An intriguing way to circumvent the problem is to pay one's respects at

Elephant Mountain. In 1963 a B-52 bomber on a training mission suffered a structural failure and crashed at the base of the mountain. Most of the wreckage was left intact as a shrine to the crewmen who perished. Mainers treat it with great reverence and ceremonies still take place there every year. Recently, the Maine Air National Guard has erected signs that direct respectful people to the site. Using these signs as navigational tools, it is possible for birders to negotiate these roads for an exploration of the area. The "B-52" signs begin on Prong Pond Road at its intersection with the Lily Bay Road. In the clear-cuts just before the crash site, Blackpolls are noteworthy among the regenerating spruce thickets.

m **Big Spencer Mountain** is a peak tall enough, at 3,230 feet, to be inhabited by Bicknell's Thrush. The strenuous climb goes through the same habitat zones as those described on Big Moose Mountain (page 168). It is one of Maine's favorite mountains to climb, particularly in foliage season.

Directions: from Kokadjo, continue ahead for 8 miles. At the bridge that crosses Bear Brook at a campsite, turn left and drive another 6 miles. Look for the trailhead on the left, and park on the right. Note that driving straight ahead at Bear Brook continues on to the Golden Road for access to Baxter State Park, the Allagash Wilderness Waterway, and the North Maine Woods forestland.

n **The Pleasant River Walk** was established in 2000 and enters the woods behind the athletic fields just north of Brownville Junction. It is a snowmobile trail in winter and a hiking path in summer. Though the first few miles provide little chance to see the river, the forest itself is decidedly mixed habitat. Many common wood warblers are observable. Red-eyed and Blue-headed Vireos sing in equal numbers. Maine's most familiar woodpeckers are present in above average numbers. It is better for Ruffed Grouse than Spruce, but either may be encountered. Veeries tend to be the most commonplace of the thrushes and Golden-crowned Kinglets are often within earshot. The trail is long and does not loop. The ball fields have portable bathrooms.

Directions: from I-95, take Exit 199 in Alton and follow Route 16 to Milo. In Milo, turn right onto Route 11 and follow through Brownville and Brownville Junction. Look for the athletic fields on the right just after crossing the Pleasant River Bridge.

o **Duck Lake** is one of the Maine Public Reserve Lands, situated just east of Nicatous Lake. It contains 24,000 acres of forest and several pristine lakes. Although this area is in Hancock County, the most reliable access is from the west, near the routes to Baxter. There is access from other directions as shown on maps and the DeLorme's Maine Atlas, but these are often rough and muddy. The allure of the Duck Lake area is the remoteness of its lakes, the variability of its habitat, and the forestry management for grouse. The primitive campsites are attractive, and are available without permit and at no charge on a first-come, first-served basis.

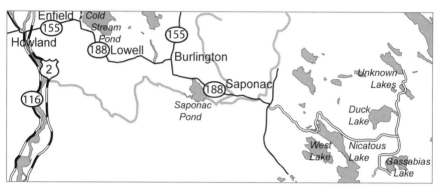

The approach to Nicatous Lake from the west is scenic and rural. The road is paved most of the way to the lake, passing such attractions as Saponac Pond and the Grand Falls of the Passadumkeag River. Once the road turns to dirt, mixed forest becomes prevalent, assuring a good variety of warblers in spring and the possibility of both species of grouse. Upon reaching the lake, turn left and pause at Nicatous Lodge. This sporting camp is of interest to birders year-round. The local warbler population is good during the summer. In winter, the chatter of American Goldfinches, Pine Siskins, and Common Redpolls can be loud, as large numbers are attracted to the openness of the lakeside, the catkins of the nearby birches and aspens, and the feeders at the lodge. Water rushing from the lake into Nicatous Stream keeps some of the water unfrozen in winter, creating the likelihood of Common Mergansers and other waterfowl, and perhaps moose. The road beyond Nicatous Lodge is a major snowmobile trail in winter. After snowmelt, it can be muddy for an extended period into the spring, made worse by logging trucks. Entry along this route should be reserved for drier seasons or high-clearance vehicles.

Gassabias, Duck, and the Unknown Lakes are pristine. Part of the reserve is managed specifically for Ruffed Grouse, but there are enough spruce bogs in the area to favor Spruce Grouse, too. The road to Gassabias Lake passes through a significant bog just before the campsite, and the boreal habitat adjacent to it is particularly good for Spruce Grouse. Canoeing on any of these lakes is prized for wildlife, scenery, and solitude. The campsites provide pit toilets.

Directions: from I-95, take Exit 217 in Howland and head east on Route 155, crossing Route 2. Turn right in Enfield onto Route 188, continue through Burlington, and follow the signs toward Nicatous Lodge. Turn left at the lake and continue past the lodge, bearing right to reach the reserve. Roads shown on older maps of the DeLorme Maine Atlas south of Gassabias Lake are inaccurate, due to a discontinued bridge over Gassabias Stream. A new road now extends south from the outlet of the lake to reach the Stud Mill Road, but this can be rough and muddy.

P **Mattawamkeag Wilderness Park** is owned and operated by the Town of Mattawamkeag. The park consists of a campground, day-use area, and 15 miles of hiking trail. It sits astride a whitewater section of the Mattawamkeag River. Campsites are well-spaced for comfort and privacy. The first three miles of the access road run through mixed forest. Hermit Thrushes, Ovenbirds, and Red-eyed Vireos predominate. Soon, balsam fir becomes more common and Swainson's Thrushes and Winter Wrens take over. Warblers include Black-throated Green, Blackburnian, and Northern Parula. At 4.5 miles, the road starts to follow the river, beginning at Lower Gordon Falls. It proceeds upriver to the increasingly dramatic Upper Gordon Falls and the Slewgundy Heater, a forceful rapid that most canoeists choose to portage. The park is rustic and the footing on trails demands attention. Fallen trees, exposed roots, and muddy spots are a challenge. But the birds are abundant and noisy. All of the common warblers are present, especially Blackburnian, Black-throated Blue, and Black-throated Green. Eastern Wood-Pewees, Scarlet Tanagers, and Blue-headed Vireos are vocal participants in the chorus. While checking in at the gate, ask for an update on trail conditions. A fee is charged for day use and camping. Visit www.mwpark.com.

Directions: from I-95, take Exit 227 toward Lincoln. Follow Route 2 through Lincoln 12 miles to Mattawamkeag. From the middle of town in Mattawamkeag, look for the sign to Mattawamkeag Regional Park and follow the access road to the park.

q **Dolby to Stacyville** traverses
a significant part of the private industrial forest east of Baxter State
Park. The unincorporated town
of Dolby lies between Millinocket
and East Millinocket along Route
157. Signs for the Dolby Log
Yard mark the entrance to the
Huber Road from Route 157.
After passing the Log Yard at 1.5
miles, boreal habitat begins to
assert itself. At a Y intersection,
the Huber Road continues left,
eventually circling back to the
Golden Road. At this split, the
Roberts Road proceeds right and
it tends to be the more productive
for birding. (Note: there are no
road signs to indicate the names

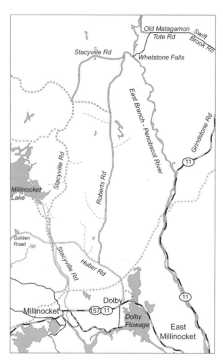

of the roads, but there are helpful mile markers along the routes.)
For the next 10 miles, Black-backed Woodpeckers and Gray Jays are
possible, especially from Mile 4 to 5. At Mile 11, a small, black spruce
bog encloses the road on both sides while a stand of white spruce
stretches up the hill behind. Throughout these logging roads, be sure
to always park out of the way of traffic. Avoid parking in hidden spots
near corners, valleys, and bridges. Stop and allow trucks to pass from
both directions. Logging trucks have the right of way on this private
road system.

Continue through a heavily logged area to Whetstone Falls, a
strong rapid that surges beneath the bridge over the East Branch of
the Penobscot River. From here northward, the road is known as the
Old Matagamon Tote Road. Less than two miles ahead, a side road
leads toward Lunksoos Camps (Lunksoos is the Algonquian name for
the Eastern Cougar), brushing a couple miles of the East Branch of the
Penobscot River. The forest along the water's edge is majestic. Eastern Wood-Pewees and Phoebes are dominant. Pine and Blackburnian
Warblers are normal occurrences. There is little traffic on this road to
spoil a bird walk. Any open spot along the river can provide a glimpse
of Common Mergansers, American Black Ducks, and Mallards.

The last mile before rejoining Route 11 in Stacyville passes fields and fruit trees. In winter it may attract Pine Grosbeaks, Bohemian Waxwings, and perhaps even the Townsend's Solitaire that stayed in this area over the winter of 2005.

Directions: from south on I-95, take Exit 244 and head west toward Millinocket along Route 11/157. Soon after crossing the Dolby Flowage, look for the right turn onto a paved road at the sign for Huber Resources Corporation. Follow the route as described above. From north on I-95, take Exit 264, turn west toward Sherman, then left onto Route 11 South along the Grindstone Road. After about five miles at a sharp bend on Route 11, bear straight onto Swift Brook Road. The road resumes its original Old Matagamon Tote Road name ahead.

r **Sawtelle Deadwater** and **Scraggly Lake** seem as if they were designed for birders. Though close to Baxter State Park, few people are aware of these sites. The entrance is about eight miles north of Shin Pond on the road to Baxter. Sawtelle Deadwater is a shallow pond encountered first, approximately 2.5 miles in length. It is also known as the Francis D. Dunn Wildlife Management Area. Maine Inland Fisheries & Wildlife maintains a water level ideal for waterfowl and moose. Ring-necked Ducks, Wood Ducks, and Pied-billed Grebes are present all summer. The best vantage point is from the boat launch adjacent to the impoundment dam at the southern tip of the lake, less than mile from the entrance. There are several more peeks at the water over the next mile, but the deadwater is best enjoyed by canoe. Moose are a common sight.

Scraggly Lake is the centerpiece of another of Maine's Public Reserve Lands. This 10,000-acre reserve contains a wealth of mature forest, marshes, and bogs, providing a variety of habitats. While the lake is marvelous, the access road is the real gem. Unlike many of the roads in the area, little logging takes place in this tract. Furthermore, the road

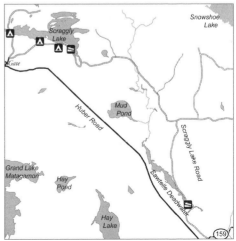

ends at the lake, so there is little traffic aside from a few sportsmen and boaters. The lack of traffic and the variety of habitat make birding from the road a pleasant experience. The road itself is uncommonly firm and smooth, even in damp seasons. The forest is mostly mixed, with enough clumps of spruce to make Boreal Chickadee and Spruce Grouse a possibility. Magnolia Warblers are particularly abundant, but Black-throated Green, Black-throated Blue, Black-and-White, Nashville, Blackburnian, Yellow-rumped, and Northern Parula are common. The road passes by the west and north sides of the lake and ends at a path to Ireland Pond.

Directions: proceed as above toward the north entrance of Baxter State Park. Just 0.7 mile after crossing the bridge over the Seboeis River, turn right at the sign for Scraggly Lake.

THE NORTH MAINE WOODS

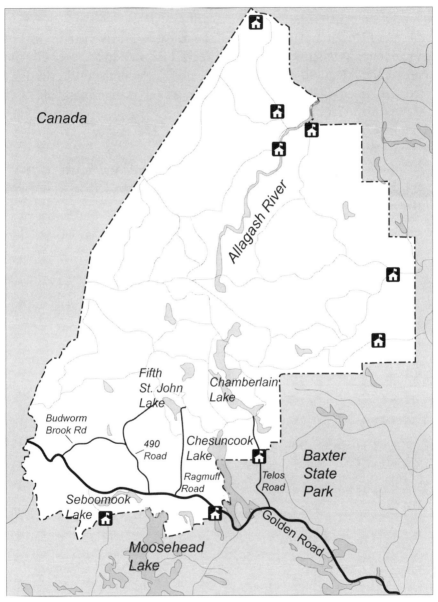

The North Maine Woods provides a unique birding experience. The region west of Baxter State Park and north of Moosehead Lake is comprised of 3,500,000 acres, owned or managed by 25 different entities, including several private family ownerships, institutional investors, private conservation organizations, and some protected by the State of

Maine as Public Reserved Lands. North Maine Woods, Inc. (NMW) is a non-profit association of these owners and managers formed in 1972 to oversee recreational use of these properties. Birders who venture into this region are participating in a centuries old tradition of public access on private lands and must recognize that this is an industrial forest, and respect its rules. The association charges small fees for day and overnight use to fund recreation management and campsite maintenance.

Trip planning: www.northmainewoods.org or 207-435-6213

★ **79** The pleasures awaiting adventurous birders in the **North Maine Woods** are innumerable. Lakes, ponds, and rivers are undeveloped. Moose, coyotes, and bears roam at will. Populations of the rare Canada Lynx have increased. Forestry practices have defined the habitat for some bird populations. This is an area that has been logged repeatedly over 200 years and the species that reside here are those that have adapted to it. All of Maine's boreal species are present. Gray Jays and Black-backed Woodpeckers are most commonly found in open areas where boreal forest is regenerating, while Boreal Chickadees gravitate to the thick spruce stands that surround waters and wetlands or that have been actively replanted. Ruffed Grouse inhabit dense mixed forest while Spruce Grouse are specialists of spruce-fir. Olive-sided Flycatchers populate areas opened by logging while Yellow-bellied Flycatchers occupy boggy areas protected from cutting. American Kestrels haunt clear-cuts while Merlins prefer mature coniferous stands along water bodies. Look for Mourning Warblers and Common Yellowthroats in early succession brambles that follow recent clear-cuts. In the next stages of forest regeneration, Chestnut-sided Warblers, Nashville Warblers, and American Redstarts are abundant. As stands mature, Black-throated Blue Warblers move into the birches and beeches while Bay-breasted and Blackburnian Warblers inhabit the more coniferous stands. Black-throated Green Warblers and Northern Parula do well in mixed forest types. Red-eyed Vireos do better among mature deciduous trees while Blue-headed Vireos tolerate emerging mixed forest. Understanding the habitat types and their characteristic foliage is an important key to birding the North Maine Woods.

Spruce trees are the key indicators for finding target boreal species. Due to the region's latitude, spruce and fir are usually intermingled in the hardwood tracts, so boreal species may be encountered anywhere.

There are three species of native spruce in Maine. White spruce retains the most conical shape. It is not shade tolerant and does not grow well in the understory. It is typically found along Maine's coast, approaching the tree line in mountains, and along roadsides and water bodies in the North Maine Woods. Black spruce tolerates the moist, acidic soils of peat bogs and swamps. Growth is slow and stunted in this type of habitat and the trees seldom grow to substantial heights. Their presence is a good indicator of habitat for Yellow-bellied Flycatchers and Lincoln's Sparrows, as well as the boreal specialties. Maine also has a good population of red spruce. This species is shade tolerant and more often grows in moist, mature forests, especially on mountainsides. It hybridizes with black spruce, and they are not easily distinguished from each other, though red spruce can grow significantly taller. Cedar, balsam fir, and tamarack are typical companion species to the spruce trees in boreal forests.

Anywhere there are thick concentrations of spruce trees, Boreal Chickadees may be found. They sometimes flock with Black-capped Chickadees, and may follow them into the open. Their lazy, slurry "Chickadee" call is easily distinguished from that of the Black-capped.

Areas that feature spruce, plus sphagnum moss, laurel, and Labrador tea are particularly well-suited to Spruce Grouse. Spruce Grouse primarily feed on conifer needles. They are sometimes seen in small flocks, perched in spruces in late winter and early spring. Later, they use the dense growth of spruce stands to shield them from predators, particularly Northern Goshawks. They can be difficult to find while incubating in June. As summer progresses, they are regularly seen on roadways, picking up gravel and allowing chicks to feed on insects that may be more abundant in drainage ditches.

Black spruce is a good indicator of Black-backed and Northern Three-toed Woodpeckers because wet areas often provide a good supply of dying trees. These trees are more prone to infestation by insects and grubs and it is easier for woodpeckers to flick bark from unhealthy trees—the primary means of foraging for these two species. Where these woodpeckers have been foraging recently, the trees will be mottled with flaked patches that look shiny. Black-backed Woodpeckers defend a territory of about 75 acres, and looking for a good concentration of woodpecker damage frequently yields the bird itself. They are noisy in June when feeding nestlings, and tend their young all summer, making them somewhat conspicuous.

Gray Jays enjoy a wide range of boreal habitat, but in the North Maine Woods they are easiest to find in spruce stands. They are noisy before nesting, and protective of curious juveniles afterwards, so they are readily observable when present. For anyone camping in the region, they may even perch on a shoulder or steal breakfast.

There are two distinct sections of the North Maine Woods. The bulk of these lands lies north of Moosehead Lake. Another section between Millinocket and Greenville is managed separately, and is called the Jo-Mary/Katahdin Ironworks Area. Each is described separately. Both areas are rich in sporting camps, some over a century old. These traditional camps are invariably remote, and range in amenities from rustic to elegant. Many have their own private trail systems and access to spots hidden away from the rest of the world. Long treasured by hunters and anglers, birders have recently begun to appreciate their total solitude.

North Maine Woods

The network of logging roads in the North Maine Woods is served by a system of well-traversed arteries. These gravel roads accommodate heavy trucks at high speed. These arteries traverse good habitat on their own, and provide access to secondary logging roads that offer additional opportunities. All major roads and many of the secondary routes provide convenient mile markers to enable rudimentary navigation, and this guide refers to them often.

The Golden Road is the most famous of the artery routes. It begins outside of Baxter State Park near Millinocket, and extends westward over the top of Moosehead Lake all the way to the Canadian border, passing several other wilderness lakes on its winding course. The woods consist of mixed forest, and this section is renowned less for its birding than for the scenery of the falls and gorges along the West Branch of the Penobscot River. Special stops include Nesowadnehunk Falls and Big Eddy. This stretch of river contains the most difficult whitewater rafting in a state known for its rafting challenges. Shortly after Big Eddy (at the intersection with the Telos Road), the Golden Road bends southward, skirting the shores of Ripogenus, Chesuncook, and Caribou Lakes. At the bottom tip of Caribou Lake, the Greenville Road enters from the east side of Moosehead Lake. North Maine Woods territory begins about five miles west at the Caribou Checkpoint.

At Mile 53, the southerly route to Lobster and Seboomook Lakes splits from the Golden Road. This road accesses some good canoe launch sites and passes south of Seboomook Lake to Pittston Farm. However, the driving can be rough during much of the year.

Just before Mile 55, the West Branch of the Penobscot River passes under the Golden Road at a place called Hannibal's Crossing. Spruce dominates this stretch of river. Boreal Chickadees and Gray Jays are common, Spruce Grouse less common. Black-backed Woodpeckers work the edges of this habitat. There is ample room to park out of the way of heavy truck traffic, but it can be dusty. Just a mile farther west, there is a logging road to the left that provides exceptional birding. This 1.5-mile road passes through an area of regenerating spruce, ending in a bog that is good for all of the boreal specialties, including unusual flycatchers and conifer-loving warblers.

At Mile 56, Ragmuff Road turns north to shadow the West Branch for awhile. It can be used to create a loop by traveling above Chesuncook Lake, east to Chamberlain Lake, and back south on the Telos Road. Over the first few miles of Ragmuff, there are several seldom-used logging roads that offer easy walks through coniferous habitat.

At about Mile 62, the 490 Road enters from the north. The first few miles of this road are excellent for Gray Jays and Boreal Chickadees. The next mile of the Golden Road shares the same spruce characteristics. Another good boreal section occurs around Gulliver Brook at Mile 72.

Near Mile 77, the access road from the west side of Moosehead Lake enters the Golden Road. The first few miles of this access road and the surrounding area on the Golden Road are thick with spruce, and it's a great place to search for the boreal specialties. Mourning Warblers and Lincoln's Sparrows breed in adjacent cut-over areas.

The Pittston Farm area is excellent. It lies just below Mile 77 of the Golden Road, nestled between Seboomook Lake and the South Branch of the Penobscot River. It is reached from the south by the 20-Mile Road on the west side of Moosehead Lake. Pittston Farm was first built in 1850 as a way station for sportsmen on their way to Canada along the old Indian Trail. Later, it served as the hub of operations for forestry in the region. Nowadays it is a getaway for sportsmen, snowmobilers, boaters, . . . and birders. At first glance, it seems an anachronism to have such a large farm and pasture this deep in the working forest. But it provides such a variety of habitat that birders could easily spend all day in the area. Pittston Farm is open year round. For more information: 207-280-0000, www.pittstonfarm.com

A quick side trip to Canada Falls is enjoyable. From Canada Lake, the South Branch of the Penobscot River cascades toward Seboomook Lake through a gorge that is easily accessed from a marked side road just north of Pittston Farm.

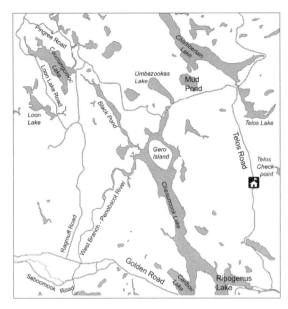

Six miles west of the Pittston Farm access road, the Golden Road crosses the North Branch of the Penobscot River over Cement Bridge. A northward turn onto Budworm Brook Road enters good boreal habitat and also initiates a fine 32-mile loop. Black-backed Woodpeckers are present along the 10 miles to Big Bog. Big Bog itself is created by a deadwater section of the North Branch of the Penobscot River. Sedge Wrens and Yellow Rails have been recorded here, though the birds are rare and canoe access is challenging. Canoeing may be more easily achieved from the north end at Mile 13.5 at an obvious intersection. The river is 1.1 miles down the hill from the intersection. (While doing this loop, another good boreal hotspot is off the beaten track along the Brailey Brook Road. Just past Fifth St. John Pond, turn left and follow about 4.5 miles to an intersection. The right fork leads to Baker Lake. Instead, choose the left fork and enjoy the first six miles of Brailey Brook Road. A good spruce/bog mix provides a wide variety of warblers, flycatchers, woodpeckers, and boreal specialties, especially Gray Jays.) Past the St. John intersection, the loop route becomes the 490 Road. As noted earlier, the last few miles are spruce-laden before reentering the Golden Road.

Approximately 15 miles beyond Budworm Brook Road, the Golden Road enters Canada. Much of the West Branch of the Penobscot River adjacent to the Golden Road has been placed under the conservation of the Forest Society of Maine, ensuring that it will remain a working, multiple-use forest. (Visit www.fsmaine.org.)

The Telos Road leads due north into one of Maine's most memorable outdoor adventure areas. The Allagash Wilderness Waterway flows north 96 miles to the St. John River on the Canadian border. It flows gently for much of its journey, but offers Class I & II rapids on occasion. The river is state-owned and federally protected, and it is one of the most popular wilderness camping rivers in America. The Telos Road departs from the Golden Road at Big Eddy, along the West Branch of the Penobscot River. After about 17 miles, it enters North Maine Woods territory at the Telos Checkpoint, then travels to Chamberlain Lake. From there, it splits into other roads leading still farther north.

Mixed forest is the rule over most of the route, though at Mile 48 there is a boreal section that holds some promise for variety and specialties. It's always a pleasure to explore the area around Chamberlain Bridge, a launch site for both the lake and the Allagash Waterway. Canoes and kayaks outnumber powerboats so it retains a strong wilderness sensibility.

For a better shot at boreal habitat, take the road that leads west from Chamberlain toward Umbazooksus and Chesuncook Lakes. Over the next 20 miles, there are several areas and side roads that are thick with spruce and moose, and it is one of the more likely places to find a Spruce Grouse in the road. If time allows, it is possible to follow this road north of Chesuncook and Caucomgomoc Lakes, connecting onto Loon Lake and Ragmuff Roads for the southbound return. However, the roads are narrow in spots, speeds are slow, and it takes quite a bit of northbound travel to get around the lakes before heading south. This route can add several hours to the return trip to the Golden Road, especially because of the characteristic scenery of the uninhabited lakes along the way.

Katahdin Iron Works/Jo-Mary

The Katahdin Iron Works/Jo-Mary area is a different kettle of fish. The North Maine Woods Association also manages recreational access in this area, though for a different mix of federal, state, and private landowners. Some of the fees used for recreation management may be different, but the rules of the road are the same as for the rest of the North Maine Woods.

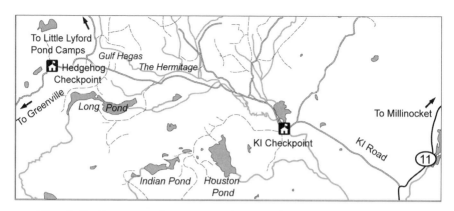

Katahdin Iron Works is a popular area because it contains parts of the Appalachian Trail, the Gulf Hagas Reserve, The Hermitage, and several ponds and streams.

From Greenville to Brownville stretches a road known as the Katahdin Iron Works Road or simply "KI." It starts in Greenville on Pleasant Street just beyond the center of town, and enters North Maine Woods land at the Hedgehog Checkpoint 9 miles east of town. Follow the signs toward Greenville Airport. From the other end, the entrance is 2.5 miles north of Brownville Junction on Route 11. Here, the checkpoint is at Katahdin Iron Works, which was a pig-iron smelting operation that thrived in the 1880s. Some of the ruins are still remarkably well preserved. "The Katahdin Trail" bisects working forest, so much of it is in secondary regrowth, but there are several major attractions.

Gulf Hagas is a 3.5-mile gorge through slate bedrock, often called "The Grand Canyon of Maine." It is part of the Appalachian Trail system and is federally owned and managed as a National Landmark. The hiking trails are popular, but seldom crowded. Trails are moderately strenuous and can be slippery. Extensive hiking in this area requires proper footwear, clothing, maps, adequate food and water, and a compass.

The Hermitage is a 35-acre stand of towering pines protected by the National Park Service, just 0.75 mile from the trailhead. Screw Auger Falls is just a mile farther. Reaching both requires fording a cold stream. To explore these areas, it is best to pick up maps and the latest information at the NMW checkpoints. The forest is mostly hardwood, with hemlock and white pines interspersed. There are few specialties here, but the normal birds include a good assortment of deciduous-loving warblers, Least Flycatchers, Eastern Wood-Pewees, Ruffed Grouse, Hermit Thrush, and Veery.

Within the KI expanse, the Appalachian Mountain Club has taken considerable steps towards providing additional conservation and recreation opportunities compatible with the working forest. AMC's Maine Woods Initiative has acquired 37,000 acres of land, adjacent to and connected with Gulf Hagas. Holdings are centered around Little Lyford Pond Camps. This is one of the oldest sporting camps in Maine, dating back to the late 1800s. Over ten miles of trails have been added or improved for hiking, snowshoeing, and cross-country skiing. Special wetland habitats are in the process of being evaluated for increased protection and access, where appropriate. In the process of conducting inventories of biological diversity, AMC naturalists have discovered many uncommon species within its property boundaries, notably Northern Goshawk, Spruce Grouse, Black-backed Woodpecker, Olive-sided Flycatcher, Gray Jay, Boreal Chickadee, Lincoln's Sparrow, Rusty Blackbird, and both species of crossbill.

One of the best stands of spruce straddles the intersection where the road to Little Lyford Pond Camps diverts north from the KI Road not far east of the Hedgehog Checkpoint. Currently, the roads to Long Pond are rough and offer little more birding than can be found on the KI Road. However, Indian Pond has revealed itself to have good species diversity, particularly on the west end, which can be accessed by intrepid canoeists. It lies adjacent to Caribou Bog, a 300-acre peat bog believed to be the last refuge of wild caribou in Maine before the species was hunted out a century ago.

The Jo-Mary Road departs from Route 11 midway between Brownville Junction and Millinocket. It is the principal access to the Maine Public Reserved Lands that surround beautiful Nahmakanta Lake, and the historic Nahmakanta Lake Camps. Along the way, it provides access to Upper Jo-Mary Campground, a terrific camping area and day-use beach on an otherwise undeveloped lake, featuring spectacular views of water and mountains. Nahmakanta Lake is embedded in the largest tract of Maine Public Reserved Lands, totaling 43,000 acres. The lake is surrounded by one of Maine's finer hiking trail systems. This is a multiple-use area allowing hunting, trapping, and snowmobiling. The Appalachian Trail crosses the reserve and there are several high-quality, primitive campsites located throughout the area. Though the traditional access is through NMW lands, requiring the normal fee, the tract itself is not within this jurisdiction.

A traditional sporting camp located on the northwest corner of the lake is the only facility on the water. Nahmakanta Lake Camps was established shortly after the Civil War. Don and Angel Hibbs have continued to modernize the cottages and grounds so that they offer one of the best remote experiences in northern Maine.

The first few miles of the Jo-Mary Road have been extensively logged. Early succession brambles provide habitat for Mourning Warblers and Common Yellowthroats.

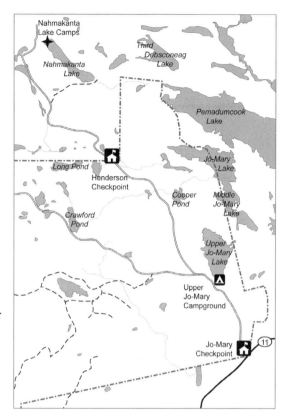

The road splits after 6 miles, with the left fork heading toward remote ponds and campsites. The right fork continues to Nahmakanta. Most of the area is hardwood and mixed forest. There is a stand of balsam fir immediately after the Henderson checkpoint at Mile 14, but the area is not promising for boreal specialties. Rather, it is rich in Ruffed Grouse, Red-eyed and Blue-headed Vireos, several species of flycatcher, and warblers such as Black-throated Green, Black-throated Blue, Northern Parula, Blackburnian, Black-and-white, Magnolia, Nashville, Ovenbird, Yellow-rumped, and American Redstart.

AROOSTOOK COUNTY

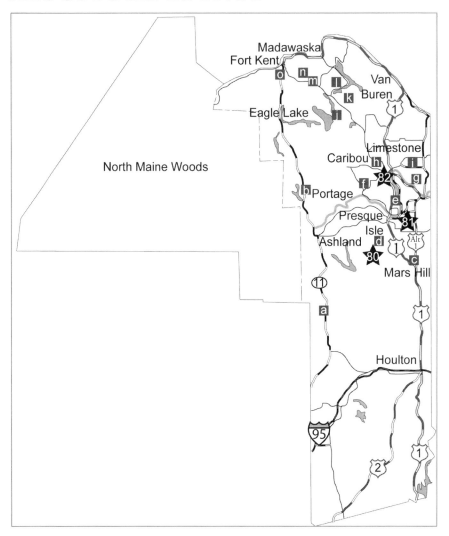

Birding in Aroostook County is like birding another country. In fact, if not for a favorable resolution of the bloodless Aroostook War of 1839, much of it would be in Canada today. Aroostook is so distinctive that Mainers refer to it as "The County" without fear of confusion with the other 15 counties. Winters are long; breeding seasons are short. Where hardwood once grew on well-drained soils, agricultural fields now prevail. Much of Maine's agricultural heritage has receded into regenerated forest, but not here. Throughout most of Maine, birders relish the pockets of spruce-fir they can find. In

Aroostook County, these are common, and it is the mature hardwood stands that are uncommon.

In 2005, nesting Northern Shovelers were joined by Maine's first-record breeding Ruddy Ducks at Lake Josephine in Easton. In 2008, Redheads were also confirmed as first-in-the-state breeders, demonstrating that typical Canadian nesters show little regard for the border in Aroostook. Pine Grosbeaks are possible at any time. Horned Larks nest in the agricultural fields of the Saint John Valley, joined later by post-breeding American Pipits, Snow Buntings, and Lapland Longspurs. Rough-legged Hawks drift across the border at will, and both species of crossbills breed here. Wintering Bohemian Waxwings and Northern Shrikes arrive first in Aroostook County and are among the last to leave in spring.

If Aroostook County can claim a special birding niche, it is waterfowl. Lake Josephine and Christina Reservoir are renowned for both abundance and variety. Furthermore, an astonishing number of geese stop over at many of the smaller ponds and marshes for a leisurely stay through late summer and autumn. With such abundance, rarities such as a Barnacle Goose are always possible. The bigger lakes experience the seasonal migrations of Arctic breeders like eiders, scoters, grebes, and scaup.

Culturally, Aroostook County is a fascinating place. French is the first language for many families through the St. John River Valley. A Swedish population also ended up here, settling in towns such as Stockholm and New Sweden. The county's isolation has helped preserve many cultural and economic traditions. Residents remain close to the land, sustained by forestry and agriculture. While traveling on Route 1, watch for the Maine Solar System Model: a 40-mile-long, scale model of the solar system. Pluto is at the Houlton Information Center. The sun is located at the Northern Maine Museum of Science at the Presque Isle campus of the University of Maine. The remaining planets are strung out along Route 1, in exact proportion to their real sizes and orbits.

There are two major access routes into northern Aroostook County, a configuration that has significant historical roots. The road that is now Route 1 was the major thoroughfare, but it ran directly through territory disputed by the British. The Fish River Road, now Route 11, was the key link for supplying American outposts during the Aroostook War, including the blockhouse known as Fort Kent. Unfortunately, the topography of this road was horrific. In summer, U.S. forces preferred supply routes along the St. John River—despite the potential for depre-dation by the British   to the marshes, swamps, bogs, and thick boreal forest of this road. In other words, what made it bad as a supply route makes it wonderful as bird habitat.

Trip planning: www.VisitAroostook.com or 888-216-2463.

➤➤-0-◄◄

Official Maine Birding Trail Sites

⭐80 **Aroostook State Park** was the first state park established in Maine, when citizens of Presque Isle donated 100 acres in 1938. Today, its expanded 800 acres offer a beach, two peaks, miles of nature trails, and idyllic camping. Campsites are roomy and well spaced. The for-est is a strong mix of spruce, fir, birch, and beech, which provides a remarkable variety of warblers, vireos, thrushes, and other songbirds. Echo Lake is productive for diving ducks and gulls.

Directions: from Route 1, just about three miles south of Presque Isle, turn left onto Spragueville Road. This road may not be marked, but it is just beyond the Aroostook Union Grange building. There is also a road sign pointing toward the Transatlantic Balloon Flight site. In just over a mile, turn left onto State Park Road. From Presque Isle, the park may also be reached by following Chapman Road to Niles Road and continuing to a right turn onto State Park Road.

➤➤-0-◄◄

⭐81 **Lake Josephine and Christina Reservoir** are owned by McCain Foods, one of the chief potato processors in Maine and Canada. Both are extraordinary for birding. Signs on McCain property warn against trespassing, but birders are allowed to travel along the town-owned road. Stay on roads and avoid active farming and harvest operations.

Lake Josephine is shown as an Industrial Waste Pond on the De-Lorme Maine Atlas. At one time, it was a sewage lagoon for the potato processing plant, but now it is used primarily to impound water for use by the plant. In species quality and quantity, it resembles some of America's best national wildlife refuges. Look for Mallards, American Black Ducks, American Widgeons, Blue-winged and Green-winged

Teal, Pied-billed Grebes, Wood Ducks, and Ring-necked Ducks throughout summer. Northern Shovelers are rare nesters in Maine, but they breed here. Breeding Redheads and Ruddy Ducks have been recently documented, the first to be confirmed in Maine. Great Blue Herons and American Bitterns lead the list of potential wading birds, while Merlins are among the raptors sighted most often. Look for shorebirds in migration, and Spotted Sandpipers throughout summer.

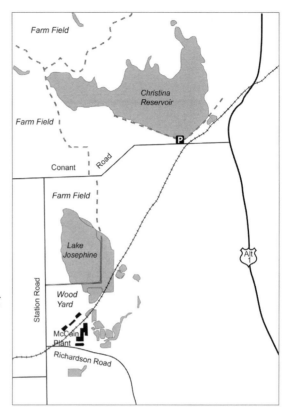

Christina Reservoir provides a reliable water supply for the processing plant and a reliable water level for nesting birds. The reservoir is larger than Lake Josephine, and views of waterfowl are sometimes more distant. But the dike extends more than a mile along the southern edge, providing plenty of observation points. A spotting scope is handy. The brush along the water's edge and the trees behind the dike are excellent for warblers and sparrows.

Directions: from Presque Isle, take Route 10 at Academy Street east toward Easton. At 1.4 miles, bear left onto Conant Road. After about 4 miles, turn right onto Station Road, then left for access to Lake Josephine just before the wood yard. A perimeter road follows the dike around the south and east side and exits north through a farm field. (Avoid this area during active operations.) Christina Reservoir is on Conant Road 2 miles beyond the Station Road turnoff. Park at the entrance road, and hike the levee on foot. The road around Lake Josephine is public, but is maintained by McCain. Stay on roadways, obey signs, and avoid private property.

82 **Caribou's Collins Pond** is particularly productive in late summer and autumn. For some reason, Canada Geese are reluctant to get shot and eaten, and they have clearly grasped that municipal ponds are off limits to firearms. There are several secluded feeding areas near town, and the geese flock to the safety of the pond when not foraging. Their presence encourages many other species of waterfowl and shorebirds, despite the popularity of the park's walking trail. Hooded Mergansers and Ruddy Ducks join the more common waterfowl, while Short-billed Dowitchers, and Greater and Lesser Yellowlegs number among the shorebirds. Collins Park has picnic tables, but the rest rooms are usually locked except during events.

Directions: a few miles south of Caribou, traffic splits off onto two parallel roadways along Routes 1 and 164. Take Route 164 to Collins Pond, turning left onto Roberts Street just before the center of town and proceeding to the Lions Club Park.

Additional Sites:

a **Route 11 between Masardis and Ashland** is laced with logging roads, all of which give access to fine boreal habitat, good for Boreal Chickadees, Black-backed Woodpeckers, Gray Jays, and Spruce Grouse. As always on all logging roads, pull over to the side and allow logging trucks to pass from both directions. Do not park on corners, below hilltops, and in other blind areas. Do not block side roads. Be patient when encountering loading operations in the road. Expect dust. In all of Aroostook County, vehicle collisions with moose are a threat because of the immense size of the animal. These crashes are sometimes fatal. Route 11 has a particularly bad reputation, especially through the swampy lowlands. Use extreme caution and do not exceed speed limits, especially at night.

b **Portage Lake** is a great reason to own a canoe. This shallow lake, part of the Fish River watershed, is endowed with substantial wetlands that are ideal for waterfowl, wading birds, and rails. Some of these may be viewable from the boat launch site just north of the town of Portage, but nothing beats a quiet paddle into these waters. Common Loons,

Common Mergansers, Ring-necked Ducks, and Pied-billed Grebes are usually observable at a distance, but other dabblers present are more likely to be discovered by canoe.

Directions: just north of Portage on Route 11, turn west onto Hathaway Road and follow to the end.

c **Mars Hill** contains one of several promising waterfowl ponds close to Route 1. A small park at the outlet dam in the center of town provides good views. Besides Canada Geese, this pond is a good bet for breeding Ring-necked Ducks, Mallards, and Wood Ducks, with a smattering of Blue-winged and Green-winged Teal.

Directions: turn onto Route 1A in the center of Mars Hill, then look for an immediate entrance to the park behind the American Legion.

d **Arnold Brook** is another interesting site, reached by continuing the drive from Aroostook State Park. The route passes a historical marker on the launch site of the first successful trans-Atlantic balloon flight, completed in 1978. A dike impounds Arnold Brook, creating a significant pond of reliable depth, ideal for migrating waterfowl. A secluded community park provides both boat access and a lakeside picnic area.

Directions: from downtown Presque Isle, turn west onto Chapman Street. After a few miles, turn left onto Niles Road. The park entrance is less than a mile ahead, but the sign is removed in winter. Continue along this route to reach Spragueville Road and Aroostook State Park. From Aroostook State Park, follow Spragueville Road to Niles Road.

e **The Aroostook River** is a magnet for ducks in migration. Bald Eagles are likely any time of year. In Fort Fairfield, the oxbow of the river just east of downtown is particularly good for waterfowl and eagles. About 3 miles west of town along Route 161, Bald Eagles have historically nested on an island in the stream opposite the intersection with Green Ridge Road. In Presque Isle, the best spot is along Route 167 opposite Burlock Road. In Washburn, not only is the river particularly marshy and productive, but also the surrounding fields have been good for American Pipits, Horned Larks, and Snow Buntings over the years.

f **Washburn** also has a productive pond with a multitude of Canada Geese in season. Behind this pond, just a few steps down the ATV trail, is a smaller pond with a greater variety of waterfowl, particularly Pied-billed Grebes. These wetlands are obvious, as they are located in the middle of town on Route 164.

g **Caribou Dam** is excellent for Common Mergansers, Double-crested Cormorants, and wintering Common Goldeneyes. Fast water below the dam guarantees open water in winter. Large flotillas of Common Mergansers often linger just below the dam in late summer as July's family groupings merge into one flock.

Directions: several streets on the east side of Route 1 lead to the river, including Lower Lyndon Street behind the cemetery. A left turn along the river leads downstream to a boat launch; a right turn leads upriver to the dam. (A sign in the parking lot of the hydroelectric plant discourages unauthorized visitors but this is, in fact, a public way and birders can drive beyond the plant for a scan of the impoundment lake.)

h **Trafton Lake** is formed by a dammed stream just south of Limestone. It can be good for waterfowl and shorebirds in migration, and a fair number of ducks may be observable in breeding season. The best viewing is at a park reached from Ward Road, which runs for three miles between Routes 89 and 223 near Limestone. A large sign marks the access road.

i **The Aroostook National Wildlife Refuge** is currently in its infancy. The new refuge is being developed on land left over from redevelopment of the former Loring Air Force Base in Limestone. One 1.5-mile nature trail has already been laid out next to the visitor center, traversing mixed habit and skirting several marshes. Other interesting sections are expected to become available to the public on the west side of the refuge, including a tract on the bank of the Little Madawaska River. Check for the latest information at the visitor center.

Directions: Aroostook NWR is near the entrance to the Loring Commerce Center, reached from Route 89 between Caribou and Limestone. Enter on Loring Commerce Road and bear right toward the visitor center. (At present, there are no signs for the NWR from the main road.)

j **Madawaska Lake**, like many of the larger lakes in Aroostook County, surprises birders with occasional flocks of sea ducks in migration. These lakes, and several major rivers to the north, serve to funnel the ducks through the region on their way to and from Hudson Bay. Eiders, scoters, and grebes habitually turn up in early spring and late autumn. It takes little time to veer off Route 161 in Stockholm onto Lake Shore Road for a quick scan of the lake. The road returns to Route 161 after two miles.

k **Sullivan Road** is a major logging road about three miles north of Madawaska Lake that winds eastward from Route 161. Its length traverses a diverse mixed forest. It is particularly productive to drive a short loop through the best habitat, entering at the Sullivan Road, continuing 2.6 miles to the Coulombe Road, and following Coulombe Road 3.1 miles back to Route 161. Besides presenting a variety of breeding warblers, this route is better than average for raptors.

l **Long Lake** lies eight miles due north of Madawaska Lake, and it is much larger. Sea ducks visit this lake, and Common Terns and Ring-billed Gulls have colonized here. It would be well worth the drive along Route 162 to St. Agatha (pronounced Saint a-GAT) for the scenery alone, but there are additional incentives. The first several miles of the route brush good spruce-fir habitat. The best place to try for Boreal Chickadees and Black-backed Woodpeckers is along the access road to the Sinclair Sanitary Wastewater Treatment Facility. The road is blocked by a locked gate. Park by the gate, out of the way of entering trucks, and enjoy the walk along the paved road. Spruce-loving warblers can be abundant from May through July. Just beyond, the vacation hamlet of Sinclair separates Mud Lake from Long Lake. It contains a boat ramp from which good views of Long Lake are possible. Continuing northwest along the lakeshore, look for the town park shortly after passing the town line of St. Agatha. It lies opposite an island that is nesting habitat for Common Terns. These terns, and small flocks from Maine's biggest inland colony of nesting Ring-billed Gulls, are often seen along the near shore, roosting on rocks and docks. From downtown St. Agatha, continue along Route 162 to Frenchville or loop back to Route 161 through the Back Settlements.

m **Daigle Pond** is always worth a stop because it is attractive to both diving and dabbling ducks. Ring-necked Ducks are a common sight in the center of the pond throughout much of the summer. Hooded Mergansers flock to the edges in autumn. Mallards, American Black Ducks, and Wood Ducks are likely along the rushes, joined by teal in migration. Daigle Pond is on the east side of Route 161 in Daigle.

n **The Back Settlements** refers to an area of the St. John River Valley that has a long agricultural history. The region is bounded by Routes 1, 161, and 162. It remains under widespread cultivation, even though there are fewer farmhouses remaining today. A drive around these dirt roads is an invitation to see rap-

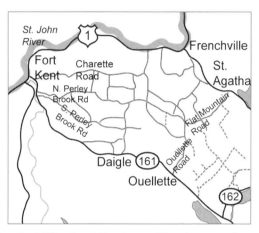

tors and grassland birds. Red-tailed Hawks, Northern Harriers, and American Kestrels are most likely, but Merlins and Red-shouldered Hawks are occasional. Great Horned Owls sweep these same fields at night. Rough-legged Hawks are no surprise in the colder months and some may drift across the border even in summer. Pockets of Horned Larks breed here, joined by American Pipits, Snow Buntings, and a few Lapland Longspurs in mid-Autumn. After August harvest, tilled fields entice flocks of Black-bellied Plovers, with the possibility of a few American Golden Plovers interspersed. This is the first place in the state where Common Redpolls sneak in from the north in search of the seeds abundant in grassy fields. They mingle with their American Goldfinch and Pine Siskin cousins. It's also the first place where irruptions of Pine Grosbeaks and Bohemian Waxwings are likely to occur, drawn by the fruit of old orchards and roadside berries. Be sure to bring along the DeLorme Maine Atlas or a good map, as many identical dirt roads criss-cross these fields, creating a maze for the unprepared. Road names may appear on maps, but seldom appear on the roads themselves.

Directions: there are many entrances and exits, but some of the normal routes include Flat Mountain Road in St. Agatha, Caribou Road in Ouellette, and Cemetery Hill Road in Daigle. From the east side of Fort Kent,

Charette Hill Road, North Perley Brook Road, and South Perley Brook Road offer access to the Back Settlements.

0 **Fort Kent** is nestled on the bank of the St. John River, which forms Maine's border with Canada. It is the educational and cultural hub of northern Aroostook County and is home to a branch of the University of Maine. Recently, it also became home to the 10th Mountain Ski Area—a world-class nordic facility that hosts international biathlon competitions and cross-country ski events. Snow covers the trail loops through much of the year, but from late May through June, warblers breed here in good numbers, grateful for its hardwood forest in a land otherwise filled with conifers. On most summer days, the trails are quiet, except for occasional athletes in training and dog-walkers.

Directions: the entrance to 10th Mountain Ski Area is on Route 11 just south of Fort Kent. The sign marking the entrance is not easily visible from the south, but is obvious from the north. Bear right and uphill to the parking lot.

CAMPOBELLO

A visit to Campobello Island in New Brunswick is a natural extension of any visit to the Down East Maine coast. Because the island is Canadian, it is on Atlantic Time—one hour later. Also, remember that proper ID—a birth certificate or other document proving citizenship in addition to a driver's license—is required for border crossings. Many Americans came to know the island as the summer home of President Franklin D. Roosevelt, and his home is now part of Roosevelt Campobello International Park—a unique park that is jointly owned and managed by the governments of the United States and Canada. The visitor center and the Roosevelt home are open from mid-May through Columbus Day. A tour of both is worthwhile. The natural area of the park is open year-round during daylight hours. There are eight miles of roads and another eight miles of walking trails within the park. As befits an international park, there are no fees.

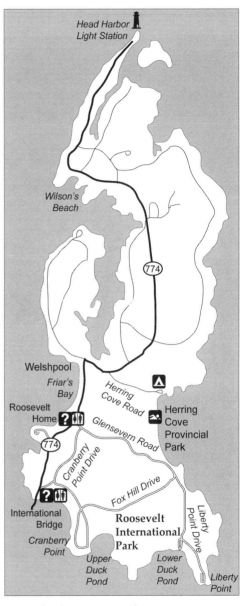

The 2,800-acre park contains many diverse habitats. In fact, it is a microcosm of all the habitats that may be found in the region, including rocky coast, beach, deciduous forest, boreal forest, bogs, wetlands, fields, and orchards. Leave plenty of time for a thorough exploration.

• The visitor center can be loud with birds in early summer. Compare the trills of the Chipping Sparrows and Dark-eyed Juncos. Expect Northern Parula and Black-throated Green Warblers, and virtually any of the boreal warbler species that pass through the parking lot in May.

• A footpath to **Friar's Head** exits from the southern end of the visitor center parking lot. Although it is only 0.6 mile long, expect to spend a lot of time because of the abundance of birds in early summer. Golden-crowned

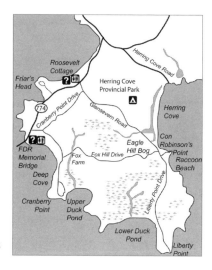

Kinglets are likely, and a Nashville Warbler is often heard shortly after entering the path. Very quickly, the trail crosses a small side road. The shrubbery here is normally alive with Common Yellowthroats, American Redstarts, and Black-and-white Warblers. The footpath leads downward, over a wetland boardwalk where Canada Warblers and Northern Waterthrushes reside, and then back uphill through a forest that contains Black-throated Green, Black-throated Blue, and Yellow-rumped Warblers. The trail levels off through a mature patch of forest that shelters Hermit Thrushes and Ovenbirds, then emerges into an old orchard where Yellow Warblers take over. Eventually, the trail emerges into the open picnic area where Baltimore Orioles and Scarlet Tanagers appear. There may also be Chestnut-sided Warblers here, but they are more often found along the main road at the bottom of the drive. Continue uphill to the observation platform overlooking Passamaquoddy Bay. Enjoy the view and the interpretive signs. It's common to find raptors riding the air currents at this elevation. Visit the platform even on foggy days with no view, because under these circumstances, Friar Head often gets unusual warbler fallouts during spring migration.

• **Glensevern Road** is opposite the entrance to the visitor center and leads to more of the park's natural areas. The road is a regular corridor for marauding Broad-winged Hawks and Northern Goshawks.

• **Eagle Hill Bog** has one of the best boardwalks in the northeast. Interpretive signs alert visitors to the rare and unusual plants that typify bog life. Stay alert for the breeding Lincoln's Sparrows, Palm Warblers, Dark-eyed Juncos, Nashville Warblers, and Purple Finches that are often visible. Possible flycatchers include Yellow-bellied, Alder, and Olive-sided. The boardwalk ends at an observation platform that overlooks an expansive horizon. The woods surrounding it contain Hermit and Swainson's Thrushes, and Scarlet Tanagers. Watch the flocks that fly over for crossbills or Pine Siskins. Train binoculars on the distant cove and perhaps become one of the few people in the world to view Northern Gannets from a bog!

• **Con Robinson Point** and **Raccoon Beach** are scanning points for sea ducks. Besides the Common Eiders that are usually present, look for all three scoters, Black Guillemots, and Red-breasted Mergansers. Note the Bank Swallows that nest here.

• **Liberty Point's** exposed location presents an awesome view of the channels between Campobello and West Quoddy Head, and Grand Manan. Two observation decks overlook waters that are rich in seals, porpoises, and whales. Look for the seals, Common Eiders, and Black Guillemots close by. Northern Gannets, shearwaters, and whales are all possible in the distance. The road to Liberty Point passes through several forest habitats. Ruffed and Spruce Grouse can be found in mixed forests, especially near Lower Duck Pond. In areas where yellow birch trees dominate, look for Black-throated Blue Warblers, Ovenbirds, and woodpeckers.

• **Lower Duck Pond** overlooks a combination saltwater cove, tidal beach, and sphagnum moss bog. American Black Ducks and Blue-winged Teal breed in the estuary. On the beach, shorebirds gather in small numbers beginning in late July. Whimbrels and Hudsonian Godwits are possible, especially after Labor Day.

• **Fox Hill Drive** contains significant tracts of boreal habitat. A Spruce Grouse in the road is not uncommon, especially after the chicks hatch in June. Drive slowly and stay alert to movements.

• **Fox Farm and Cranberry Point** provide open, brushy habitat. Both are good places to look for Ruby-crowned Kinglets, American Redstarts, and Chestnut-sided, Magnolia, and Yellow Warblers. American Woodcocks occupy low, wet areas but stay well concealed. Scan the channel between the point and the U.S. mainland. Scoters are very common in the off-season, sometimes even in the summer. Mergansers are also likely.

• **Upper Duck Pond** is actually a saltwater cove, making it a good place to look for shorebirds. Although August and September are the best months for shorebirding, non-breeding Black-bellied Plovers may be present in early summer. Migrating waterfowl pass through in early spring and late autumn, though a few ducks can be present year-round. Northern Harriers are a common sight over the marsh for much of the year.

• **Herring Cove Provincial Park** is next door to the international park. Glensevern Road is the dividing line. The birds and views are the same, especially the view of the mile-long cobblestone beach and sheltered bay. The park provides 100 campsites, almost half with electrical hookups.

• **Friar's Bay** lies west of the main road on Route 774, just beyond Roosevelt's summer home. Shorebirds often forage the cobblestone beach in August, and it's a good place to scan for scoters in any season.

• **Welshpool** is on the west side of the island. It faces the Passamaquoddy Bay channel between the U.S. and Canada. In August and September, this channel fills with thousands—perhaps tens of thousands—Bonaparte's Gulls and Black-legged Kittiwakes. Minke Whales are also drawn into the channel in chase of the same food. Wharves in this area provide some viewing points for the channel. The ferry to Deer Island disembarks vehicles near these wharves.

• **Wilson's Beach, Cook's Point Road, and Pollock Cove** are located on the north end of the island on Route 774. Look for opportunities to pull off the road and scan the channel, or continue on to Head Harbor Light Station.

• **Head Harbor Light Station** stands on East Quoddy Head at the north end of the island. This is where the best oceanic birding action is. Gulls roost in abundance on the rocks. Herring and Black-backed Gulls are the largest but Bonaparte's Gulls and Black-legged Kittiwakes should also be easy to see in late summer. Rarities like Common Black-headed and Little Gulls show up intermittently. Roosting shorebirds are also possible, including Ruddy Turnstones. Northern Gannets may be seen plunge diving offshore, occasionally rather close. These are the waters of Humpback, Fin, and Minke Whales and they can sometimes be seen at a distance. Minkes even come close to shore occasionally. Greater and Sooty Shearwaters are not far offshore and may approach the coast when breezes and food supplies warrant it. Be sure to check the treetops around the parking area. Several warbler species are present, and it's also a likely spot for finches. Even crossbills are possible. At low tide, it is pleasant to walk across the sand bar to the head and the lighthouse, but be sure to beat the incoming tide back to the mainland.

GRAND MANAN

Grand Manan is nine miles across the channel from the United States mainland, southeast of Lubec. It is closer to the U.S. mainland than to any mainland location in Canada. Nonetheless, it is one of the best-known birding locations in New Brunswick. Of the 391 bird species currently accepted for New Brunswick, 363 have occurred on Grand Manan. The only access to the island is on board one of the finest pelagic birding rides by ferry in North America. The island is more than 15 miles long and 11 miles across at its widest point.

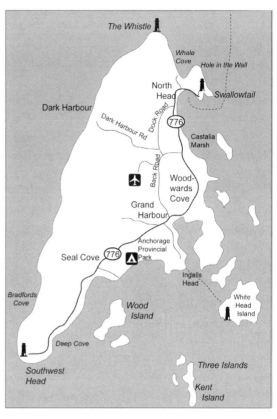

In the northeast corner of Maine, the border crosses through Calais into St. Stephen, New Brunswick. From here, it's about a forty-minute drive to Blacks Harbor, though it's always wise to get in line for the ferry an hour in advance, especially in the height of tourist season. Don't rush. The ocean pushes inland in several spots along the coast, each one more scenic than the next.

A better reason to leave plenty of time is that Blacks Harbor itself is a great birding spot. From the dock (or the top deck of the ferry) the harbor is noticeably full of gulls. The sardine plant in Blacks Harbor draws many, as does the bountiful food supply in the cold harbor water. In the winter and early spring, be alert for Iceland Gulls and the less common Glaucous Gull. From mid-summer through autumn, Bonaparte's gulls are plentiful. Check their numbers in August and September for Common Black-headed Gulls. Common Terns are also present through the latter half of the summer. The harbor waters are home to Common Eiders, Black Guillemots, Long-tailed Ducks, Horned Grebes, Common Loons, Red-throated Loons, Double-crested Cormorants, and Buffleheads in varying concentrations through the year. In August and September, check for shorebirds along the tidal margins. The common peeps are often present, as are Greater and Lesser Yellow-legs. Stay alert for Whimbrels in late summer and early fall.

At the top of the hill above the harbor, where the road makes its final turn down toward the docks, there is a gated dirt road that provides a short and very rewarding half-mile hike to a lighthouse. The path begins through some close secondary boreal growth that is good for Black-capped Chickadees, Red-breasted Nuthatches, Golden and Ruby-crowned Kinglets, and Canada Warblers. Soon the growth on the left side of the path thins and mixes with secondary stands of hardwoods, giving way to a mossy wetland. This area is particularly good for American Redstarts, Common Yellowthroats, and White-throated Sparrows. As the path continues toward the ocean, it extends through taller patches of jack pine, home to other warbler species such as Blackburnian. Hermit and Swainsons Thrushes may be observed anywhere along the path. At the end of the path, the tall conifers are attractive to crossbills. They can be present at any time of year. A spit of land connects the lighthouse island with the mainland at low tide. It is a welcome spot for Whimbrels in August and September.

Dress warmly for the ferry. The birding is often so good from the top passenger deck of the ferry that it is hard to tear away to the warmth and comfort of the lounge. Even in a dead calm, the speed of the ship can cause a dank draft on the deck. Two ferries alternate during the height of tourist season. The *Grand Manan* is the smaller of the two, offering good views from the front of the boat as well as from the rear deck. On the *Grand Manan V*, there is nowhere to stand in the front of the boat, nor is it easy to move quickly from one side to the other. This ferry is better birded from the top deck in the rear, and there is a particularly comfortable viewing spot, standing out of the wind, behind the starboard smokestack. (The port stack has a noisy vent.)

The ferry ride is 90 minutes. Ledges at the harbor entrance usually feature a large number of cormorants, Double-crested in summer, and Great Cormorants in winter. After leaving these behind, there is a 30-minute lull where nearly every bird turns out to be a disappointing

Herring Gull. Over the middle thirty minutes, the variety of species should increase. White-sided Dolphins often become apparent, and Humpback Whales are seen regularly. Minke Whales also cruise the open waters. From mid-July through Labor Day, Greater and Sooty Shearwaters fill the channel, sometimes by the thousands. Manx Shearwaters are much less common, but they still can be seen regularly. Black Guillemots are the most common alcid, but this crossing also produces sightings of Common Murres and Razorbills, especially when seas are calm. Parasitic and Pomarine Jaegers are less common, but possible in the second half of summer. Northern Gannets may be expected at any time except in the dead of winter. They grow numerous from mid-August to late November . . . then start popping up again in April. Wilson's Storm-petrels make their appearance in the second half of summer, though they are not common on this passage, unlike in Maine waters farther south.

In the last 30 minutes the ferry slowly passes the north side of Grand Manan, rounding the point at Swallowtail Lighthouse to enter the ferry terminal at North Head. Dolphins, harbor porpoises, and occasional whales remain possible sightings right up until the ship sounds the warning horn. Note the harbor seals around the herring weirs. In season, shearwaters may remain numerous right up until the ferry makes the final turn. Common Terns also pop up in the last third of the crossing.

Upon nearing the island, it becomes easy to see what makes Grand Manan so special. The island does not lie in the ocean so much as it stands upright over it, with towering cliffs around three-quarters of its circumference. Most of the inhabitants live on the east side of the island simply because the land is too rugged everywhere else. The exception is Dark Harbor, a most unusual village chiseled into the one crevice on the otherwise unbroken escarpment of the island's west side.

The cliffs give the island much of its unique habitat. Common Ravens and the occasional Peregrine Falcon nest on the ledges, while Black Guillemots nest in the crevasses. Gulls nest anywhere tumbled rocks have created tiny islets. Bald Eagles take command of the more prominent trees while Merlins breed in the lower shoreland conifers. Grand Manan is situated in the middle of the Bay of Fundy, home of the world's highest tides. The cold currents that sweep by all sides of the island are rich with food for the bird species that nest on the smaller islands nearby.

In summer, note the tents on the nearest cliff as the ferry approaches the island. This is "Hole in the Wall," a private camping and hiking area with rigorous trails and phenomenal campsites. Throw open the tent flap in the morning and scan for whales.

Next, the ferry passes Swallowtail Light. It's one of the island's most popular scenic areas, and it is impossible to exaggerate the birding potential of this promontory. Shearwaters, terns, gulls, eiders, Black Guillemots, Long-tailed Ducks, Red-breasted Mergansers, and passing gannets and jaegers are all observable from this cliff in their proper seasons. So are whales, dolphins, porpoises, and seals.

The ferry docks in North Head, home to most of the inns, gift shops, and restaurants on the island. Many of the homes have bird feeders that attract Purple Finches and American Goldfinches. Pheasants are backyard birds here, often seen and heard. From here, it is a short walk to Swallowtail Light and only a moderate hike to Hole in the Wall. It's also a short walk to bike and kayak rentals, and to the boat tours that go out of the harbor. It is possible to experience Grand Manan without a car.

Route 776 runs the length of the island, along the eastern shoreline. Just south of North Head, look for Whale Cove Road and Whistle Road. Whale Cove is picturesque, quiet, and secluded. Noted American author Willa Cather spent many summers in a quiet cottage in this cove. Whistle Road is just beyond Whale Cove Road. It leads three miles to The Whistle, one of three lighthouses on the island. There is a low observation platform adjacent to the lighthouse. The seascape is exceptional. On calmer days, porpoises and seals are impossible to miss in the eddy that surges around the northernmost point of the island. Even Minke Whales come in close to feed along the tide line. Greater and Sooty Shearwaters come within binocular range here. It's a great spot for a picnic lunch and one of the best spots for sunsets. At the end of Whistle Road, the beach is typical of the rocky beaches on the west side of the island. In later summer, a few shorebirds sometimes poke around the water's edge.

There are many private drives and a few public roads that branch off Whistle Road. Any of these can be rewarding for warblers and woodland species. Indian Beach and Eel Brook Roads are two that can be walked for some distance without worries about traffic. Look for them about two miles from the turnoff on Route 776. Swainson's Thrushes are common in these woods.

Castalia Marsh is farther down Route 776. A large sign now marks the once obscure entrance. It is one of the reasons why the island is known for its birding diversity. Shorebirds gather in August and September. Of these, perhaps 10% of the sandpipers will be White-rumped and nearly as many will be Least. The Least Sandpipers are amazingly tame, sometimes scurrying underfoot along the edges of the marshside mud. On average, they work themselves up the ocean-side beach farther than their Semipalmated cousins. Shorebirds are most abundant at the far end of the spit at high tide. This is also when Peregrines and Merlins are most likely to buzz the flock.

The walk to the end of the spit is nearly as entertaining as the destination. Song and Savannah Sparrows occupy the grassy areas. Common Yellowthroats reside in the large bushes. In fringe seasons, Vesper Sparrows, Horned Lark, Lapland Longspur, and Snow Buntings occur regularly, usually along the margins of the beach grass or in the jeep path. At higher tides, the usual sea ducks should be in evidence. At low tide, check the distant rocks for Black-crowned Night-herons, especially at dusk.

The marsh always contains a few waterfowl, usually Canada Geese, Mallards, American Black Ducks, Red-breasted Mergansers, and Buffleheads. In shorebird season, Short-billed Dowitchers are inevitable, though not in big numbers. Greater and Lesser Yellowlegs are usually apparent. Killdeer and Willets are not secretive and will be obvious, if present. Tree Swallows share the air with Barn Swallows, the latter often nest under the eaves of the picnic table shelters. Be alert for Bank Swallows. They nest in the banks just north of the marsh, and their buzzy call is easy to pick out as they pass.

Woodward Cove is the next southbound landmark on Route 776. There's something strange about the water in this cove at low tide: there isn't any. Though the cove is actively used to moor fishing vessels, any boat anchored away from the pier will be resting on its hull at low tide. Naturally, shorebirds can be found poking around these mudflats at that time. Scan for Ruddy Turnstones in migration. Some non-breeders may stay here all summer.

Grand Harbour contains the Grand Manan Museum. It displays artifacts from the island's history and is also home to the Allan Moses Bird Collection. Moses was one of the most prolific taxidermists of his day. He bequeathed his collection of 300+ specimens to the museum in 1953.

Here's a chance to note the size difference between Greater and Lesser Yellowlegs at arm's length, and examine every feather of all the local sea ducks. It was Moses who convinced J. Sterling Rockefeller to purchase Kent Island in 1935 to create one of the earliest seabird restoration facilities in North America. Moses deserves much of the credit for rescuing the Common Eider from possible extinction when its downy feathers were discovered to possess marvelous insulating qualities.

To reach Ingalls Head take a left turn off Route 776 in Grand Harbour. A free ferry to White Head Island operates regularly from the dock. The ferry ride is sheltered from prevailing winds in fair weather, allowing for steady hands on your binoculars. Common Terns are often visible during the short passage and Bald Eagles love to perch on shoals in the channel. Leach's Storm-petrels nest on nearby Kent Island. On rare occasions, they can be seen in daylight returning to their burrows, especially on the first and last ferry runs of the day. These nocturnal birds have also been observed flying through the lights at Ingalls Head harbor on occasional summer nights.

Plan on spending a half-day or more on White Head Island. It is scenic, uncrowded, and birdy. Upon disembarking from the ferry, turn right and follow the road to a parking lot barely large enough for three cars. The lighthouse will be visible a mile away. It is possible to drive to the lighthouse, but walking is preferable. On the left, this stony road leads past low brush, good for Common Yellowthroats, and roadside wetlands, good for Solitary Sandpipers, Greater and Lesser Yellowlegs, Killdeer, and Yellow-bellied Flycatchers. Grasslands are good for Song and Savannah Sparrows. Pheasants are frequently heard and infrequently seen, just off the road in the thicker grassy areas bordering the trees. On the right side, the intertidal zone borders the road all the way to the lighthouse. Some of the smaller shorebirds may be present, and this is a favored feeding ground for Black-bellied Plovers, Whimbrels, and Great Blue Herons. Double-crested Cormorants are always in view, except when replaced by Great Cormorants in winter.

The lighthouse is taller than any on Grand Manan, yet it is still smaller than the lighthouse 10 miles offshore on Gannet Rock and 20 miles offshore on Machias Seal Island. It occupies a promontory worth scanning. Of particular note, a small group of islands noted on nautical charts as Three Islands is southwest across the channel. On the largest of the three—Kent Island—a permanent research station is set up under the auspices of Maine's Bowdoin College. Kent Island is home to one of the largest breeding colonies for Leach's Storm-petrels on the eastern seaboard.

The road continues beyond the lighthouse. The woods thicken on the left, and a sheltered beach appears on the right. A few shorebirds may turn up, but mostly this is a beach for roosting gulls. After the beach, the path winds through Golden-crowned Kinglet and Boreal Chickadee habitat. This is a pleasant hike, and it is possible to see a variety of warblers. The only drawback is that the trail is shared with all-terrain vehicles, which tend to churn up muddy spots, creating uneven footpaths.

Elsewhere on White Head, shorebirds are numerous in the harbors and along the beaches. A left turn off the ferry leads quickly through the village area. Around a corner, there is a small wetland drained by a culvert under the road. The birds here are more noteworthy for their quality than their quantity. Medium-size shorebirds make regular appearances, including Short-billed Dowitchers, Pectoral and Solitary Sandpipers, Greater and Lesser Yellowlegs, and Willets. Killdeer are common. Scan carefully before getting out of the car because Green-winged and Blue-winged Teal are often present and can be spooked easily. Scan from the breakwater on the left side of the road, where the tidal change is substantial, and the birds can change with the tide every 15 minutes.

At the height of tourist season, return to the ferry terminal well before its scheduled departure. Capacity is limited and stragglers may have to wait for the next run.

Back on Grand Manan and continuing south on Route 776, Anchorage Provincial Park is 1.5 miles ahead. Turn left toward the park. Within a mile, the road splits. The right fork leads into the camping area, featuring its spacious campsites and hot showers. The shrubs and bushes are loaded with songbirds in the morning. A left turn at the fork leads to another of Grand Manan's premier birding opportunities. The road splits at a nice stretch of beach, with Long Pond on the left. On a typical day, gulls will be abundant on both the salt- and the freshwater side. Careful observation may reveal freshwater ducks on the far side of the pond. Common Terns often forage at the distant end of the pond.

By car or by foot, continue past Long Pond. Along the way, Song and Savannah Sparrows flit among the grasses. At any time, the oceanside beach will have many gulls, the potential for shorebirds (especially Sanderlings), and occasional dabbling ducks. Before Big Pond, there is a small parking lot and a nature trail on the left. This short, easy loop offers pure boreal habitat. Blackpoll Warblers breed here. Boreal Chickadees are occasional among the more common Black-capped. In the earliest spring season, Yellow-rumped and Palm Warblers fill the treetops. Throughout the summer, Cedar Waxwing whistles are routinely heard, and Golden and Ruby-crowned Kinglets are common.

Just beyond the loop trail is Big Pond. This pond tends to be more promising for freshwater ducks, and perhaps a few Buffleheads. Most retire to the far side of the pond, making a spotting scope helpful. American Widgeons, Blue-winged Teal, Green-winged Teal, Mallards, and Black Ducks regularly occur, and Canada Geese are almost always present. The road ends at Big Pond, but there is a footpath that continues to Ox Head.

Seal Cove on Route 776 is the departure point for the only Canadian boat tour to Machias Seal Island, located just ten miles to the southwest of Grand Manan. Sea Watch Tours visits the Atlantic Puffin colony six days a week from late June to early August. It also offers whale-watching and pelagic birding tours through September. Visit www.seawatchtours.com or call 506-662-8552.

Deep Cove is 3 miles below Seal Cove. It is the best beach on the island. In fact, at low tide, it's the biggest beach in lower New Brunswick. For the best birding results, take a long look at the ocean, then turn around. The dunes and surf-tossed stones have isolated a nice freshwater pond that regularly contains American Black Ducks and Common Mergansers, and perhaps a few other species, notably Wood Ducks. This has been a favorite spot for nesting Merlins. They are lively and noisy for much of the summer once the young are hatched in late June. Boreal Chickadees also show up in the conifers several times a day. The parking lot for the beach is just beyond Driftwood Cottage.

On Route 776, opposite the freshwater pond and north of the beach parking for Deep Cove, there is a dirt road on the right that leads ultimately to Bradford Cove. This is one of the better woodland warbler walks on the island. Common warblers are numerous. Both species of chickadees and nuthatches are present, and the woods contain both Hermit and Swainson's Thrushes. In irruptive years, both species of crossbill are seen here regularly.

Southwest Head is the last stop on Route 776, and it is dramatic. The lighthouse on this cliff is relatively short, because the land itself is already 200 feet above sea level. The entire head consists of a precipitous cliff that is rare in nature, although common on Grand Manan. Unlike other cliffs on the island, the upland is open and fully exposed, allowing grand views. Black Guillemots nest in the crevasses and are always present in the waters below.

The trail leading along the edge of the cliff is required birding. Northern Gannets pass close to the cliffs in April and May, and come close again from August through November. Peregrine Falcons nest on the cliff in some years. The bushes along the trail contain Common Yellowthroats, Song Sparrows, and White-throated Sparrows, while the grasslands are home to Savannah Sparrows. After less than a mile, the trail leads into the woods, making for a pleasant hike to Bradfords Pond and Hay Point. Wear waterproof footgear. All-terrain vehicles have left deep muddy ruts in places. These coniferous woods are home to Pine and Blackburnian Warblers, as well as Swainson's and Hermit Thrushes. Blue-gray Gnatcatchers are uncommon this far north but they have turned up here.

It's about a mile to Bradford Pond. Approach cautiously, in case freshwater ducks are present. The best way to bird this pond is to sit quietly on the beach near the solitary cottage and wait for things to happen. Warblers and flycatchers work the trees bordering the pond, while shorebirds work the mudflats. Killdeer and Spotted Sandpiper are the most likely of the latter group, though Yellowlegs and Solitary Sandpipers are possible. Stay alert for Boreal Chickadees, which are common in the thick firs behind the cottage. Cedar Waxwings are obvious almost all summer, and crossbills are likely in good cone years.

The six-mile road that leads to Dark Harbor passes through both hardwood and boreal habitat, each with its particular preferred songbirds. Just before the road takes its final plunge to the village, the birding is especially rewarding because of the sudden and dramatic changes in both vegetation and elevation. Dark Harbor Road is reached from Route 776 by taking Dock Road from North Head or Back Road from Castalia. Follow the signs.

Dark Harbor lives up to its name. Mother Nature carved out the initial notch in the otherwise unbroken cliff face of Grand Manan's west side. The tiny community of fishermen and dulse harvesters finished the job. Dulse is a dark, rich seaweed that is pulled from the ocean at low tide and sun-dried. It is prized as a delicacy in many cultures and there is none better in the world than here. The huge natural lagoon around which the camps and shanties are built makes a perfect impoundment for lobsters, trout, and salmon. The lagoon always contains cormorants and gulls. Mergansers, Buffleheads, and Common Loons are also likely. The basin on the south side empties at low tide and the walk around the edge can be interesting, though sometimes slippery. Black-crowned Night-herons are regularly found here.

Appendix A: Maine Audubon Field Checklist of Maine Birds

ALCIDS (ALCIDAE)
Atlantic Puffin
Black Guillemot
Common Murre
Dovekie
Razorbill
Thick-billed Murre

BITTERNS and HERONS
(ARDEIDAE)
American Bittern
Black-crowned Night-Heron
Great Blue Heron
Great Egret
Green Heron
Least Bittern
Little Blue Heron
Snowy Egret
Tricolored Heron
Yellow-crowned Night-Heron

BLACKBIRDS (ICTERIDAE)
Baltimore Oriole
Bobolink
Brown-headed Cowbird
Common Grackle
Eastern Meadowlark
Orchard Oriole
Red-winged Blackbird
Rusty Blackbird

BOOBIES (SULIDAE)
Northern Gannet

CARDINALS and ALLIES
(CARDINALIDAE)
Blue Grosbeak
Dickcissel
Indigo Bunting
Northern Cardinal
Rose-breasted Grosbeak

CHICKADEES (PARIDAE)
Black-capped Chickadee
Boreal Chickadee
Tufted Titmouse

CORMORANTS
(PHALACROCORACIDAE)
Double-crested Cormorant
Great Cormorant

CRANES (GRUIDAE)
Sandhill Crane

CREEPERS (CERTHIIDAE)
Brown Creeper

CUCKOOS (CUCULIDAE)
Black-billed Cuckoo
Yellow-billed Cuckoo

FALCONS (FALCONIDAE)
American Kestrel
Merlin
Peregrine Falcon

FINCHES (FRINGILLIDAE)
American Goldfinch
Common Redpoll
Evening Grosbeak
Hoary Redpoll
House Finch
Pine Grosbeak
Pine Siskin
Purple Finch
Red Crossbill
White-winged Crossbill

FLYCATCHERS (TYRANNIDAE)
Alder Flycatcher
Eastern Kingbird
Eastern Phoebe
Eastern Wood-Pewee

FLYCATCHERS (TYRANNIDAE)
- Great Crested Flycatcher
- Least Flycatcher
- Olive-sided Flycatcher
- Willow Flycatcher
- Yellow-bellied Flycatcher

GEESE and DUCKS (ANATIDAE)
- American Black Duck
- American Wigeon
- Barrow's Goldeneye
- Black Scoter
- Blue-winged Teal
- Brant
- Bufflehead
- Cackling Goose
- Canada Goose
- Canvasback
- Common Eider
- Common Goldeneye
- Common Merganser
- Gadwall
- Greater Scaup
- Green-winged Teal
- Harlequin Duck
- Hooded Merganser
- King Eider
- Lesser Scaup
- Long-tailed Duck
- Mallard
- Mute Swan
- Northern Pintail
- Northern Shoveler
- Red-breasted Merganser
- Redhead
- Ring-necked Duck
- Ruddy Duck
- Snow Goose
- Surf Scoter
- White-winged Scoter
- Wood Duck

GNATCATCHERS (SYLVIIDAE)
- Blue-gray Gnatcatcher

GREBES (PODICIPEDIDAE)
- Horned Grebe
- Pied-billed Grebe
- Red-necked Grebe

GROUSE (PHASIANIDAE)
- Ring-necked Pheasant
- Ruffed Grouse
- Spruce Grouse
- Wild Turkey

GULLS and TERNS (LARIDAE)
- Arctic Tern
- Black Tern
- Black-headed Gull
- Black-legged Kittiwake
- Bonaparte's Gull
- Caspian Tern
- Common Tern
- Forster's Tern
- Glaucous Gull
- Great Black-backed Gull
- Great Skua
- Herring Gull
- Iceland Gull
- Laughing Gull
- Least Tern
- Lesser Black-backed Gull
- Little Gull
- Parasitic Jaeger
- Pomarine Jaeger
- Ring-billed Gull
- Roseate Tern

HAWKS and EAGLES (ACCIPITRIDAE)
- Bald Eagle
- Broad-winged Hawk
- Cooper's Hawk
- Golden Eagle

HAWKS and EAGLES
Northern Goshawk
Northern Harrier
Osprey
Red-tailed Hawk
Red-shouldered Hawk
Rough-legged Hawk
Sharp-shinned Hawk

HUMMINGBIRDS
(TROCHILIDAE)
Ruby-throated Hummingbird

IBISES (THRESKIORNITHIDAE)
Glossy Ibis

JAYS and CROWS (CORVIDAE)
American Crow
Blue Jay
Common Raven
Fish Crow
Gray Jay

KINGFISHERS (ALCEDINIDAE)
Belted Kingfisher

KINGLETS (REGULIDAE)
Golden-crowned Kinglet
Ruby-crowned Kinglet

LARKS (ALAUDIDAE)
Horned Lark

LOONS (GAVIIDAE)
Common Loon
Pacific Loon
Red-throated Loon

MIMICS (MIMIDAE)
Brown Thrasher
Gray Catbird
Northern Mockingbird

NIGHTJARS (CAPRIMULGIDAE)
Common Nighthawk
Whip-poor-will

NUTHATCHES (SITTIDAE)
Red-breasted Nuthatch
White-breasted Nuthatch

OLD WORLD SPARROWS
(PASSERIDAE)
House Sparrow

OWLS (STRIGIDAE)
Barred Owl
Great Gray Owl
Great Horned Owl
Long-eared Owl
Northern Saw-whet Owl
Short-eared Owl
Snowy Owl

OYSTERCATCHERS
(HAEMATOPODIDAE)
American Oystercatcher

PIGEONS and DOVES
(COLUMBIDAE)
Mourning Dove
Rock Pigeon

PIPITS (MOTACILLIDAE)
American Pipit

PLOVERS (CHARADRIIDAE)
American Golden-Plover
Black-bellied Plover
Killdeer
Piping Plover
Semipalmated Plover

RAILS and ALLIES (RALLIDAE)
American Coot
Common Moorhen
Sora

RAILS and ALLIES
Virginia Rail

SANDPIPERS (SCOLOPACIDAE)
American Woodcock
Baird's Sandpiper
Buff-breasted Sandpiper
Dunlin
Greater Yellowlegs
Hudsonian Godwit
Least Sandpiper
Lesser Yellowlegs
Long-billed Dowitcher
Pectoral Sandpiper
Purple Sandpiper
Red Knot
Red Phalarope
Red-necked Phalarope
Ruddy Turnstone
Sanderling
Semipalmated Sandpiper
Short-billed Dowitcher
Solitary Sandpiper
Spotted Sandpiper
Stilt Sandpiper
Western Sandpiper
Whimbrel
White-rumped Sandpiper
Willet
Wilson's Phalarope
Wilson's Snipe
Upland Sandpiper

SHEARWATERS
(PROCELLARIIDAE)
Greater Shearwater
Manx Shearwater
Northern Fulmar
Sooty Shearwater

SHRIKES (LANIIDAE)
Northern Shrike

SPARROWS (EMBERIZIDAE)
American Tree Sparrow
Chipping Sparrow
Clay-colored Sparrow
Dark-eyed Junco
Eastern Towhee
Field Sparrow
Fox Sparrow
Grasshopper Sparrow
Lapland Longspur
Lark Sparrow
Lincoln's Sparrow
Nelson's Sharp-tailed Sparrow
Saltmarsh Sharp-tailed Sparrow
Savannah Sparrow
Snow Bunting
Song Sparrow
Swamp Sparrow
Vesper Sparrow
White-crowned Sparrow
White-throated Sparrow

STARLINGS (STURNIDAE)
European Starling

STORM-PETRELS
(HYDROBATIDAE)
Leach's Storm-Petrel
Wilson's Storm-Petrel

SWALLOWS (HIRUNDINIDAE)
Bank Swallow
Barn Swallow
Cliff Swallow
N. Rough-winged Swallow
Purple Martin
Tree Swallow

SWIFTS (APODIDAE)
Chimney Swift

TANAGERS (THRAUPIDAE)
Scarlet Tanager

THRUSHES (TURDIDAE)
American Robin
Bicknell's Thrush
Eastern Bluebird
Gray-cheeked Thrush
Hermit Thrush
Swainson's Thrush
Veery
Wood Thrush

VIREOS (VIREONIDAE)
Blue-headed Vireo
Philadelphia Vireo
Red-eyed Vireo
Warbling Vireo
White-eyed Vireo
Yellow-throated Vireo

VULTURES (CATHARTIDAE)
Black Vulture
Turkey Vulture

WAXWINGS (BOMBYCILLIDAE)
Bohemian Waxwing
Cedar Waxwing

WOOD WARBLERS (PARULIDAE)
American Redstart
Bay-breasted Warbler
Black-and-white Warbler
Black-throated Blue Warbler
Black-throated Green Warbler
Blackburnian Warbler
Blackpoll Warbler
Blue-winged Warbler
Canada Warbler
Cape May Warbler
Chestnut-sided Warbler
Common Yellowthroat
Louisiana Waterthrush
Magnolia Warbler
Mourning Warbler

WOOD WARBLERS
Nashville Warbler
Northern Parula
Northern Waterthrush
Orange-crowned Warbler
Ovenbird
Palm Warbler
Pine Warbler
Prairie Warbler
Tennessee Warbler
Wilson's Warbler
Yellow Warbler
Yellow-breasted Chat
Yellow-rumped Warbler

WOODPECKERS (PICIDAE)
American Three-toed Woodpecker
Black-backed Woodpecker
Downy Woodpecker
Hairy Woodpecker
Northern Flicker
Pileated Woodpecker
Red-bellied Woodpecker
Red-headed Woodpecker
Yellow-bellied Sapsucker

WRENS (TROGLODYTIDAE)
Carolina Wren
House Wren
Marsh Wren
Sedge Wren
Winter Wren

MAINE AUDUBON works to conserve Maine's wildlife and wildlife habitat by engaging people of all ages in education, conservation, and action.

For more information or to become a member of Maine Audubon, call 207-781-2330 or visit www.maineaudubon.org.

Maine Audubon
20 Gilsland Farm Rd.
Falmouth, ME 04105

Appendix B: Trip Planning

The southern portion of Maine is well developed, with plenty of inns and restaurants. Much of the birding takes place on beaches, in parks, and within land trusts. The northern portion of the state is wild and remote, where birding takes place mostly on private lands among the undeveloped lakes, rivers, and woods of the industrial forest, and in primitive public areas like Baxter State Park and the Allagash Wilderness Waterway.

The area between these two is a transition zone. It borders the wilder areas, but still provides good accommodations and tourist amenities. The zone runs from a range of mountains in southwestern Maine to sparsely developed lakes in Down East Maine. It is roughly from the White Mountain National Forest near Bethel, to Rangeley Lake, to the Bigelow Preserve near Kingfield, across to Moosehead Lake, over to Baxter State Park, and from there on to the Down East interior of Washington County. The west side of Aroostook County is the wildest, most remote part of the state. The east side of the county is flat agricultural land, with wetlands similar to the potholes of the central plains of the United States and Canada.

In breeding season, any location is good for Maine's wealth of songbirds. Typically, visiting birders are interested in enjoying certain experiences. Here are a few.

Wake Up to Loons. Common Loons reside on most of Maine's lakes in summer. For an opportunity to hear them calling through the bedroom window, select accommodations in one of Maine's many lake regions. The Sebago Lake area in the southern portion of the Maine Lakes & Mountains Region provides a large choice of accommodations and dining, close to theaters, amusements, and other tourist attractions. The Belgrade Lakes area in the Kennebec and Moose River Valley Region also provides a good choice of accommodations and dining. For a more remote experience, plan a vacation around Rangeley Lake, Moosehead Lake, or Grand Lake Stream. To enjoy complete solitude and get away from it all, check into one of the sporting camps in northern Maine.

Breathe Salty Air. The Maine Beaches region in the southern part of the state is developed, with many amusements and amenities. It provides a good base of operations for exploring some of Maine's best birding sites. The Mid-Coast region is quieter. The small towns along Route 1 have plenty of food and accommodation choices to offer visitors. The windjammer fleet of Rockland, Rockport, and Camden makes them a good place to visit for sailing enthusiasts. The smaller villages off Route 1, on the peninsulas of the uneven coastline, are tucked away from the bustle. Acadia National Park on Mount Desert Island is suitable for hiking and biking, but the best kayaking is around Castine, Deer Isle, and Stonington, located just east of MDI. The coast is much less developed east of Ellsworth. In Washington County—a county the size of Delaware—there are only two McDonald's Restaurants, and no national brand-name hotels. However, the birding opportunities are first-class.

Watch Puffins. There are five Atlantic Puffin colonies along the coast. Three are reached from the Mid-Coast area, although only Eastern Egg Rock can be visited daily. This island is also the best bet for Roseate Terns. In the Down East and Acadia Region, the whale-watch boat from Bar Harbor visits Petit Manan Island each morning. Farther up the coast, puffin tours from Jonesport and Cutler go out to Machias Seal Island. This is the only puffin-nesting island that allows the public to land, when weather conditions permit, but the boats are relatively small and the trip to the island is longer than the other daily trips. It's a challenge for anyone prone to seasickness. This is one of the best birding experiences in Maine. Details about these trips, and several limited seabird trips that visit Matinicus Rock and Seal Island, are explained in Appendix D.

Stay on an Island. At least once in a lifetime, visit Monhegan Island during migration season. Check Maine Audubon's latest field ornithology offerings on Hog Island. Tour Grand Manan. Stay with the Elderhostel on Campobello during peak warbler season. For more flexibility, drive onto an island that can be reached by bridge or causeway, such as Deer Isle and Mount Desert Island, both in the Down East and Acadia Region.

Smell the Balsam. On safari for Spruce Grouse, Gray Jays, Boreal Chickadees, and Black-backed Woodpeckers on a damp morning, the scent of balsam fir hangs sweetly in the air. Target the northern portion of the Maine Lakes and Mountains region or the upper stretches of the Kennebec and Moose River Valley Region. The Maine Highlands is an excellent choice for boreal species around Moosehead Lake and Baxter State Park. Pockets of boreal nesters can even be found close to Bangor around Sunkhaze Meadows National Wildlife Refuge. Down East and Acadia have the same birds, though the bulk of these specialized habitats tend to be along the northern coastal trails or the interior portions of Washington County. Here are some good destinations to consider when chasing boreal birds: Bethel, Rangeley, Stratton, Kingfield, Jackman, The Forks, Greenville, Millinocket, Grand Lake Stream. In Aroostook County, consider Houlton, Presque Isle, Caribou, and Fort Kent.

Climb. Go looking for Bicknell's Thrush at Grafton Notch State Park, not far from Bethel, on Saddleback Mountain near Rangeley, or any of the high peaks around the Bigelow Preserve. All are in the Maine Lakes and Mountains Region. In the Maine Highlands, Big Moose Mountain and Big Spencer Mountain near Moosehead Lake are known to have nesting populations, and the tallest peaks in Baxter State Park do too. The dining and accommodations in these areas are excellent.

Don't Climb. It is possible to take long bird walks that are more horizontal than vertical. In the Maine Beaches region, try Marginal Way in Ogunquit, Laudholm Farm in Wells, or Kennebunk Plains. Acadia National Park's carriage trails are easy to walk for long distances. The coastal trails of Down East Maine can be rugged but change little in elevation. Visit the Pine Tree State Arboretum in Augusta or Moxie Falls in The Forks, at opposite ends of the Kennebec River Valley Region. Despite all the mountains in Baxter State Park, many of the choices for bird walks are on level ground along the roads and trails of the Maine Highlands.

Go Wild. The southern half of the state has everything a visitor could want. The towns bordering the Maine woods have everything a visitor could need. Northern Maine has the woods, the waters, and the wildlife. However, except for the sporting camps in the region, visitors must bring everything with them. Much of this region is managed by North Maine Woods, Inc. Visit www.northmainewoods.org or call 207-435-6213. To stay in Baxter State Park, visit www.baxter stateparkauthority.com. To paddle the Allagash Wilderness Waterway, look up information at the Maine Department of Conservation Web site: www.maine.gov/doc.

The Appalachian Mountain Club purchased its first sporting camps as part of its Maine Woods Initiative in 2003. The camps and trails involved with the project are simply outstanding. Click on www.outdoors. org. The new Northern Forest Canoe Trail stretches from western New York to northern Maine. Visit www.northernforestcanoetrail.org. A new hut-to-hut trail system is now under development in Maine. Get updates at www.mainehuts.org.

Stay Wild. Many visitors to Maine expect the creature comforts offered by upscale hotels and inns. There is no shortage of these in the cities, along the coast, near ski mountains, and along developed lakes. But birders who like to get close to nature and "away from it all" can truly appreciate the remoteness and tranquility of Maine's traditional sporting camps. Many were originally established to support logging activities. Later, they principally served hunters and anglers. Today, Maine sporting camps cater to all who love the outdoors, especially those who enjoy rustic simplicity without intrusion from the outside world. The Maine Sporting Camps Association maintains a Web site at www.mainesportingcamps.com. It provides more information about all of its member camps throughout Maine. A number of these camps were visited as the Maine Birding Trail was being researched. The following are a representative sample of the sporting camp experience:

The Appalachian Mountain Club's **Little Lyford Pond Camps** is located off the Katahdin Iron Works Road between Greenville and Brownville Junction in the KI/Jo-Mary area, just west of Gulf Hagas. Established in 1874, there are seven log cabins sleeping 1-6 people each, and a bunkhouse with 12 bunks. A modern lodge features a kitchen, activities center, and library. Miles of hiking trails are available on site and the camp's location puts it conveniently between Moosehead Lake and Baxter State Park.

Medawisla is the Native American name for the Common Loon. It's also the name of AMC's best sporting camp for birding. Its seven pine-paneled cabins are located on Second Roach Pond east of Moosehead Lake, the only structures on the lake. Because the camp borders the outflow of the lake, it is an exceptional place to watch moose from the cabin window. The location is also ideal for chasing Maine's boreal specialties. Spruce Grouse are seen nearby, and Black-backed Woodpeckers nested in the camp's driveway in 2004. Bald Eagles and Common Loons nest on the lake and both are easily encountered while paddling. Medawisla is only a half hour from lands managed by the North Maine Woods, both north and south. It is even closer to Nahmakanta Lake, and closer still to Moosehead Lake. A trail network is maintained on site. Cabins are fully furnished for up to 10 with gas stoves, gas and electric lights, propane refrigerators, linens and towels, dishes, cooking utensils, screened porches, and hot showers.

Nahmakanta Lake Camps have been so well maintained that it is hard to believe they have such a long history. Dating to the 1870s the camps earned their renown from the extraordinary fishing in the area. Nowadays, a host of winter activities, including dog-sledding, make the camps a year-round destination. For birders, there are many attractions. Located in Maine's 100-Mile Wilderness, the camps are near the Appalachian Trail and the trails of the Nahmakanta Maine Public Reserved Lands. Canoeing is fabulous. The area is rich in moose and other wildlife. Eight guest cabins accommodate 2–8 people each. All have picture windows facing the lake and screened porches. There is no electricity and you won't miss it. Gas provides the light, cooking, refrigeration, and hot showers. Cook in cabins or have Don and Angel Hibbs feed you.

The first cabin at **Spencer Pond Camps** was built a hundred years ago. The camps are still the only buildings on Spencer Pond, 14 miles from any neighbor. The current owners, Bob Croce and Jill Martel, are avid birders and maintain an excellent trail system around the camp. Their bird feeders attract a stunning array of sparrows and finches. Merlins have nested among the cabins in the last couple of years and Black-backed Woodpeckers are seen nearby. Hot spots for Spruce Grouse dot the area map. The camps are just south of the North Maine Woods lands on the Golden Road. They are very near Big and Little Spencer Mountains, where Bicknell's Thrush may be found near the summits. Six rustic lakeside cabins offer exceptional views of Little Spencer Mountain and the pond. Each is fully equipped for housekeeping.

The Birches has its roots in Maine's sporting camp tradition, though it offers a greater variety of accommodations than most. Fifteen rustic waterfront cabins, six exclusive private home rentals, cabin tents, wilderness yurts, and rooms in the main lodge at The Riverview are all available. In addition, casual lakeside dining and a lounge are provided. There is a beach, hot tub, dry sauna, and a new fitness center, so The Birches may be regarded as a complete destination resort, even though it retains its rustic character. For birders, a trail system built for cross-country skiers in winter proves to be a boon for warbler watching in summer, winding through a variety of habitats. The moose-watching expedition offered by The Birches is among the best in the state.

Pittston Farm is notable for its elegant simplicity. A variety of accommodations is available in the lodge, cabins, and carriage house. The location is exceptional. The complex is on the shore of Seboomook Lake, at the confluence of the North and South Branches of the Penobscot River. Although it is deep in the woods, it is just 20 miles from Rockwood and the west side of Moosehead Lake, and minutes from all of the North Maine Woods to the north. It is a mere three miles from the Golden Road and borders excellent boreal habitat. The birding variety is outstanding. Pittston Farm is open year round.

Penobscot Lake Lodge is so remote that "you can't get there from here" except by boat or float plane. Located only one mile from the Quebec border, it is one of the most secluded spots in Maine. Fortunately, it is also one of the most luxurious sporting camps, with comfort, amenities, and great food that are routine. For birders, the habitat is terrific. Miles of trails lie outside the cabin door. One trail leads west toward Canada through a variety of mixed habitats that assures Ruffed Grouse, and possibly Spruce. Another trail through thinned hardwoods provides opportunities for most of Maine's woodland warblers. A beaver flowage on the east side of the lake is a haven for waterfowl, bitterns, and raptors. Moose are a certainty. Rather than using a traditional gas-powered generator, electricity is provided through quiet solar power. Penobscot Lake Lodge is in the northwest corner of North Maine Woods lands, which means that any day trip from the lodge will be through unoccupied wilderness in some of the best NMW territory.

Other Resources:
The state clearinghouse for visitor information is operated by the Maine Office of Tourism at www.visitmaine.com. The Maine Department of Transportation provides information about getting around the state at www.exploremaine.org. Also, visit the Maine Tourism Association site at www.mainetourism.com.

Regional links:
- The Maine Beaches: www.MaineBeachesAssociation.org
- Greater Portland and Casco Bay: www.VisitPortland.com
- Mid-Coast: www.MainesMidCoast.com
- Down East & Acadia: www.DownEastAcadia.com
- Maine Lakes & Mountains: www.WesternMaine.org
- Kennebec & Moose River Valey: www.KennebecValley.org
- The Maine Highlands: www.TheMaineHighlands.com
- Aroostook County: www.VisitAroostook.com

Accommodations:
- Maine Innkeepers Association: www.maineinns.com.
- Maine Sporting Camps Assn.: www.mainesportingcamps.com.
- Maine Campground Owners Association: www.campmaine.com.
- Maine State Parks: www.maine.gov/doc/parks/programs/index.html
- Acadia National Park Campgrounds: www.nps.gov/acad/planyourvisit/campgrounds.htm

Dining:
- Maine Restaurant Association: www.mainerestaurants.com

Boating:
- Windjammer Sailing in Mid-Coast: www.sailmainecoast.com
- Windjammer Sailing in Acadia: www.downeastwindjammer.com
- Sea Kayaking: www.maineseakayakguides.com

Outfitters and Guides:
- Adventure Outfitters: www.maineoutdoors.com
- Registered Maine Guides: www.maineguides.com
- Professional Wilderness Guides Assn.: www.maineguides.org

Ferry Services:
- High-speed Ferry to Nova Scotia: www.catferry.com
- Maine State Ferry Service: Several state-run ferries to offshore islands. www.state.me.us/mdot/opt/ferry/maine-ferry-service.php
- Ferry Service and Cruises in Casco Bay: www.cascobaylines.com
- Ferry Service to Monhegan Island: www.monheganboat.com
- Hike and Bike Service to Isle au Haut: www.isleauhaut.com and www.oldquarry.com

And finally, the authoritative resource for printed and electronic information about the great state of Maine is *Down East* at www.downeast.com.

Appendix C: Bird Finding

Residents and birders planning a visit to Maine often consult a state checklist, compile a "wish list," and seek bird-finding advice from Maine Audubon and state experts. The following species are regularly requested, though some are rarely seen in Maine.

Terms:
  Abundant: certain to be seen, very numerous
  Common: certain to be seen in suitable habitat
  Locally common: normally seen at limited, site-specific habitats
  Uncommon: might be seen in suitable habitat
  Occasional: seen only a few times each season
  Irruptive: highly nomadic and varies from year to year
  Vagrant: wanders into Maine, outside of its normal range
  Rare: not seen every year

American Woodcock: Widespread, common breeder readily seen while displaying at dawn and dusk in May. Secretive afterward, but may flush underfoot during a hike.

Atlantic Puffin: Abundant breeder on five islands off the Maine coast. Rarely seen from land.

Barrow's Goldeneye: Uncommon winter resident, but favors particular spots. Reliable sites: Winslow Park in Freeport, Kennebec River in Bath and Waterville, Belfast Harbor, Penobscot River in Bangor and Orono, open water below large dams in winter.

Black Guillemot: Common breeder on mainland and island cliffs. Seen easily in many harbors and along rocky shorelines.

Black-legged Kittiwake: Common in Down East Maine after breeding. Abundant from West Quoddy Head in Lubec through Eastport and Campobello in late summer. Regularly seen at Monhegan Island in autumn.

Bohemian Waxwing: Irruptive winter resident, recently abundant in most winters. Large flocks descend on fruit trees.

Boreal Chickadee: Locally common breeder in boreal areas, though silent while nesting in June. Prefers thick, impenetrable spruce stands.

Red Crossbill: Nomadic winter irruptive not seen every year. Lingers to breed in good cone years, especially in coastal, alpine, and northern areas.

White-winged Crossbill: Nomadic winter irruptive not seen every year. Lingers to breed in good cone years, especially in coastal, alpine, and northern areas. Slightly more common than Red Crossbills.

Black-billed Cuckoo: Uncommon breeder in southern and central Maine, primarily around deciduous woodlands and agricultural areas. Try Brownfield Bog and Fuller Farm in Scarborough.

Yellow-billed Cuckoo: Uncommon breeder in southern and central Maine, primarily around deciduous woodlands and agricultural areas. Range extends farther north. Try Brownfield Bog and Fuller Farm in Scarborough.

Dovekie: Uncommon vagrant in migration. Sometimes forages or is blown close to shore in late autumn. Try Dyer Point in Cape Elizabeth and Marginal Way in Ogunquit.

Alder Flycatcher: Common empidonax flycatcher throughout Maine, heard often through breeding season.

Willow Flycatcher: Uncommon empidonax flycatcher throughout Maine, occupying similar open habitats. More common in southern Maine.

Yellow-bellied Flycatcher: Uncommon empidonax flycatcher found around bogs and alpine areas where it is easily located by voice.

Olive-sided Flycatcher: Uncommon tyrant flycatcher found around wetlands, bogs, and northern forest clear-cuts.

Barnacle Goose: Vagrant in autumn, found very rarely in association with Canada Geese.

Cackling Goose: Vagrant in autumn, found rarely in association with Canada Geese.

Gray Jay: Locally common breeder in boreal areas, noisy and inquisitive. Prefers tall, sparse spruce stands, gliding from perch to perch.

Great Cormorant: Common in winter: a few pairs nest near the puffin colonies on Matinicus Rock and Seal Island. Associates with Double-crested Cormorants on Monhegan Island in autumn.

Evening Grosbeak: Uncommon Maine breeder, mostly in boreal areas, but wanders throughout the state.

Pine Grosbeak: Winter irruptive not seen every year. May be abundant in fruit trees during peak years.

Ruffed Grouse: Widespread, common resident. Seen regularly on hikes and on roadways, especially with chicks in July.

Spruce Grouse: Widespread, uncommon resident. Seen regularly on coastal trails in Washington County, mountain trails above 2,500 feet, logging roads in boreal areas around Rangeley, Moosehead Lake, and Baxter State Park.

Common Black-headed Gull: Uncommon vagrant seen annually in Maine, generally associating with Bonaparte's Gulls. Try Pine Point in Scarborough, Rockland Harbor, and the channel between Eastport and Campobello.

Lesser Black-backed Gull: Uncommon vagrant seen annually in Maine.

Little Gull: Uncommon vagrant seen annually in Maine, generally associating with Bonaparte's Gulls. Try Pine Point in Scarborough, Rockland Harbor, and the channel between Eastport and Campobello.

Iceland Gull: Uncommon in winter all along the Maine coast wherever large gatherings of gulls roost.

Gyrfalcon: Rare winter visitor.

Hudsonian Godwit: Uncommon in autumn migration. Try Fortunes Rock Beach in Biddeford and Pine Point in Scarborough.

Long-tailed Jaeger: Rare in autumn, seen from whale-watching and pelagic boats.

Parasitic Jaeger: Uncommon in autumn, seen regularly from whale-watching and pelagic boats. Seen close to shore more often than Pomarine. Try Dyer Point in Cape Elizabeth.

Pomarine Jaeger: Uncommon in autumn, seen regularly from whale-watching and pelagic boats. Seldom seen close to shore.

Common Murre: Breeder on several offshore islands. Abundant on Machias Seal Island. Seen regularly from Grand Manan ferry. Sometimes seen from shore at rocky promontories along the entire coast, especially Down East.

Thick-billed Murre: Uncommon winter visitor where it can sometimes be seen close to shore. Try Cliff House in Wells, Marginal Way in Ogunquit, Dyer Point in Cape Elizabeth, Pemaquid Point, Thunder Hole in Acadia NP, and Blueberry Hill at Schoodic Point.

Northern Fulmar: Uncommon. Seen on *The Cat*, whale-watching, and pelagic birding trips. Rarely seen from shore.

Northern Gannet: Commonly seen offshore. Often seen from shore at any spot offering extensive views of open ocean, such as southern Maine beaches and Acadia National Park. Abundant from the cliffs of Monhegan Island, often close to shore.

Northern Goshawk: Common but secretive breeder throughout the state. Found in Baxter State Park and Moosehorn NWR.

Boreal Owl: Rarely heard, very rarely seen. May wander south to Maine during post-breeding dispersal, generally from late July through autumn.

Great Gray Owl: Rare winter irruptive. Not seen every year.

Long-eared Owl: Rare breeder.

Northern Hawk-owl: Very rare winter irruptive. Not seen every year.

Saw-whet Owl: Common but hard-to-see breeder. Widespread in mixed and boreal forest. Some migrate in October but return very early in spring. Others remain resident all winter.

Short-eared Owl: Rare breeder. Crepuscular—seen before dusk while hunting low over large fields and marshes.

Snowy Owl: Uncommon winter irruptive. Usually seen every year.

Philadelphia Vireo: Uncommon breeder in deciduous areas near mountains. Try Grafton Notch State Park at the Appalachian Trail parking lot, campgrounds in Baxter State Park, and the Bigelow Preserve.

American Golden-plover: Uncommon. Seen regularly during migration, primarily in autumn. Try Fryeburg Harbor in Fryeburg, Biddeford Pool, Fortunes Rocks, Green Point WMA in Dresden, Pine Point in Scarborough, and the South Lubec Sand Flats.

Piping Plover: Endangered nester on southern Maine beaches. Try Laudholm Farm in Wells, Fortunes Rocks in Biddeford, Popham Beach State Park, and Reid State Park.

Razorbill: Common breeder on seabird islands except at Eastern Egg Rock. Seen on puffin trips and from Grand Manan ferry. Seen from shore at Quoddy Head State Park.

Common Redpoll: Winter irruptive seen in most years. Travels in large, noisy flocks.

Hoary Redpoll: Rare winter irruptive associating with Common Redpolls.

Rough-legged Hawk: Uncommon winter resident. Favors open islands and coastal marshes. Scope Richmond Island from Kettle Cove and the Scarborough Marsh.

Rusty Blackbird: Uncommon breeder seen regularly in migration. Nests in northern forest wetlands. Current decline in population is alarming.

Purple Sandpiper: Common winter resident along rocky shores next to the waterline.

Upland Sandpiper: Uncommon nester in sand plains, blueberry barrens, and agricultural areas. Try Kennebunk Plains, Clarry Hill in Union, and the blueberry barrens Down East.

White-rumped Sandpiper: Mixes with autumn migration flocks of Semipalmated Sandpipers.

Scarlet Tanager: Common breeder in mature hardwood stands but, despite it bright color, tends to stay out of sight in the top of the canopy.

Cory's Shearwater: Occasional. Rarely seen in the Gulf of Maine. Prefers the warmer waters of the Gulf Stream and is seen on pelagic trips to the southern part of the gulf off Georges Bank.

Greater Shearwater: Seasonally abundant. Seen on *The Cat*, whale-watching, puffin, and pelagic trips, sometimes in large numbers. Often abundant along the ferry crossing to Grand Manan in July and August. Seldom seen from shore. Try Dyer Point in Cape Elizabeth, Pemaquid Point in Pemaquid, and The Whistle on Grand Manan.

Snow Bunting: Winter irruptive sometimes found in large flocks over weedy fields and blueberry barrens.

Leach's Storm-petrel: Abundant nester on offshore islands, but nocturnal and seldom seen. Best bet: post-breeding dispersal in August, notably from whale-watching boats out of Bar Harbor.

Manx Shearwater: Uncommon North Atlantic breeder. Seen on *The Cat*, whale-watching, puffin, and pelagic birding trips, usually singly. Seldom seen from shore. Try Dyer Point in Cape Elizabeth.

Sooty Shearwater: Seasonally abundant. Seen on *The Cat*, whale-watching, puffin, and pelagic birding trips, sometimes in large numbers. Often abundant along the ferry crossing to Grand Manan in July and August. Seldom seen from shore. Try Dyer Point in Cape Elizabeth, Pemaquid Point in Pemaquid, and The Whistle on Grand Manan.

Wilson's Storm-petrel: Often abundant offshore from June through September. Commonly seen from ferries and daytrip boats.

Fox Sparrow: Uncommon breeder in northern Maine seen often beneath feeders in migration. Regularly heard singing in boreal areas of Baxter State Park.

Lincoln's Sparrow: Common breeder in bogs and in damp clear-cuts of boreal forest.

Nelson's Sharp-tailed Sparrow: Common breeder in salt marsh wetlands from Scarborough Marsh north. Overlaps and interbreeds with Saltmarsh Sharp-tailed Sparrows in Scarborough and Weskeag Marshes. Occasional breeder at inland freshwater marshes.

Salt-marsh Sharp-tailed Sparrow: Uncommon breeder in salt marsh wetlands north to Weskeag Marsh.

Seaside Sparrow: Rare breeder. Occurs almost annually at Scarborough Marsh.

Arctic Tern: Abundant nester on offshore islands. Seldom seen from shore.

Least Tern: Endangered nester on southern Maine beaches. Try Laudholm Farm in Wells, Pine Point in Scarborough, Popham Beach State Park, and Reid State Park.

Roseate Tern: Uncommon nester on offshore islands. Usually seen on seabird trips to Eastern Egg Rock; infrequently seen on seabird trips to Petit Manan Island. Nests on Stratton Island near Scarborough Marsh and forages at Pine Point.

Bicknell's Thrush: Uncommon alpine breeder, limited to stunted spruce zones above 3,000 feet. Found on mountaintops in a band from Mahoosucs and Grafton Notch State Park to Saddleback and the Kennebagos near Rangeley, Mount Blue State Park, Bigelow Preserve, Moosehead Lake, and Baxter State Park. Hike Saddleback ski area trails for the best concentration.

Gray-cheeked Thrush: Rarely seen during spring migration.

Bay-breasted Warbler: Uncommon breeder in boreal areas. Tolerates mixed forest vegetation.

Blackpoll Warbler: Locally common breeder in spruce stands. Tends to prefer higher elevations where it is common, but can be found at sea level.

Canada Warbler: Common but secretive breeder in wet tangles of most forests.

Cape May Warbler: Very uncommon breeder in boreal areas. Prefers tall conifers, often near streams.

Mourning Warbler: Uncommon breeder. Skulks in the low underbrush of regenerating maples and brambles in northern forests.

Tennessee Warbler: Very uncommon breeder in boreal areas.

Wilson's Snipe: Widespread common breeder in wetlands. Noisy through breeding season, especially during aerial display flight.

Whimbrel: Uncommon in autumn migration. Try Biddeford Pool, Pine Point, Scarborough Marsh, Weskeag Marsh in South Thomaston, and Little Machias Bay in Cutler.

Black-backed Woodpecker: Uncommon breeder in boreal regions. Favors disturbed areas where it strips bark from dead and dying conifers.

Northern Three-toed Woodpecker: Rare breeder in boreal regions of northern Maine. Habits and habitats same as the Black-backed Woodpecker.

Yellow Rail: Rare, secretive breeder. Very seldom reported.

Appendix D: Atlantic Puffins and Pelagic Birding

There are five Atlantic Puffin colonies off the Maine coast: Eastern Egg Rock, Matinicus Rock, Seal Island, Petit Manan, and Machias Seal Island. Adult puffins come ashore to breed in late April, and begin returning to the sea in August. Some linger into September, but the fruitful season for visitation is only about a dozen weeks long. Once they leave their islands, puffins disperse across the ocean and are seldom seen, even from boats. Puffins are not often seen from the mainland.

• **Eastern Egg Rock** is the southernmost colony of Atlantic Puffins in the world. The 11-acre island is located six miles from the shore in New Harbor. Common, Arctic, and Roseate Tern colonies are also established on the island and it is one of the most reliable places to see Roseate Terns in Maine. As of this writing, the island is visited every day during puffin season by the *Hardy III*, docked at New Harbor. Visit www.hardyboat.com or call 800-2-puffin. Cap'n Fish circles the island four times a week from Boothbay Harbor. See www.puffins.capnfishs.com or call 800-633-0860. Maine Audubon offers a number of trips during the summer, either as part of its ornithology camps on Hog Island in Bremen, or as field trips for the general public. Visit www.maineaudubon.org or call 207-781-2330 for the current schedule.

• **Matinicus Rock** is three times the size of Eastern Egg Rock, but it is also three times farther out to sea. Visits are irregular. Currently, Maine Audubon leads several excursions per summer to the island. These trips have become very popular because the day trip travels through waters rich in pelagic species. Matinicus Rock, unlike Eastern Egg Rock, has a population of Razorbills, and may host Great Cormorants in summer. Visit www.maineaudubon.org or call 207-781-2330 for the current schedule. Charter trips are also available from Matinicus Excursions. Visit www.matinicusexcursions.com or call 207-691-9030.

• **Seal Island** is three times the size of Matinicus Rock. It lies 22 miles off the mainland. Besides the abundant puffins, it is home to a large number of Razorbills, and supports a few breeding pairs of Great Cormorants. Black Guillemots are abundant on the way to the island, and the trip passes through waters that are good for pelagic species. Captain Bill Baker of Old Quarry Adventures makes regular trips to the colony beginning in May, and additional visits are available by charter. Visit www.oldquarry.com or call 207-367-8977.

• **Petit Manan Island** is a 16-acre island covered in birds. It supports a large population of Laughing Gulls and Common Terns, almost as many Arctic Terns, and several dozen pairs of Roseate Terns. Many pairs of Razorbills visit the island, and actual nesting began in 2007. Leach's Storm-petrels, Black Guillemots, and Common Eiders also nest on the island. Bar Harbor Whale Watch makes daily morning trips to the island before heading out to the whaling grounds. The large, stable boat is great for people who suffer from seasickness. Visit www.barhar borwhales.com or call 207-288-2386. Robertson Sea Tours and Adventures in Milbridge visits the island in summer. The smaller, shallow-draft boat is capable of maneuvering close to the island for excellent viewing. Visit www.robertsonseatours.com or call 207-482-6110.

• **Machias Seal Island** is the granddaddy of puffin islands. Huge numbers of Atlantic Puffins populate the 20-acre island, accompanied by plenty of Razorbills and Common Murres. Large colonies of Common and Arctic Terns also nest here, though their nesting success in recent years has been diminished by gull predation. Ownership of the island is contested between the United States and Canada. However, Canada built the island's lighthouse in 1832 and staffs the research facility today. Two American companies and one from Canada visit the island. The Norton family of Jonesport has offered tours since 1939. Visit www.machiassealisland.com or call 207-497-2560. Captain Andy Patterson operates Bold Coast Charters and visits the island daily. Visit www.boldcoast.com or call 207-259-4484. The Wilcox family has provided daily trips from Grand Manan since 1969. Visit www. seawatchtours.com or call 877-662-8552.

PELAGIC BIRDING

Currently, the number of boat tours to pelagic waters is increasing in Maine. Maine Audubon offers the largest tour in autumn. Its annual trip on the whale-watch catamaran from Bar Harbor attracts birders from all over the world. In 2007, Maine Audubon acquired a larger boat to serve its Hog Island facility. Several tours are now offered to Matinicus Rock and other destinations in pelagic bird waters. Check the current schedule at www.maineaudubon.org or call 207-781-2330.

See Life Paulagics is a tour company that schedules pelagic tours along the eastern seaboard. In 2007, the company began partnering with Freeport Wild Bird Supply to offer occasional tours from Portland on board the *Odyssey*. Check for current offerings at www.paulagics.com or www.freeportwildbirdsupply.com.

Whale-watch tours search waters that are typically good for shearwaters, storm-petrels, gannets, jaegers, and phalaropes. Currently, these whale-watch tours operate in Maine:

• The *Deborah Ann* docks at Perkins Cove in Ogunquit. This 40-foot boat is among the smallest whale-watching boats. Though this may cause some motion discomfort on rough days, it also assures close views without having to fight for a spot on the rail. Visit www.deborahannwhalewatch.com or call 207-361-9501.

• First Chance Whale Watch in Kennebunk upgraded to an 87-foot boat in 2006, with ample viewing space on two decks. Visit www.firstchancewhalewatch.com or call 800-767-2628.

• The *Odyssey* in Portland can accommodate up to 85 passengers. The vessel boasts a nearly 100% whale sighting record on Jeffrey's Ledge and the Sagadahoc Grounds. Visit www.oldportmarinefleet.com or call 207-775-0727.

• Captain Fish's Whale Watch originated whale-watching from Boothbay Harbor and is now in its third generation of family operation. Its vessels are among the most modern and well-equipped. Besides whale-watching trips, the company provides weekly trips to Eastern Egg Rock for Atlantic Puffins. Visit www.mainewhales.com or call 800-636-3244.

• The *Harbor Princess* in Boothbay Harbor ventures forth daily to find whales. At 100 feet long and 24 feet wide, she can accommodate 149 passengers in comfort. The bottom deck allows passengers to walk 360 degrees around the vessel for good views in all directions. Visit www.whaleme.com or call 888-WHALE-ME.

• Bar Harbor Whale Watch is a real favorite for pelagic birding. The morning cruise makes a side trip to Petit Manan Island for Atlantic Puffins, Razorbills, and breeding colonies of Common, Arctic, and

Roseate Terns, before continuing the search for whales in an area called "the Ball Park." The *Friendship V* is a fast catamaran that covers a lot of ocean in a hurry, yet is big enough to be stable in rough weather. Visit www.barharborwhales.com or call 888-WHALES-4.

• The *Sylvina W. Beal* in Eastport is a unique windjammer that sails out to the feeding grounds of Finback and Minke Whales just beyond East Quoddy Lighthouse. In later summer, expect to sail through thousands of Bonaparte's Gulls, Black-legged Kittiwakes, and rafts of seabirds feeding on the same abundance that attracts the whales. The vessel does not typically get far enough into open ocean for shearwaters and storm-petrels. Visit www.eastportwindjammers.com or call 207-853-2500.

Appendix E: Pests and Hazards

There are two pieces of good news regarding pests in Maine: 1) there are no poisonous snakes or spiders, and 2) if it weren't for all the insects, there wouldn't be as many birds. Blackflies and mosquitoes are the top two complaints among Maine birders, but both are controllable problems.

Everybody in the world knows about mosquitoes, but Maine's blackfly comes as a sorry surprise to some. For those not used to them, the bites can be all the more irritating. Furthermore, they are harder to deter with head nets because they will land on clothing and crawl under hoods, under waistbands, and up sleeves. At their worst, they swarm in distressing numbers. Fortunately, they have a short season, generally a month that begins in mid-May through southern Maine, starting a week later in northern Maine. They are deterred by repellents. Unlike mosquitoes, they require moving streams to breed and are less prevalent in cities and along the ocean shore.

Maine's mosquitoes are no worse than in many other places. Indeed, compared to the Florida Everglades in wet season or the summer Arctic, they are insignificant and merely annoying. They may swarm during a day of birding in May and June, as well as during the hours of darkness in mid-summer. They, too, are controllable with repellents, and they are much easier to dissuade with head nets and hooded sweatshirts, or even a good sea breeze.

The no-see-um is sometimes called a midge in other northern regions, though "midge" is a name given to a variety of biting insects. The Maine version is less than an eighth-inch long, and most victims don't even know the culprit is around until they feel the slight itching of a bite in progress. The itch seldom lasts long and these critters are a minor nuisance except when camping. They can make a night in the sleeping bag miserable. No-see-ums are nocturnal and cannot stand even a slight breeze, so they are seldom encountered while birding in daylight hours.

Horseflies and deerflies prefer hotter weather and, of the two, deerflies are more numerous. They don't usually become a problem until the dog days of summer. Their bite is painful and annoying, but it is their incessant buzzing around the head that is most distracting. They prefer to attack the highest point of their targets and are easily deterred by a hood or hat.

Ticks are a growing problem. They are found statewide, though the majority are confined to southern coastal areas. Wood ticks (also known as dog ticks) are the largest. They readily feed on humans and are also the easiest to detect. "Deer" ticks are smaller, no bigger than 1/16th inch. These are the ticks that carry Lyme Disease. The early signs of the disease show up as a rash at the bite site and then flu-like symptoms. Untreated cases can lead to arthritic conditions and possible neurological problems. Not all deer ticks carry Lyme Disease and a tick must remain attached to the host for at least 24 hours in order to cause infection. It is worth being aware of their presence, but they are still an uncommon occurrence. Repellents are available, but tucking pant legs into boots and socks, and frequent checks, continues to be an effective approach in tick-prone areas.

Maine has its fair share of stinging insects. Bees, wasps, and yellow jackets are common in summer. The latter are most aggressive around sweet liquids. Otherwise, they all tend to leave people alone. Honeybees are commonly imported to pollinate crops, particularly blueberry fields. When venturing upon blueberry barrens in late May and early June looking for Upland Sandpipers and Vesper Sparrows, expect to see swarming hives surrounded by electrified fences to keep the bears out.

The only poisonous plant in Maine is poison ivy, which thrives along some roadsides and stream edges. Some offshore islands are completely covered in it. Sufferers are familiar with its bright green color and "leaves of three—let it be."

Now the really good news: while winter birding at 20 degrees below zero, none of these pests is a problem.

HAZARDS:

Heavy Trucks: The industrial forest is a network of dirt roads, including major arteries with heavy traffic. Other roads range in size from secondary routes to discontinued jeep paths. Logging trucks weigh 100,000 pounds. Drivers are paid by the load and it is important to them to be able to make their runs quickly and without impediment. Always obey the rules of the road:

- *Give all trucks the right of way. Pull over and stop for trucks in both directions.*
- *Obey posted speeds; maximum is 45 mph.*

- *Never stop in the middle of the road. Never stop on a corner or below a hill crest.*
- *Never block side roads, even those that look abandoned.*
- *Do not linger on bridges.*
- *Avoid active logging areas, where possible. Avoid roads that are too narrow for two vehicles.*

Other considerations:

- *Roads can be very, very dusty—obscuring driver's vision and choking hikers.*
- *All roads are gravel surfaced, which can be tough on tires. Be prepared and have at least one spare.*
- *In wet periods, side roads can be muddy, rutted, and often impassible.*
- *Speeding vehicles can kick pebbles into windshields—another reason to stop for trucks.*
- *Signage has improved in recent years, but many roads and intersections are unmarked. Always have a good map—preferably two: an updated DeLorme Maine Atlas and the latest North Maine Woods map, available at checkpoints.*
- *Gas up. There are few services in the North Maine Woods. There is seldom cell phone service.*
- *Bicycles, motorcycles, ATVs, and horses are prohibited.*
- *North Maine Woods supports the principles of "Leave No Trace." Pack it in and pack it out.*

Moose Collisions: The seriousness of moose collisions cannot be understated. Maine averages hundreds of personal injuries and several fatalities annually due to accidents involving moose. Their dark coloration makes them very difficult to see at night. Slow down in moose areas and heed warning signs.

Cell Phone Coverage: While communications are improving all the time, many of Maine's rural areas and most of the remote regions are currently without signal coverage. Don't rely on cell phones in emergencies.

Appendix F: American Birding Association's Code of Ethics

Everyone who enjoys birds and birding must always respect wildlife, its environment, and the rights of others. In any conflict of interest between birds and birders, the welfare of the birds and their environment comes first.

CODE OF BIRDING ETHICS
1. *Promote the welfare of birds and their environment.*
   (a) Support the protection of important bird habitat.

   (b) To avoid stressing birds or exposing them to danger, exercise restraint and caution during observation, photography, sound recording, and filming.

   Limit the use of recordings and other methods of attracting birds, and never use such methods in heavily birded areas, or for attracting any species that is threatened, endangered, of special concern, or is rare in your local area.

   Keep well back from nests and nesting colonies, roosts, display areas, and important feeding sites. In such sensitive areas, if there is a need for extended observation, photography, filming, or recording, try to use a blind or hide, and take advantage of natural cover.

   Use artificial light sparingly for filming or photography, especially for close-ups.

   (c) Before advertising the presence of a rare bird, evaluate the potential for disturbance to the bird, its surroundings, and other people in the area, and proceed only if access can be controlled, disturbance minimized, and permission has been obtained from private landowners. The sites of rare nesting birds should be divulged only to the proper conservation authorities.

   (d) Stay on roads, trails, and paths where they exist; otherwise keep habitat disturbance to a minimum.

2. *Respect the law and the rights of others.*
   (a) Do not enter private property without the owner's explicit permission.

   (b) Follow all laws, rules, and regulations governing use of roads and public areas, both at home and abroad.

   (c) Practice common courtesy in contacts with other people. Your exemplary behavior will generate goodwill with birders and nonbirders alike.

3. *Ensure that feeders, nest structures, and other artificial bird environments are safe.*

(a) Keep dispensers, water, and food clean, and free of decay or disease. It is important to feed birds continually during harsh weather.

(b) Maintain and clean nest structures regularly.

(c) If you are attracting birds to an area, ensure the birds are not exposed to predation from cats and other domestic animals, or dangers posed by artificial hazards.

4. *Group birding, whether organized or impromptu, requires special care.*

Each individual in the group, in addition to the obligations spelled out in Items #1 and #2, has responsibilities as a group member.

(a) Respect the interests, rights, and skills of fellow birders, as well as people participating in other legitimate outdoor activities. Freely share your knowledge and experience, except where code 1(c) applies. Be especially helpful to beginning birders.

(b) If you witness unethical birding behavior, assess the situation, and intervene if you think it prudent. When interceding, inform the person(s) of the inappropriate action, and attempt, within reason, to have it stopped. If the behavior continues, document it and notify appropriate individuals or organizations.

Group leader responsibilities [amateur and professional trips and tours].

(c) Be an exemplary ethical role model for the group. Teach through word and example.

(d) Keep groups to a size that limits impact on the environment and does not interfere with others using the same area.

(e) Ensure everyone in the group knows of and practices this code.

(f) Learn and inform the group of any special circumstances applicable to the areas being visited (e.g. no tape recorders allowed).

(g) Acknowledge that professional tour companies bear a special responsibility to place the welfare of birds and the benefits of public knowledge ahead of the company's commercial interests. Ideally, leaders should keep track of tour sightings, document unusual occurrences, and submit records to appropriate organizations.

PLEASE FOLLOW THIS CODE, DISTRIBUTE IT, AND TEACH IT TO OTHERS

The American Birding Association's Code of Birding Ethics may be freely reproduced for distribution/dissemination. Visit www.americanbirding.org.

Appendix G: Acknowledgements

I'm bound to have forgotten someone who provided invaluable assistance during the five years and tens of thousands of miles I logged to research and assemble the *Maine Birding Trail*. There is no surer way of remembering that person than to commit all the other contributors' names to paper and then, once the names appear in print, realize in shock who got left out. To you, I apologize.

Thanks to Bob Cash and Lynn Vernon, two Maine Audubon trustees who first put this notion in my head. Maine Audubon staffers Bill Hancock, Judy Camuso, and Susan Gallo were instrumental in the early phases of the project, and Bill has been a contributor ever since its inception. Bill Sheehan is the fount of all birding knowledge in Aroostook County, and he proved it repeatedly. Norm Famous knows all and sees all in Down East Maine and was invaluable in documenting some of the more remote parts of the state. Jeff Wells is the birder I wanted to be when I grew up. Or maybe I'm thinking of Seth Benz.

The accounts of birding in southern Maine are much better because of advice from Derek Lovitch, Scott Cronenweth, Joanne Stevens, Scott Richardson, Don Tucker, and Turk Duddy. Thanks to Jeff Tarling, whose early support on behalf of the City of Portland demonstrates that some communities truly "get it" in terms of enhancing their natural resources. I spent pleasant days in the Mid-Coast area accompanied by Bob Brooks, Carol Jack, and Pete Darling. Mike Fahay, Mark Mahnke, Nancy Bither, Jay Adams, Stella Walsh, Kristen Lindquist, and Chad Dorsey filled in the gaps.

In the Acadia region, Leslie Clapp, Chip Moseley, Sal Rooney, Ken Crowell, Rich MacDonald, Michael Good, Zack Klyver, Chuck Whitney, and Ed Hawkes added their knowledge. Farther Down East, Bill Kolodnicki and Maurry Wills must have lived right in a past life, because they're spending this life at Moosehorn National Wildlife Refuge. Marion Bates is a good birder and is just fun to be with.

Stan DeOrsey, Susan Hayward, Peter Kallin, Herb Wilson, Don Mairs, and Don Smith can take credit for improving accounts in the central part of the state. Tom Henderson, Bob Crowley, J. Dwight, Wendy Howes, Jennifer Perry, Jean Preis, and Nancy Perlson get the nod for advancing my understanding of western Maine.

U.S. Forest Rangers Katie Stewart and Leslie Rowse corrected my draft for the White Mountain National Forest. Judy Markowsky, Tom Comish, Barry Burgason, and Ron Joseph guided my thoughts in many of the areas north of Bangor. Shannon LeRoy of the Appalachian Mountain Club has been priceless in helping uncover birding opportunities in the Moosehead Lake area. Chief Naturalist Jean Hoekwater fleshed out my understanding of the birding in Baxter State Park. Sarah Medina reviewed the descriptions for the North Maine Woods. I am indebted to The Nature Conservancy, especially Nancy Sferra, for advice on developing better description for TNC properties.

Paul Garrity deserves a special note of appreciation. His Web site at mainebirding.net and its e-mail list-serve have enabled birders to communicate statewide for over a decade. He has been generous in his support for this project. Julie Suchecki's e-mail list also tipped me off to new sightings and new sites to go explore and research. Several folks volunteered to provide photography, particularly Bob Malbon and Garth McElroy.

A birding trail needs the support of the statewide tourism community. Donna Fichtner, Bob Smith, and Vaughn Stinson have been most helpful. Janice Dyer, Mike McCabe, Christina Shipps, Mark Robie, and Laurie Cormier enabled me to put birding tourism into practice. In Maine, nobody captures the essence of this state better than Down East Books and *Down East* magazine. I greatly appreciate their support and the encouragement of editor Michael Steere.

The Maine Birding Trail belongs to the people of Maine. I am grateful to the elected and appointed officials who made it possible. Early in his administration, Governor John Baldacci made nature-based tourism a key priority. Eliza Townsend, deputy commissioner of the Department of Conservation, Tom Hodgman from the Maine Department of Inland Fisheries & Wildlife, and Phil Savignano from the Maine Office of Tourism, with the counsel of Maine Audubon's Eric Hynes and Bill Hancock, joined me in shepherding the final project to a successful launch.

Finally, with the completion of this guide, my wife, Sandi, is very much looking forward to getting her husband back.

Index